Astrology for the
Light Side of the Brain

ASTROLOGY
FOR THE
LIGHT SIDE
OF THE BRAIN

Kim Rogers-Gallagher

International Standard Book Number 0-935127-35-6

Printed in the United States of America

· Published by ACS Publications
5521 Ruffin Rd
San Diego, CA 92123-1314

First Printing, October 1995

Thanks and Appreciation

There are lots of wonderful people in the world, and I've been blessed by knowing many of them. All of them provided their charts, their experiences, their friendship and their support during the time this book was being written. Most of them understood when I stopped going out. Some of them came over and dragged me out anyway. So... since being a Sag gives me license to be excessive, I'm going to mention every last one of 'em:

First, to my Extended Family at the Seacoast Family "Y"— mostly for their ongoing love, but also for tolerating my schedule... Most especially with love and respect to The Commander, for five years worth of wonderful chats, and for getting the show on the road as only a Gemini can.

To The Inner Circle, the Tightest of the Tight, the wonderful, wonderful friends my Aquarian Moon just adores —First of all, to "The Wife", the one and only Sharon Ann. To Deb and Tim, medieval playmates, much-loved friends, Sunday dinner companions. To Dottie, a fine Gemini, the only person who sees my Moon in all her phases... For Julie Baby Mama Sweetheart Honey, Angel-Pie. For Bonnie, for deep psychological Mexican conversation. For Michael Q.—for um... oh, for everything. For Michael B., the darling of the Sag Squad, and the other Michael B., for late-night chats at The Brewery. For Jean, the most efficient Leo around, and the very best (and happiest) camper I've ever known. For Sabrina, The, um.... Queen—for simply being Herself. For Kristin, who selfishly sleeps an hour longer one night a year—and enjoys it. For Kitty, for being herself under all circumstances— the best thing she could possibly do.

To Mr. Frank, my partner in crime, a truly special gift from the Universe whose last name I promise never again to forget. In public.

To The Monday Night Discussion Group—MWAH!!!!

To The SAA...so many wonderful people.

To The Girls—Charlotte, Chris, Chris, Judy, Robin, Marty, Elaine, Laney, and, of course, Hope, without whom we would all be truly Hopeless....

To Anji and Rick Levine, my West Coast family, for opening up their fire-sign hearts and their wonderful, wonderful nest to me—and my pets—when the Universe relocated me to Seattle. Special love to Anji for the giggles, and to Rick for the "Sshhh's." I love you guys to pieces.

To Mark Lerner, the owner/operator of the best little astrology magazine around, *Welcome to Planet Earth*, for taking a chance on a new writer back in January 1991. Many thanks, much love and blessings always.

To Ray Merriman, my very favorite Capricorn kinda guy, for the myriad of ways he has extended me his kindness and support.

Special, special wicked thanks to the Mighty Editress.

To my sisters, Kathy, Polly, and Lisa—welcome home, ladies.

To Rob, much-loved Merlin, for wonderful, long talks.

With all the love and respect and admiration possible to Dusty, for soothing the Moon/Neptune square...

To Lorraine, for Mooning me when I need it.

To Nick, for friendship, inspiration, and travelogues.

To Angel, Ginny, Demetra, Ann, Suzie, Lee, and Barbara—astrological Girlfriends extraordinaire.

To all the critters who own me. Most especially to Kate, my 17 year-old calico (and co-author) who sat with me daily through every page, proof-read with me each evening, and added a few comments of her own en route from a nap on the printer, where she should never sit, across the keyboard, where she should never walk, to my lap, where she is always welcome.

To Helen, for laying a solid IC.

To Papa Bob. That's all.

To Damon. Thank you, thank you, thank you...

Table of Contents

INTRODUCTION

Playful Astrology

Well, hello. Welcome to my book. Forgive me for being so pushy this early in our relationship, but I really must insist that you read this page before you go anywhere else—please—even though I know "Introductions" are not notoriously interesting passages, and being a Sag, I've certainly ignored my share. This one will be fun—honest—and I promise the rest of the book will be, too. So before you flip to the chapter on "Venus through the Signs" (to look up your own and see if this thing's any good), give me just a couple of paragraphs to clue you in on who I am and what the point of this book really is. Because if you don't, you might not get all the best from it. And I want you to get as much out of this baby as you possibly can.

See, I love astrology. It's the only thing I've ever found that's absolutely consistent, and my skittish Aquarius Moon really appreciates consistency—in an odd kind of way. Since you wouldn't have made it this far if you weren't looking for some answers yourself, you really ought to hang around and learn a little more. You're on to something here. This stuff is great, and I'd like to help you learn it.

There are a couple of things you ought to know, however, before we go any further. Like, for starters, if you're here because you want to know your lucky numbers or your lucky colors or your lucky days, you're going to be disappointed. That's Zolar, not me. I'm also not going to predict earthquakes, the end of the world, or how long Liz and Larry will stay married. That's Jeanne Dixon.

You won't find any damaging generalizations in here, either—not even about Virgos and their psychotic obsession with details, or Sag's notorious Lack o' Grace. Nope. This is one o' them New-Age-type astrology books, see, and that means that I make it a rule never to be pessimistic, never to believe that any planet or sign is inherently "malefic" or "benefic," (that's Astrologese for "bad" and "good"), and never, never, to start a sentence with "The native...." (That's an inside joke you'll understand later on.)

You also have my word there are no tables in the back of this book to terrify you, and no "simple" instructions on How To Calculate Your Own Chart—so don't be scared. If you'd like a chart done, I strongly suggest having it calculated for you by a professional astrologer or chart service. Until you have a real "feel" for what astrology is, it won't do you any good to struggle with the mechanics. So what you will find in the back of this book is a place to send your data off to, that will calculate your chart and have it back to you before the Moon's next phase. Having your chart done professionally, at least at first, ensures that you'll never have to contend with the heartache of discovering that the Capricorn Ascendant you knew, loved, and owned for the past two years was miscalculated—and you're really Sag Rising (which would explain how you made that mistake to start with).

I'm also not going to try to convince you to "believe" in astrology, because it's not a religion, and it has nothing to do with religion. You can feel free to continue believing—or disbelieving—in whatever you like. You see, astrology is a system, a perfectly logical system that's often described as equal parts "science" and art. Whatever you call it, it works. Honest. So it's not about believing. It's about understanding. About drawing parallels between the movements of the planets in the heavens and conditions Down Here—and that's not a new concept. It's called seasons, and gardeners have been working with them for years. Well, astrologers are gardeners, too. We just use all the planets, and the Moon, too, when we plant our seeds.

Now, it's not like I'm asking you to chant, or rub herbs into your navel. And nobody's going to channel a Being from Another Plane. Promise. We're dealing with the planets here, and planets are real. I've seen them. So have you. NASA's even got snapshots. Planets are so "real," in fact, that they follow real orbits, consistent enough to be put into mathematical tables. Planets don't need you or me to "believe" in them, and I think it's safe to say that they won't disappear if you don't clap your hands. That's Tinkerbell, not Saturn.

So if you came for lottery numbers, you're in the wrong department. If, on the other hand, you want to learn a brand-new way to describe everything you already know in a language that will fascinate, befuddle, educate, and entertain you, then sharpen your pencils. Because that's what astrology really is, and we're going to talk real astrology here.

If you're a beginner, it's very important that you read this book in the order it's presented. I tend to build one fact on another, so if you don't read Chapter Three, you'll think I'm speaking an obscure foreign language in Chapter Four. I promise to keep your attention, however, and I'm reasonably sure you'll have a good time. Being a Sag, I'm of the belief that learning anything can be fun—and that goes double for astrology.

You can also learn astrology from different voices. So you'll find that whenever I've quoted other astrologers throughout this book, I've tried to include "directions" for you, ways for you to find more of what the author or speaker has done. If you like what you read, go check out their books, or try to get to a conference where they're speaking. There are so many good astrologers out there—find as many as you can.

One more thing—thanks for making an investment in this book. I appreciate the time you spent earning the pesos to buy it. I'd love to hear your comments, too—my Mercury in Sag loves long-distance mail—and I welcome you to contact me at the address below:

PO Box 141, Ridgeway, CO 81432-0141.

That said, I thank you for your patience and I invite you to turn the page.

CHAPTER ONE
TAKING THE CHART APART

An Overview—
Let's See What This Thing Can "Do"

Your chart is a map that freeze-frames the galaxy, a Cosmic photograph that pinpoints exactly where everything Up There was— every star, planet, asteroid, and comet—from the perspective of your location, at the moment you made your planetary debut. Since the Earth, the Moon, and all the planets are constantly in motion, no two charts are ever exactly alike—just as each of us and, in fact, each moment in time, is absolutely unique.

Most charts are calculated in what's called a Geocentric format, which means they're "earth-centered"—constructed as if the earth were at the center of the universe, that is. The spot in the center of the chart that may have your name printed on it is like a trap door—it's the "You Are Here" of the chart. When you peer out at the world, it's through this circular "lens."

So your chart is **your view of reality**. Your own personal tool-kit. Everybody's got one, as does every event, every question, and every thought. Everything that ever **began** has a chart, in fact. The magic of astrology is that it allows us to understand **how** that view of reality affects our lives. We can look at a chart, rub our chins, step through that trap door, and come away knowing what type of **potential** the chart contains—what it's capable of. Once you've got your chart, you know your **Highest** Potential. So rather than allowing patterns that aren't constructive to continue repeating in your life, you've got an "answer key" to work with. You can choose to use difficult energies in more positive ways, which is where growth comes from. By the same token, knowing your chart also gives you the ability to make the most of your innate "gifts."

The Four Basic Food Groups

There are four basic categories to astrological interpretation, what I like to refer to as the Four Astrological Food Groups. There are planets, signs, houses, and aspects. Learn all four and you'll have the means to understand any type of astrological technique.

The first "food group" is **planets**. They represent the **urges** or **needs** we've all got, just by virtue of taking up residence inside a human body. Like I said, they're our tools. When we need to do a particular job, we reach for one of our planets. For example— Venus is what we reach for when it's time to love, Mars is what we pull out for a fight, Mercury is how we communicate—our own personal switchboard—and the Moon is the piece of us that feels. Each of these inner bodies provides the energy or impetus for those particular activities.

Now, it's important here to keep in mind that planets don't "do" anything. **We** do. You may become quite tired of me saying that, actually, but I can't impress that on you enough. The planets are symbols for our inner needs and drives. Astrologically, as with the rest of life, it's all in the playing. We use the energies our inner planets supply us with, ideally to accomplish the tasks our Sun sets out. Think of the planet as the verb in a sentence: Mercury is how we say "I Communicate," Venus is how we say "I love," and so forth.

The second "food group" is the **signs**. If planets are like verbs, signs are like adjectives. **Signs** tell **how** a planet will express itself—how it's going to operate. They're like "**flavors**" or "**styles**" a planet "filters" through. Yes, you'll get mad—everybody does, because everybody's got an internal Mars, and "I express my anger" is Mars' job. But **how** do you express your anger? Immediately and spontaneously—despite the fact that you might get fired for it? Or do you pout and "tsk" and carry on, refusing to divulge your problem for days? The sign a planet "wears" is like its **cos-**

tume. So a planet "wearing" Aries is all done up in red—and it
acts red, too. Fiery. Feisty. Impulsive. A planet "wearing" Scorpio, on the other hand, stalks around in black. Its energy is slower, sexier, and more calculated than Aries.

Then there's **houses**, "food group" number three. You'll notice that every chart is divided into twelve pieces, just like the
face on a clock. These wedges are the **houses**, and inside every
house is a **piece of your personality**, a "side" of you that steps
out when a particular Life Situation presents itself. Think of how
different you are when you're at work than when you're out on a
date. That's the difference between your sixth house "side" and
your fifth house "side," respectively. There are twelve "sides" to
each of us—one to a house. So your chart is really like one **big**
house, with twelve **rooms** where you stash different **sides of your
personality**.

Aspects ("food group" number four) are angles, pure and simple. Most are measured in multiples of 30 degrees. Since there
are 30 degrees in every sign, aspects are most easily found by
counting signs. A square, for example, exists when two planets
are at right angles to one another—three signs, (or 90 degrees)
apart. An opposition occurs when two planets are six signs (or
180 degrees) apart—literally opposite to one another. Aspects
describe the nature of the relationship between two planets—
whether they make life "cushy" or challenging for each another.

There. Now. If I've done my job right, all that should sound
familiar, like something you already know. In fact, there's **nothing** in this book that you **don't** already know. Nothing. You
know what it's like to love someone, which means you're already
familiar with using your Venus. You also know that people express their anger in very different ways—which means you know
how Mars differs from one sign to another. You know there are
many different facets to your personality, too, that you're not at
all the same person when you're with your Mom as you are when
you're at work. That's what the houses describe. You also know
what it's like to feel "torn" about something—to want to do something and yet not want to do it—and that's what aspects like
squares and oppositions often feel like.

Getting Started

THE TOOLS OF THE TRADE

So you're "sold," then. You're in. You want to know more about this stuff. You're thinking you may even want to **be** an astrologer when you grow up. Well, wonderful. We're always looking for A Few Good People. You'll need two things to get started Astrologizin'. First, get your own chart, if you don't already have one. (For ways of ordering charts, see "Where to Find It," in the back.) If you can get a few other charts of folks you're especially close to, that will help, too.

You'll want an **ephemeris**, too. The sooner the better. What's an **ephemeris**? Well, um, it's a book of tables. Now, I know I promised there'd be **no numbers**, and that a book of tables **is** numbers, but this is a wonderful book of numbers. It shows the whereabouts of the planets on any given day, and they're usually assembled in 100-year batches. So if you've got one for this century, you can look at any day from January 1, 1900, to December 31, 2000 and see where the planets were. The day you started high school. The night you met your wife. The moment you found out you were pregnant. They're all In There. I promise you, once you get over the mental block about the numbers, you'll never be without it. Never. Not even camping. Now, I promised not to scare you with too many tables, but being able to read an ephemeris is really important—and really **easy.** If it wasn't, **I** certainly wouldn't have made it this far. So. Check out Figure 1 and trust me... you'll be writing in the margins and using it for a diary in no time.

MAKING SENSE OF YOUR COMPUTER CHART

The Outside

Now, once you've got your birth chart in your hands, you'll need to figure out how to use it. So our next quest is to take you on a guided tour of your birth chart, to show you where everything's kept.

First of all, you'll notice that the circle you have in front of you is divided into twelve sections. These are the twelve **houses** we talked about earlier. As you can see, the houses are numbered counterclockwise, beginning at the spot where you'd find nine

JULY 1995 — LONGITUDE

Day	Sid.Time	☉	0 hr ☽	Noon ☽	True ☊	☿	♀	♂	♃	♄	♅	♆	♇
1 Sa	18 34 19	8♋43 21	11♌39 29	17♌48 2	3♏ 8.0	16♊57.6	24♊46.3	18♍22.0	7♐ 6.5	24♓43.7	29♑18.1	24♑35.6	28♏12.3
2 Su	18 38 16	9 40 34	23 59 5	0♍12 53	2R 58.6	18 1.1	25 59.6	18 55.1	7R 1.0	24 44.2	29R 15.9	24R 34.1	28R 11.2
3 M	18 42 12	10 37 47	6♍29 42	12 49 52	2 51.6	19 8.6	27 13.0	19 28.3	6 55.7	24 44.6	29 13.7	24 32.5	28 10.1
4 Tu	18 46 9	11 35 0	19 13 43	25 41 36	2 47.2	20 20.1	28 26.3	20 1.7	6 50.6	24 44.9	29 11.5	24 31.0	28 9.0
5 W	18 50 5	12 32 12	2♎13 55	8♎51 2	2D 45.2	21 35.6	29 39.7	20 35.2	6 45.5	24 45.0	29 9.2	24 29.4	28 7.9
6 Th	18 54 2	13 29 24	15 33 17	22 21 0	2 44.8	22 55.1	0♋53.1	21 8.8	6 40.6	24R 45.1	29 6.9	24 27.8	28 6.9
7 F	18 57 59	14 26 36	29 14 26	6♏13 46	2R 45.0	24 18.4	2 6.5	21 42.5	6 35.9	24 45.1	29 4.6	24 26.2	28 5.9
8 Sa	19 1 55	15 23 47	13♏19 3	20 30 12	2 44.7	25 45.5	3 19.9	22 16.4	6 31.3	24 45.0	29 2.3	24 24.6	28 4.9
9 Su	19 5 52	16 20 59	27 46 59	5♐ 8 59	2 42.8	27 16.4	4 33.3	22 50.3	6 26.9	24 44.8	29 0.0	24 23.0	28 3.9
10 M	19 9 48	17 18 10	12♐35 33	20 5 53	2 38.5	28 51.0	5 46.7	23 24.4	6 22.6	24 44.5	28 57.7	24 21.4	28 3.0
11 Tu	19 13 45	18 15 21	27 38 59	5♑13 41	2 31.6	0♋29.2	7 0.2	23 58.6	6 18.5	24 44.0	28 55.3	24 19.8	28 2.1
12 W	19 17 41	19 12 33	12♑48 45	20 22 49	2 22.4	2 10.8	8 13.7	24 32.8	6 14.6	24 43.5	28 53.0	24 18.2	28 1.2
13 Th	19 21 38	20 9 44	27 54 36	5♒22 50	2 12.0	3 55.8	9 27.2	25 7.2	6 10.8	24 42.9	28 50.6	24 16.6	28 0.4
14 F	19 25 34	21 6 56	12♒46 24	20 4 20	2 1.5	5 44.1	10 40.7	25 41.7	6 7.2	24 42.2	28 48.3	24 15.0	27 59.6
15 Sa	19 29 31	22 4 8	27 15 52	4♓20 27	1 52.2	7 35.4	11 54.2	26 16.4	6 3.8	24 41.4	28 45.9	24 13.3	27 58.8
16 Su	19 33 28	23 1 20	11♓17 45	18 7 40	1 44.9	9 29.5	13 7.8	26 51.1	6 0.5	24 40.5	28 43.5	24 11.7	27 58.0
17 M	19 37 24	23 58 33	24 50 14	1♈25 43	1 40.0	11 26.3	14 21.4	27 25.9	5 57.4	24 39.5	28 41.1	24 10.1	27 57.3
18 Tu	19 41 21	24 55 47	7♈54 28	14 16 58	1 37.5	13 25.5	15 35.0	28 0.8	5 54.4	24 38.4	28 38.7	24 8.5	27 56.6
19 W	19 45 17	25 53 1	20 33 46	26 45 30	1 36.7	15 26.8	16 48.6	28 35.9	5 51.7	24 37.2	28 36.3	24 6.9	27 55.9
20 Th	19 49 14	26 50 16	2♉52 47	8♉56 19	1 36.6	17 29.9	18 2.2	29 11.0	5 49.1	24 35.9	28 33.9	24 5.2	27 55.2
21 F	19 53 10	27 47 32	14 56 45	20 54 45	1 36.2	19 34.5	19 15.9	29 46.2	5 46.7	24 34.5	28 31.5	24 3.6	27 54.6
22 Sa	19 57 7	28 44 49	26 50 57	2♊45 56	1 34.4	21 40.3	20 29.6	0♎21.6	5 44.4	24 33.0	28 29.1	24 2.0	27 54.0
23 Su	20 1 3	29 42 6	8♊40 17	14 34 30	1 30.4	23 46.9	21 43.3	0 57.1	5 42.4	24 31.4	28 26.7	24 0.4	27 53.5
24 M	20 5 0	0♌39 25	20 29 4	26 24 23	1 23.6	25 54.1	22 57.1	1 32.6	5 40.5	24 29.7	28 24.3	23 58.8	27 53.0
25 Tu	20 8 57	1 36 44	2♋20 51	8♋18 45	1 14.1	28 1.5	24 10.8	2 8.3	5 38.8	24 27.9	28 21.9	23 57.2	27 52.5
26 W	20 12 53	2 34 3	14 18 21	20 19 52	1 2.4	0♌ 8.9	25 24.6	2 44.0	5 37.3	24 26.0	28 19.5	23 55.6	27 52.0
27 Th	20 16 50	3 31 24	26 23 29	2♌29 19	0 49.1	2 16.0	26 38.4	3 19.9	5 36.0	24 24.1	28 17.1	23 54.0	27 51.6
28 F	20 20 46	4 28 45	8♌37 28	14 48 0	0 35.5	4 22.6	27 52.2	3 55.9	5 34.8	24 22.0	28 14.7	23 52.4	27 51.2
29 Sa	20 24 43	5 26 7	21 1 0	27 16 32	0 22.6	6 28.4	29 6.1	4 32.0	5 33.9	24 19.9	28 12.3	23 50.8	27 50.8
30 Su	20 28 39	6 23 29	3♍34 38	9♍55 23	0 11.6	8 33.3	0♌19.9	5 8.1	5 33.1	24 17.6	28 9.9	23 49.2	27 50.5
31 M	20 32 36	7 20 52	16 18 53	22 45 16	0 3.2	10 37.2	1 33.8	5 44.4	5 32.5	24 15.3	28 7.6	23 47.6	27 50.2

Figure 1

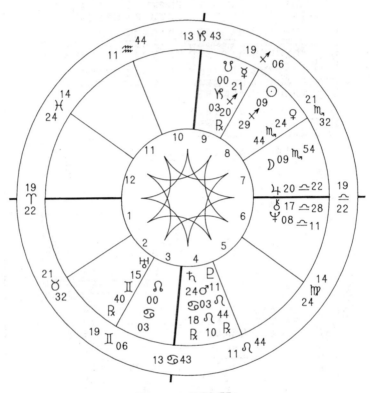

Bette Midler

Figure 2

o'clock on a clock face. Although the signs that appear on each house will vary, the **order** of the houses will never change. The first house on any chart is always the first house, the second house is always the second house, and so forth.

The lines that separate one house from another are called **house cusps**; the line that **precedes** a house is its cusp. So the line that separates the 2nd house from the third is the **third house cusp**, and the line that separates the fifth house from the sixth is the **sixth house cusp**, and so forth.

House cusps show how the time and location of your birth reflected your view of the galaxy. They describe, both literally and figuratively, your "slant" on Things.

Think of your chart as one big house, of houses as rooms, and of cusps as the doors to those rooms.

Okay. On each house cusp, you'll see an abbreviation like this one: 13 ♋ 43. Translated into English, that means that the "door" of that "room" opens onto 13 degrees and 43 minutes of Cancer (♋). (Again, remember that the circle is 360 degrees, and that there are 30 degrees in every sign and 60 minutes in every degree.)

Although the "average" size of a house is 30 degrees, in actual practice, houses come in varying sizes, depending on how far from the equator you were born. (Folks born very far north or very far south have the greatest variations in house size, since their position along the slant of the Earth's axis causes their "view" of the Sun to be from an extreme angle.)

Ordinarily, all of the signs of the zodiac will appear **in order, one to a "door,"** around the outside of your chart wheel. If you notice, however, that you've got two signs missing and two signs repeated, you've got what's called an **interception**—which sounds a lot worse than it is. Interceptions aren't fatal and they're not uncommon. They also don't work alone—like all the house cusps, you'll only find them in opposite pairs. See, what happens is that instead of having a "door," or house cusp, to call their own, all 30 degrees of each intercepted sign are contained within a house. So, since it's the preceding sign that appears on that house cusp, and the following sign that appears on the next house, intercepted signs **seem** to "disappear." They don't. Trust me.

Think of intercepted signs as being antechambers, or rooms within rooms.

Astrologers have different opinions as to the significance of interceptions, and we'll discuss all that later on. For now, your mission is simply to understand that intercepted houses are automatically much larger than other houses since they contain not only all 30 degrees of the intercepted sign, but also pieces of both the sign before and after.

In a nutshell, the "job" of the houses is to provide a framework, a place for the signs and the planets to set up shop.

THE MIDHEAVEN AND THE ASCENDANT

There are two Very Special House Cusps that you may have heard about at one time or another. (See Figure 3.) These two House Cusps are the main points of access to your chart. They're "entrances" to you. There's the Ascendant, or Rising Sign, which is the first house cusp, and the Midheaven, or "MC," which is the cusp of the tenth house. These particular points are very important, for reasons we'll discuss in depth later. For now, think of them as "exit points," (as Karen Hamaker-Zondag puts it so well), as spots where our charts "open" to the world, where we mingle and mix with others and with our environments.

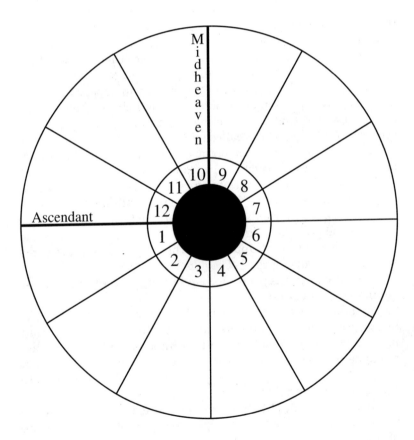

Figure 3

The Inside

So. That's the outside of the wheel. On the inside, you'll find the planets, written out in a series of half-sentences like this one: ☿ 21 ♐ 20. That translates into "Mercury is at 21 degrees of Sagittarius (♐) and 20 minutes." Which means that if you'd been looking for Mercury in the sky at that moment, you would have found it by first locating the section of the sky given to the sign Sagittarius, and then finding the twenty-first degree of that sign. Each planet, as well as the Sun and the Moon, will appear inside your chart wheel, in the same abbreviated form. Here's a list of abbreviations for the planets and the signs, and the symbols—or **glyphs**—for each, just in case you've got a chart that's hand-drawn.

SU	☉	SUN	AR	♈	ARIES
MO	☽	MOON	TA	♉	TAURUS
ME	☿	MERCURY	GE	♊	GEMINI
VE	♀	VENUS	CN	♋	CANCER
MA	♂	MARS	LE	♌	LEO
JU	♃	JUPITER	VI	♍	VIRGO
SA	♄	SATURN	LI	♎	LIBRA
UR	♅	URANUS	SC	♏	SCORPIO
NE	♆	NEPTUNE	SG	♐	SAGITTARIUS
PL	♇	PLUTO	CP	♑	CAPRICORN
			AQ	♒	AQUARIUS
			PI	♓	PISCES

There are also symbols for each of the aspects (such as ♂ □ △ ☍). They'll be completely introduced in Chapter Six.

RETROGRADES IN THE CHART

Depending on the type of program you use and whether or not you have a hand-drawn chart, you'll see "R" or "ʀ" written in occasionally after one of the planetary sentences I mentioned above. That "R" stands for "Retrograde," and yes, you do need to know this, because retrograde planets have special behavior patterns. (We'll cover Retrogrades in Chapter Two, The Planets.)

STRAY ABBREVIATIONS YOU MIGHT ALSO FIND INSIDE THE WHEEL

Okay. You've successfully interpreted each abbreviation or glyph and linked it with the appropriate planet on the inside of your wheel. This thing's starting to make sense after all. But some charts have a couple of "extra" glyphs in there, too, stuff like "P," "V," "EP," and "N." "What the heck are those?" you'd like to know. Well, they're not asteroids, and they're not mistakes. "P" means "Part of Fortune," "V" means "Vertex," "EP" means "East Point," and "N" means "North Node." All of these are mathematically calculated points and, although we will eventually give each of them the air time they deserve, it's way too early to even attempt to explain them to you. I promise we'll come back to them, however, in Chapter Ten "Exclamation Points." But no fair flipping ahead.

Well, now. Look how far you've come already. You've only been here for a few pages, and already you know your way around an astrology chart. You also know the difference between signs, planets, houses, and aspects, and you're an expert on where to find the Midheaven and the Ascendant. So. Now that you've got the basics down, let's go a little deeper. Let's talk about the planets.

CHAPTER TWO

THE PLANETS

Okay. This is the most basic of all the food groups, and a very important section to understand. So get yourself a drink of water, pick a comfortable spot, and let the dog in now.

First off, always keep in mind that your chart is a map of the Cosmos as it was when you arrived, a stellar photograph that freeze-frames the galaxy. So logically, you'll always find every planet, as well as the Sun and the Moon, in every chart. Each planet represents the **source** of a particular type of energy within us. Mercury's where we get our communication energy, Venus is where love and appreciation originate, and so forth. There are no "good" energies or "bad" energies, and no "good" or "bad" planets. And I repeat, the **planets don't "do" anything**. **We do.** We use our planets as we see fit. They're the cookie jars we stick our hands into when we're attending to a particular human **urge** or **need**. It's not their doing when things go well, and it's not their fault when things don't.

The Initial Disclaimer

My style of teaching is to create a mental picture for you, to paint a portrait of a planet by reminding you of a type of person I know you're familiar with, who I feel best embodies most of the qualities and energies of a particular planet. Call them Archetypes, if you like—or cartoons. Regardless, these images come with genders attached, so most of my planetary portraits do, too. However—just because I've described a planet by using a masculine or feminine character doesn't mean you can't operate yours unless your gender "matches." You can, and you do. All the time. Both men and women are built with both masculine and feminine "parts," and we do a nice job with all of them. The idea behind the Planetary Caricatures I've drawn is simply to make you **feel** a planet's energies—and some planets inarguably "feel" more "masculine" or more "feminine" than do others.

You may also find that my descriptions of the planets are somewhat lighter in tone than others before me. That's probably true. Please don't imagine that I don't take astrology seriously because of my tone. I do. But although Counseling with astrology is a Very Serious business, Learning Astrology doesn't have to be. See, Humor conjures the Archetypes. That's what stand-up comics and sit-coms and your hysterically funny neighbor have in common: they all have a knack for recognizing an Archetype in its latest disguise, and making light of us when we act that Archetype out in dysfunctional ways. In other words, they mimic us at our worst and make us laugh. While we're laughing, we get to really "see" ourselves. To become conscious of our behavior. And that's what it's all about.

I'm also going to assign Titles to each planet to let you know which type of energy is handled by which planet. In fact, I've made each planet the head of a Department in a very busy corporation—You. The Sun, of course, is the Executive Director of You, so all of the Department Chairs, although important in their own right, absolutely must answer to the Sun. All that said, it's time to meet your staff.

The 'Inners'

The planets are traditionally divided into what we call "Inner Planets" and "Outer Planets." The "inner planets" are comprised of the Sun, the Moon, Mercury, Venus, Mars, Jupiter, and Saturn. They function like a company's shareholders, so they're concerned with your personal needs—like love, possessions, anger, and growth. For this reason, the inner planets are also known as the **personal planets**. The sign they "wear" says an awful lot about your personal style—**the way you do the things you do**.

The 'Outers' Uranus, Neptune, and Pluto

The "Outer Planets," on the other hand, function like The Board of Directors of your corporation. They're in charge of networking, mergers, and keeping the company up on current and future trends. They're not at all interested in individual personal comfort. They pull us, instead, toward Universal Concerns. So wherever the outer planets fall in our charts, we often feel a sense of "mission" or "duty." The more prominent they are in your chart, the more strongly you'll feel that you're here "for a reason."

These three are much more "driven" than the inner planets. They often take months to pass through a single degree, the same distance the Sun covers in a day. They connect us to our generations and to major life cycles. When considering the sign an Outer Planet is wearing, remember that a sign is like a costume a planet wears. Since the outers spend so long wearing a sign, they inspire a "style" of dress (sometimes quite literally), an **attitude** or **collective opinion** that's shared by that generation. Since they do represent **your interpretation** of a generational mindset, and since generational mind-sets change so drastically from one age-group to another, the **house** position of the outers is a very specific statement about how you handle change. The nature of the change described depends on which planet you're dealing with—Uranus, Neptune, or Pluto—and we'll talk about each of them in much greater detail at the end of this chapter.

Okay. That said, let's look at each of the planets—their personalities, some ways to "feel" each of them, and the parts of the body they correspond with. Since the Sun is the Executive Director, we'll go right to the top.

The Sun

Just as the Sun itself is the warmth at the center of the Solar System, the **Sun** in your chart is the spark at the center of your life. Your Sun is the piece of you that describes your *raison d'etre*— "reason for being." Although each of the other planets are important in their own right (since each symbolizes the urge or need to perform important functions), they all "take their orders," figuratively speaking, from the Sun.

You can think of the Sun as a vehicle. **We're** the drivers. The planets are different types of fuel we "feed" our vehicle as we encounter different types of terrain. Of course, as with any vehicle, the longer you own it, the better you become at knowing what type of fuel it performs best with, the more skilled you become at operating it, and the more certain you are of where to reach to find the wipers or the light switch. The word that sums all this up, of course, is maturity, and maturity is "learning" your Sun, gradually "growing into" the person you're supposed to be.

FEELING THE SUN

Let's do an exercise: pretend I just walked up to you and said, "Who are you?" First, you'd tell me your name, because it's the most basic part of your **identity**—your own personal Designer Label. Your name distinguishes you from everyone else in the town, in the club, and in the room. It gives clues to at least half of your ethnic background, and if it's hyphenated, it might even show your marital status. So there's really **plenty** in a name.

If I asked who you really **were**, though, underneath your label, you'd give me your occupation next—what you "do" on a daily basis. Since what we "do" amounts to about a third of our lives, it usually reflects **who** and **what** we think we are—how we see ourselves.

Now, if I pushed the subject past name, rank, and serial number, you'd have to concentrate on your **qualities**—your traits—and that's when all the good words would come out. So let's push it—go ahead, pick ten qualities, ten words that perfectly describe **you**, the You you'd be if you never again had to do anything you weren't really excited about doing. Those ten words will describe your Sun—by sign, especially, but also by house. Try it. It works. The reason it works is because the Sun's signature is on every corner of your chart—it pervades every planet and shows up in every house. The Sun shows your **Basic Motivation**—your life's quest.

Everyone's Sun has the same goal: to shine. To accomplish Something Important, and be recognized for it. There's a television commercial out there that's specially designed with that Need to Be Important in mind. It's the Army commercial—the one that tells you to "**BE** all that you can **BE**—Keep on reaching, Keep on growin'—Find your future...." The music is designed to get you up and out of your chair, just marching around the room, primed to **GO**, to **DO**, to **ACCOMPLISH**. It's stimulating. Exhilarating. And effective. An aerobic class for your pride. You can't help but feel your Sun rev when you hear that music and listen to the words. Leave off the last line of the song—about joining the Army—and you've got a perfect description of what it feels like to keep on reaching for **your maximum potential.** That's what life is all about—reaching and growing, constantly finding our futures—and that's what the Sun in our charts is all about; it's the side of us that's always eager for tomorrow.

Now, if you haven't lived on this corner of the planet for the last twenty years of your life, you may have avoided that commercial and its catchy little tune. In that case, think of the Sun as your Ego—your need for attention. Just as too much sun on an August afternoon gets you a sunburn, a Sun that's "over-amped" often pumps out too much personality—which translates into words like "pompous" and "egotistical," and can produce a personality that needs to grab center stage, even at the risk of "scorching" those around it; like a child misbehaving to get Dad's attention, no matter what the cost.

And speaking of Dads, since the Sun represents our Yang energy (the "masculine" side of us), it's also a good indication of the type of relationship we had with our Dad, or whoever our first male role model happened to be. See, masculine energy equates with Self-Assertion. How we assert, then, as we grow older is strongly affected by how we remember the male principle being demonstrated while we were growing up. And it's not limited strictly to ourselves, either. Whether we're male or female, we see our expectations of a male role model over and again through life in our relationships with men.

Now, each planet has "jobs" to do on the physical level—organs and body parts it's in charge of. As Executive Director of You, the Sun's job, first of all, is to represent the health of the body as a whole, and its ability to resist sickness and disease. In general, are you robust, delicate, or somewhere in between? Overall vitality—the amount of energy you're used to putting out on a regular basis—is shown by the Sun's condition.[1] The Sun also specifically "rules" (or "has jurisdiction over") the heart, the back, and the circulatory system.

---

1 "Condition" is an astrological term that describes how a planet feels about how the other planets are treating it—that is, is it being assisted or challenged by the relationships it has with the rest of the Board? (More on that in "Aspects," Chapter Six.)

Each planet also has an Earthly representative, a particular metal whose physical properties best embody the planet's **essence**. The Sun's built-in affinity is with gold, of course, that rich, royal, and regal metal. And just as pure gold is the most valuable of elements, learning to express You is the most valuable of traits. In other words, to "do" your Sun, to make yourself really happy, just do what comes naturally. As Joseph Campbell said, "Follow your bliss."

The Moon

Moonlight on the water. A silvery patch that shivers, changes, and fades. If you really want to feel the Moon, get close to some water on a clear night, and stare right up at her. The Moon **invites** us to look—especially when she's full. She hypnotizes us and makes us sigh. She's the ultimate feminine energy. She's kept us mesmerized for centuries, inspired countless love songs, and provided just the right mood for more than one tender question. And still, despite the fact that she's the Queen of subtlety, romance and dreams, her effect on human behavior is "real" enough to prompt emergency rooms and police stations to routinely schedule extra staff when she's full. 'Cause folks certainly do tend to act up.

Not bad for a satellite, hmmm?

Of course, this isn't just any satellite—she's **our** satellite. As Dusty Bunker says, the Moon "circles the earth like a protective mother hen." And just as the Sun shows how we viewed our relationship with Dad, the Moon represents the symbolic way we see our relationship with our Moms—or whoever it was that "mommed" us. The Moon is your inner mother. Your nurturer. Your caregiver. Think of her as the head of the Security Department of your corporation. She knows what's Good for you—what's "safe" emotionally and where you'll feel secure. She's what you use to gauge the "Comfort Level" of all new situations. Most of the time, she's silent, but if you ever start to imagine her as unimportant, think of how the mood you're in can either make or break your day.

In your chart, the Moon represents the inner you, the person who, rather than acting out or acting on, as the Sun does, reacts to what happens around you. The side that **feels** and responds to what happens. Your Moon shows how you cope when you're hurt—where you'll go to lick your wounds.

In addition to her role as head of the Security Department, the Moon has two "specialties:" Change and Constancy. Yes, that certainly does sound contradictory, but it's not—it's just the way she operates, somehow simultaneously erratic and stable. She grows, has her fill of the Sun's light, then wanes. She rests and hides through the New Phase, and then gradually reappears. She has moods. And mood swings. And feelings that can be hurt. She changes, certainly, but the changes are predictable. Recordable. And constant.

In the body, the Moon rules the breasts, the ovaries, and the womb, all necessary for creating and nurturing an infant. Overall, she's the planet to check for the health of the emotional body and, since she specializes in subtlety, she also rules the fluids in our bodies, the internal ocean that keeps us alive.

The Moon corresponds with silver, a metal long associated with The Goddess. The **reflective** qualities of the Moon find physical expression in the **reflective** quality of silver, too—it's the metal used to create mirrors.

Mercury

Every corporation has an Executive Secretary, an unsung hero/ine who keeps tabs on everyone in the corporation, who makes sure not only that everyone **knows** their job, but also that they **do** their job. A combination Scribe, Scriptwriter, and Spokesperson, you might say. An Internal Switchboard. Well, meet yours. If you can catch him—or her—that is. Because this is one **busy** planet. And one planet that's highly underrated, too.

It's easy to take Mercury for granted. This planet is so good at the job, you never notice it's working. Your Mercury keeps you up on What's Happening Out There around you without any **conscious** effort on your part. It's the side of you that lives totally in The Present, that's always on "Scan." Your Mercury is always alert to shifts in Your Environment. Which includes big changes—in location, for example—but more subtle changes, too. Temperature and light, for example, are under Mercury's jurisdiction. When you decide it's time to put on a sweater or take off your shades, it's your Automatic Pilot mechanism that reminded you to do it, the part of you that's got the world memorized, who performs familiar tasks without stopping to think about how.

And speaking of the telephone, think of how long it would take to answer a call, speak to the caller, and leave a message for your roommate if you had to consciously plan **every** body movement and choose every phrase, right from the time you realized what that ringing noise was. Mercury handles all that—it's a built-in Efficiency Expert, on call 24 hours a day, always familiar with Your Routine, always ready to handle the preliminary details that free you up to Cut to the Chase. Like I said, a very busy planet.

To do all this, Mercury needs to be able to help You **bridge the gap** between You and Your environment, to provide the energy that allows you to think, speak, exchange a knowing glance, walk from point A to point B, gesture, and understand a symbol. Quite the job description—and that's just for starters. See, whenever you do any of those things, you're **communicating** with your environment. Any time you have a conversation, change locations, listen, or consider something, you affect your immediate environment. And that's Mercury's specialty—the Right Here and the Right Now.

To really get at a planet's meaning, it's fun to take a peek at its myth—it's like looking at an archetype through The Story of Its Life. Mercury's story is particularly interesting because his job duties haven't changed all that much. As Messenger of the Gods, Mercury shuttled messages back and forth between Gods and Mortals. In our charts, Mercury shows how we **translate**, how we shuttle information back and forth from Out There to Here. Your Mercury shows how you think, how you reason, how you make sense of things.

Since neither Gods nor Mortals have ever been notoriously good at Patience, Mercury had to learn to move fast. In fact, since he literally had to "think on his feet," he needed wings. A pair on his head and a pair on his feet. Now, if that image sounds really familiar, but you can't quite remember from where, check out the figure on the FTD sticker next time you're in a flower shop. Yep. It's Mercury, still doing his job, "running" from one florist to another, carrying bits of information from one place and getting it to another place—ASAP. FTD is so fond of Mercury, matter of fact, that they named their computer network after him. As did GM when they decided to name a whole line of cars "Mercurys."

In the body, Mercury's job is the same—to transmit messages. It's natural, then, that it be in charge of the body's Central Nervous System, the Internal Switchboard that lets your eye and your hand collaborate.

The metal Mercury corresponds with is, of course, Mercury, and it's a great match. Next time you break a thermometer, try to pick up **only** the Mercury from the floor. And good luck. Because just as your Mercury never stops collecting data, those little beads won't ever come back without the dog hair, crumbs or grains of dirt they collected along the way.

MERCURY RETROGRADE— AND RETROGRADES IN GENERAL

Every so often the person who does the astrological forecast on the radio in the morning will announce that Mercury's about to go Retrograde. Usually this news is accompanied by a warning of some kind, a reminder to get all important papers signed beforehand, and make all your travel plans ahead of time, too. Which makes the Retrograde sound much scarier than it really is. So while we're in the neighborhood, let's talk about what "Retrograde" really means, first with respect to Mercury and then as it applies to all the other planets, too.

You'll know that a planet in your chart is retrograde if it has an "r" or an "℞" symbol printed after it. (For example: ♂ 2 ♎ 47 ℞ means "Mars is at 2 Degrees of Libra and 47 minutes, moving retrograde.) Literally, "retrograde" means "backwards," and although none of the planets really throw their engines into reverse and back up, all of them appear to, periodically, from the earth's perspective. The example astrologers are fondest of using to explain The Retrograde Phenomena is to have you picture yourself on a train, looking out the window at a person on a horse just ahead. Since the train is moving faster than the animal, it will eventually "pass" it. If you want to keep watching the horse, you'll have to turn around in your seat and look backwards to do it. And that's what happens with Mercury—every three months for three weeks, it appears to be moving backwards, and we're forced to turn around to "see" it.

And there lies the rub. Because when the Head of the Communication Department is behind us, we may not pay attention to The Details as closely as we usually do, and those details may not be tended to as well as they usually are. You can just imagine what goes on at your local newspaper, where Getting Information Out Quick is the order of the day. When Mercury's Retrograde, typos can go unseen by the Spell Checker a bit more easily because they're so cleverly disguised. (See, Hermes, the original Trickster, was one of Mercury's early aliases...)

And it's not just the written word that falls victim to the Trickster. Communication involves meeting with others, too, so when Mercury's Retrograde, our timing in general may feel "off." We miss appointments due to circumstances beyond our control. Sometimes it's because we "heard" wrong, and wrote down the wrong directions. Sometimes we were **given** the wrong directions. Or we leave them on the kitchen table and don't realize it until we're an hour away from home—and the phone number to call is on the same piece of paper. Sometimes perfectly responsible people just "forget" their appointments. Fortunately, everyone seems to have similar problems during these times, so folks tend to be a bit more sympathetic than usual when you show up a half-hour late—even if you are a Sag, and you're always, always late, anyway.

So that's what Mercury Retrograde **is**—and **why** it is. We'll also cover **how** it is, if you own it, next. But what's the point? Do we have to just find a place to hide—for three weeks—when Mercury reverses direction? Aren't all energies good for **something**? Well, they certainly are, and Mercury Retrograde is no exception. Astrologer Erin Sullivan recently noted that the ratio of time Mercury spends Direct and the time it spends in Retrograde— roughly a third of its cycle—corresponds with the amount of time we spend awake and asleep—about a third of our lives. An interesting concept.

We need to rest, because we need time to **assimilate** all the experiences we've accumulated, to shuffle data around inside our minds and get it to the right department for storage. Remember, we never truly forget anything—we just stash some things further away from the surface than we do others. So, since Mercury is in charge of Communications, its retrograde period is like a **collective** Dream-Time.

Mercury Retrograde, then, isn't "bad"—it just takes some planning to cooperate with the energies. It's meant to be spent assimilating experiences, **re**viewing the past, and **re**doing, in general. Matter of fact, if you really want to get the most out of a retrograde, confine your activities as much as possible to those that have "re" attached to the beginning of the word. **Re**-schedule appointments, repair vehicles, **re**turn to the past, **re**-write documents and agreements, and so forth.

And If You're the Proud Owner of Mercury Retrograde
Contrary to popular opinion, being born when Mercury was retrograde doesn't mean you'll automatically be quiet, shy, or tongue-tied. It **does** mean that you'll **think** before you open your mouth—maybe just a couple of seconds longer than the average bear. See, whether you realize it or not, you came in with a keen understanding of What Could Go Wrong Here. You've learned to be prepared for any eventuality. Which makes you a natural trouble-shooter.

Other Folks, however, often **aren't** into trouble-shooting. So you may notice a tendency of others around you to let you do all the planning for them. You may also notice that during Mercury Retrograde, things go more easily for you—as if the rest of the world is finally operating on the same warp speed as yours.

As for The Others...
Now, all of the **planets** have retrograde periods—the Sun and the Moon do not. We've talked about how Mercury's Retrograde affects Mercury's performance, but isn't there some type of "blanket statement" we should be able to make about Retrogrades in general, or maybe some key-words we can toss together?

Well, yes. First off, remember that when they're retrograde, planets are assimilating. Going over what's happened. Gathering their strength and filing away experiences. In a nutshell, being **born** with a planet retrograde means you're doing **internal** work with that planet. It can also mean that you're "clearing the decks" in the life department that particular planet is in charge of. You're always ready for Stage Two, in other words.

Now, since any planet is more potent when it's wearing its own sign, or a sign it's especially fond of, it stands to reason that planets "rest" easier in their own signs. So a planet that's retrograde in its own sign is "sleeping" more soundly and more comfortably in that sign, just as we sleep better in our own beds. Which means its energies may be really "withheld" during the retrograde period. Doesn't mean it's not working, however, any more than our **brains** aren't working while we're asleep. Again, it's just the **assimilation** season in the planet's cycle.

Stations—Retrograde and Direct

Now, here's a tiny lesson on Celestial Mechanics. Just a tiny one, I promise, with no calculators necessary, a quick explanation of how planets do The Retrograde, and how they do The Direct. See, before planets "change" direction, whether it be from direct to retrograde, or vice-versa, they appear to slow down to what will eventually be a complete "stop." Again, it's like driving a car— you've got to stop before you can change from reverse to drive, or drive to reverse. Well, that point of "stopping" before changing direction is called a planet's station, and that's when its significance is the strongest. Stationary planets are, in effect from Earth's perspective, standing still—so they indicate a strong focus on the spot where they've stopped.

If you were born when a planet was stationary, it's important to notice whether the planet was about to go direct or retrograde. If it's on its way to a retrograde period, it's winding down. So its attention span won't be what it usually is and matters that pertain to that planet's Department, then, may take your natal planet a little longer to "get." This is why folks often say that Natal Retrograde Planets take longer to develop their energies than Direct planets do—not because they're really "slow," but because they're a little slower to express outwardly than are Direct Planets.

On the other hand, if your stationary planet is about to go direct, it's reorienting to its environment, just like you do every morning. Understand that although this planet is going to need a jump-start to get going, matters under its jurisdiction are going to be very important to you. So pay special attention to it, always. And don't give it anything challenging to do until it's had its coffee.

See, when a planet goes direct, it symbolically signals a "new beginning." The cycle[2] isn't complete, however, until the planet returns to the degree where it originally went retrograde—'til it retraces its steps, that is. The most important thing to remember is that retrogrades happen so that we can rest after periods of

2 For more on planetary cycles, see *Astrocycles*, by Vivian B. Martin, Ballantine Books, 1990.

Forward March. So rest. Revamp. Assimilate. And, if you were born with a retrograde planet or two, make sure you give yourself plenty of Dreamtime as a matter of course.

Venus

Scientists have supposedly proved that purring doesn't mean a cat is pleased and happy. Not at all. Well, I beg to differ. In my humble opinion, purring certainly does **seem** to accompany some pretty cushy moments in a cat's life, a signal that everything's just fine, thank you, and that you, the human, have finally found the right spot behind the ear. So next time your cat starts to purr, forget What Scientists Say and, instead, try to imagine how **good** it must feel In There for that wonderful sound to just come rolling out. Because, just between you and me, I believe purring may well be the purest symptom of **contentment** out there—and that's Venus' specialty. She's the Queen of contentment, satisfaction, and pleasure. All the Nice stuff. In fact, Venus' official title is Head of the Department of All Nice Things.

Now, when I say she specializes in "Nice" things, I'm talking **really** nice. All your favorite things, in fact. Venus' spot in your chart shows what you love and how you love it. Cats, maybe. Or chocolate. Your new Significant Other. A great big pillow. Whatever. Anytime you find yourself smiling just because you feel so **good**—well, that's your Venus. Purring.

Now, since Venus is the part of us that loves to be **pleased** in some way, and since we humans do love to feel good, physically, it's not "bad"—within reason, of course—to allow our hedonistic sides to enjoy the physical and material pleasures Venus rules. Money buys experiences, and experience is why we take up residence inside these bodies. Venus is in charge of **attracting** all our favorite things for us. She holds the purse-strings, so whatever we feel **belongs** to us in some way, whatever we feel **adorns** us or makes us more beautiful also falls under her jurisdiction.

Of course, we can also be pleased aesthetically—through art, for example, and music. So whether that warmth that just spread across your chest is due to a glorious sunset, a few words from The Beloved on the answering machine, or the Firebird you just drove off the lot, if it makes your heart thump when you hear it or look at it, that's Venus.

Know how you feel when your favorite Aunt pecks you on the cheek and calls you Honey? Know how you smile when somebody walks by you on the street wearing her perfume? **That's** Venus, too. That wonderful warm buzz, that feeling that your heart's just been hugged? That's your Venus, one of the more delightful fringe benefits that come with these bodies.

Now, Feeling Nice leads to Being Nice—adapting your behavior to make it pleasing to The Other, that is. So Venus is also in charge of reminding you of Your Manners. She emerges when you need to engage in Charming Small Talk, Light Chit-chat, and Social Niceties. The Weather is a very Venusian topic. See, Venus loves social situations where folks don't come together for any other point than to enjoy each other's company. At times, that may mean Avoiding The Issue, another Very Venus Thing To Do. See, The Lady believes in Peace—at all costs. So she's not above lying if it will avoid an unsightly scene. The best thing to keep in mind when an urge like that one hits is that, with just a little more effort, you can use Venus to tell the truth—**sweetly**.

Now, Venus is also Head of the Relationship Department, since you've got to be **with** someone to **use** that Nice, polite side you've been polishing up. She's the urge that drives you out on a Saturday night to try to find your "other half." She's the inner need to couple that makes you want a partner, sometimes at any cost.

You'll recognize Venus easily at the very beginning of a relationship, when you're on your best Well-Mannered behavior, when absolutely **everything** The Beloved does is **just fine** in your mind, no matter what It is. Walk across your back? Sure, fine. Sit through a Double-Header? You betcha. Venus, matter of fact, can even be a bit deceiving at the beginning of a relationship, mainly because she completely disguises Mars.

In the body, Venus is in charge of the sensory organs, our bodies' receptors, the spots that tell us what feels good and what doesn't.

Her earthly representative is copper, a metal that mixes easily with all other metals, that wears pastels well when it's heated. Copper is a perfect "alloy"—which sounds an awful lot like "ally," you know, and the lady **is** into partnerships, after all.

Mars

Okay. It's time to meet our next contestant. Get ready, gang, because here he is, the Head of the Department of Mess With Me and You Die, the Dude with the Attitude, the guy who makes very, very sure that nobody, but **nobody** steps on your blue suede shoes—and lives to talk about it... let's have a really enthusiastic welcome for Mars, The Red Planet.

Here's the side of you who just won't take it any more, who challenges when threatened, who fights back when you feel like you're under attack. Your Mars is a One-Planet Swat Team, a warrior all done up in red, feet planted squarely in fighting stance, sword drawn and ready to go. Your Mars is your hit-man, your own personal "Rambo." Your Sigourney Weaver, even. Your Mars is brave, fearless, and courageous. When someone offends you and you're trying to decide whether to retaliate with the bomb or the pearl-handled pistol, it's Mars' call.

Now, although there's a lot more to Mars than anger, the easiest way to recognize him, at least at first, is to think of how we describe anger—because most of the images we use involve the image of fire. "Hot under the collar." "Seeing red." "All fired up." When the switch to your Mars gets flipped, you're ready to do anything to avenge yourself—regardless of whether or not you're physically strong enough to handle The Offender. Mars doesn't consider size, strength, or the odds. See, Mars is the force of your will. It's the push that gets you across the finish line because you want to finish, whether or not it's humanly possible. Your Mars is your drive to compete, your urge to win.

Like the fire element it's built of, Mars is a truly spontaneous energy, a bundle just waiting to "blow." And it's pretty easy to spot Mars even when we're not using it—when we're angry but we can't act, for example. Ever get so mad that you shake? That's Mars, too. See, Mars is in charge of adrenaline, which is manufactured by the body in times of extreme stress—so if you need an extra push of energy to take care of yourself, you'll have it. When someone yells at you, your Mars reacts as if you're about to be attacked, and turns on the adrenaline machine. You become super-charged with Fight Back energy. If you don't use that energy, it doesn't just go away.

In fact, unless you give yourself a very strenuous physical task to accomplish, unless you give your Mars a Project, that is, he'll just find a whole bunch of victims to give a little poke to, in lieu of the one who earned it. It may take him a day or even a week to get rid of all of it. Doesn't matter. Your Mars will out—no matter what it takes—one way or another.

Of course, like I said earlier, Mars isn't just how you "do" anger. Your Mars describes how you "do" all your actions—it's The Way You Take Action, matter of fact. Anytime you do anything, anytime you push, pull, yank, swim, or glide, whenever you change your environment to suit your tastes, instead of the other way around, your Mars is what you reach for. Now, since Mars rules the muscles in the physical body, Mars does have a tendency to "strong-arm" its way into a situation, to stir up a bit of dust so you can get Your Way. He does tend to get a little Pushy at times—he's even been known to shove. But nothing gets done unless he okays it. He's the spark plug that gets you going, the way you Go Off In Pursuit of what you want.

As far as metals go, there's really only one that would do for Mars. When you are a weapon, you need a good strong representative, so Mars absolutely insists on Iron and Steel. Which makes sense—guns (also known as firearms) are made of iron and steel, as are knives, machinery, and cars. All those things are used by us to exert our will over What's Out There, and that's what Mars is all about.

Jupiter

Of all the planets, Jupiter's reputation is the best. He's known as "The Greater Benefic," to start with. He's the Head of the Department of Generosity, Abundance, Joviality, and Laughter. Oh—and Excess. But we'll get to that. For now, picture Jupiter as benevolent and merry, a laughing King on his throne, an authority figure with a sense of humor who won't send you to the dungeon if you promise to tell a really good story at Court. Remember Venus, your favorite Aunt? Well, Jupiter's your favorite Uncle, the guy with the rather sizable midsection who talks too much, laughs too loud, and wears too much after-shave. The guy who, despite all that, you can't help but love—he's got a heart as big as a watermelon—and a credit-card tab to match.

Jupiter does **everything** in a very Big Way. He's all about Making Things Bigger—about pushing past walls. Jupiter represents what prompts you to take a chance, to risk, to try something new, just **because** you've never tried it. And there's a reason for that Urge To Experience New Stuff. It often comes to us disguised as a beast called Boredom, and when it rears its restless little head, it's because it's time for you to stretch, to **grow**, to **expand** your horizons. To boldly go where you've never gone before. Expansion, in fact, is one of Jupiter's **very** favorite words.

Needless to say, Jupiter is your built-in Advertising Department, the piece you take out when you extend to others. Let's go back to the corporation analogy for a minute. If you want your company to grow, you need to go out and Network. You need to mingle with other folks. So, dammit, you'll just **have** to Travel. And Confer. And Mingle. Oh, sure, it's tedious, traveling to faraway places, meeting new people every month, but, hey—somebody's got to do it. Well, that's your Jupiter's function—to get You out there, to introduce You, to "sell" You to Your World—no matter how far you have to go—literally and figuratively—to do it.

Since Jupiter's all about Reaching Out And Touching Someone, it's no wonder that his spot is a place where you'll go out of your way to be generous, where you'll give for no reason, where you'll practice Random Acts of Kindness, as they say. Consequently, when you run around acting like Santa Claus, you get treated like you're Santa Claus. So your Jupiter side will bring you luck—literally—all of the time, though oftentimes not so's you'd notice.

Now, as with all good things, there's a flip side to this coin, and, as I said earlier, it involves the matter of Excess. Of having too much, going too fast, and blowing things out of proportion. Anytime you overdo anything, it's because your Jupiter overate. So words like "Too," "Very," and "Most" are the exclusive property of Jupiter, as are "More" and "Better." Being extravagant, wasteful, and excessive are symptoms of a Jupiter that's out of control, gobbling up everything in its path.

Still, much as Jupiter certainly can be misused to the nth degree, when polled, nine out of ten folks will take a transit from Santa Claus over a transit from one of The Others any day. So although it's become quite fashionable to bash The Big Guy of late, let's let him keep his "Good" reputation. Let's try to keep our appetites in check, and not blame him when we don't. After all, it's not easy being a King.

Now, since Jupiter's so fond of expanding, he handles the growth of the physical body. Which certainly does include "growing" an extra pound or two where you don't want it. Since he's in charge of Networking, too, he correlates with the liver in the body, the organ that filters what we take in.

Saturn

Say Hello to Saturn, the Old-Nay Sayer himself, a rather gaunt gentleman who always stands with his arms folded and his hands tucked neatly under his elbows. His wardrobe consists of two very conservative suits and one Skeptical Expression, and no matter what you just said, he'll have to shake his head doubtfully before he answers. You may hear him laugh, but you'll be hard-pressed to catch him smile. He bears a striking resemblance to that schoolmaster of olde, Icobod Crane, and just like Icobod, he makes you feel like you've got to sit up really straight when he's in the room.

As per his title, Saturn's favorite word is "No"—but he likes "Wait," "Stop," and "Don't" pretty well, too. 'Course, he's in charge of Just Saying No. He's the Head of the Department of Don't you Dare, You Better Not, and Just Wait 'til I Get to Your Midheaven. He believes in thrift; his motto is "Quality doesn't cost, it pays," and he never, ever forgives a debt. Neither a Borrower nor a Lender be—that's what Saturn always says.

Now, Saturn's got a really heavy reputation to tote around. He's been delegated the rather unpopular task of uncovering our limitations, of telling us what we can't do. 'Course, we humans don't **like** that much at all, but, hey—**Somebody's** Got To Do It. Someone's got to give us a good Reality Check when we get a little too Jupiter-ized. Matter of fact, that phrase pretty much sums up Saturn and his affiliation with the "R" word—Responsibility, that is. Someone's Got To Do It—someone's got to take care of whatever It is, of the Business At Hand. And Saturn's always happy to take care of business.

Now, as I said, Saturn deals with Reality, with how life really is, **as is**—totally unembellished. It's this ability to see reality so clearly that makes him perfectly aware of just how capable you really are. So when you don't do something as well as you could have—and you know it—he shakes his finger and scolds you for it. Doesn't matter if you've done a 98% perfect job. This planet is your conscience with a capital "C," the old-fashioned, traditional piece of you that Does Things That Way because We've Always Done Them That Way, **that's** why, and he won't settle for 98%. Saturn insists that you be true to yourself, that you do absolutely everything you can to finish a job right. He's the Wilford Brimley that lives inside you, telling you whether or not your next move is "The right thing to do."

Needless to say, when it came time to decide who'd be in charge of The Rules and The Laws, Saturn raised his hand. And that's just as it should be. As resident expert on What's Normal Around Here, wherever Here is—and what's not—he frowns, Big Time, on behavior that's not Socially Acceptable. And he knows how to set penalties for breaking those Rules.

But there's a softer side to Saturn, too. Picture an Indian Grandmother, slow but strong, wise with a sureness that only the experience of many years can bring. This side of Saturn teaches us that in the long run, you get exactly what you've earned. This side of Saturn tries to teach her wayward grandchildren the virtues of patience, endurance, and self-control.

Now, sometimes that means returning you to "Go" if you don't deserve the $200 yet. Not all lessons are learned easily, you know, and unfortunately, the tough ones really are the ones that stick. Saturn's not out to be unkind to you, however. Only to teach you The Right Way. Saturn is about Decency. Respectability. Integrity, too. Saturn's in charge of all kinds of structures, from the Main Beams in a house to the bones in your body, structures that determine, in the long run, whether something stands or crumbles. That's where the Integrity comes in. If it's not done right, it'll collapse when it's tested—so it has to be done right. Pretty heavy responsibilities—so you can see why Saturn needs to be such a stickler for details. Now remember you own a Saturn, so, somewhere in life, it's your job to Do It Right, too—whatever It is.

Sometimes the weight of all those details and all that Responsibility makes us feel like there's a block in our chart wherever Saturn is, an invisible stone wall that stops us from accomplishing what we really want most to do, when in fact, it's only ourselves that stop us—our fear of failure. It may even seem easier to tell ourselves that we **can't** do what our Saturn wants us to do, rather than to try and risk failing. 'Course, the easy thing to do isn't always the **right** thing to do... is it?

The skin and the bones are the structures that keep our bodies together—internally and externally—so they're both affiliated with Saturn. Lead is the metal that works with Saturn. A rather nice fit, too, since lead is strong but malleable, dull on the outside but quite shiny when it's worked with. And there's the key to Saturn: work on it and it will shine.

THE SATURN RETURN

Now, Saturn takes 29½ years to come full circle in our charts, and it's that point that's called The Saturn Return. It's a rite of passage, you might say, a time when we symbolically take our Official Adulthood Entrance Exam. By that age, we've encountered quite a few "tests" en route to becoming a Grown Up, so Saturn's Return to its natal degree brings a test, a grade, and either a reward or a remedy. At this point you learn something about You. You're either on The Right Path—or you're not. We'll talk a whole lot more about the Saturn Return in Chapter Eight which discusses "Transits."

SATURN AND THE OUTER PLANETS

Now here's where the plot thickens, kids. See, once you've got a relatively good grip on what it is you actually need on a personal level via the Inner Planets, and once you've encountered the discipline, patience, and Reality of Saturn—which is how you earn what you need—well, once you understand all that, you're ready to experiment a little. With **Un**reality—via the Outer Planets.

I know this sounds confusing. What the heck is Unreality, for starters? Well, "Unreality" is 1) what hasn't happened yet, 2) what we don't expect to happen, and 3) what we can't control happening. "Unreality" is anything that takes us out of The Norm, in other words. So there are all kinds of experiences in our daily lives that are "Unreal." Bumping into your best friend from high school while you're off trekking in Nepal. Falling in love in an hour. Living through a divorce or the death of a loved one. And all those experiences are under the jurisdiction of The Outers, the three planets that orbit just beyond Saturn—Uranus, Neptune, and Pluto.

It's quite a club, this one. Exclusive, you might say. Just those three members (that we know of, at least), each of them a radical in their own way, each one a symbolic significator that it's time to jump-start your life—even when you don't realize, consciously, that you need it.

See, Saturn defends the existing order. That's a fine thing, of course, but we humans are not notoriously good at initiating change, so we tend to hold on to that existing order even when it's obvious that change is now necessary. That's where The Outers come in. Their contracts include a "Make Things Change" clause and that's what we all do, periodically. Basically, they all serve as antitheses to Saturn's energy. They enjoy their work, too, albeit for different reasons.

Saturn and Uranus
Uranus despises the existing order—no matter what it is. He's a Mad Professor who constantly does battle with City Hall, tilts at Power Plants, and keeps trying to get everyone else to Change, Now—While There's Still Time. Uranus also has a habit of putting that Change in effect rather **suddenly**, which wreaks havoc on Saturn's beloved schedules, but has the effect of a Wake-Up call on your future.

Saturn and Neptune
Now, Saturn likes to deal with reality, with life as it really is, totally unembellished. Just the Facts, Ma'am. Neptune, on the other hand, hates facts. Facts make life dreary. There's no room for dreams in the Real World, no castles, knights or magic—and that's Neptune's specialty. She's a visionary, a mystical Goddess who can make something that's not real **seem** real—which makes Saturn crazy.

Saturn and Pluto
Saturn's a Wall-Builder, too, a reinforcer, constantly tending to a structure, firming, tightening up, and preserving The Past—at all costs. Pluto's idea of a Good Time is to toss the baby, the bath water, the tub the kid had the bath in, and maybe even the apartment where the bath took place. Saturn handles change by Just Saying No. Pluto, on the other hand, insists that we Just Let Go.

The job of The Outers, then, is to happily topple The Existing Order Saturn guards whenever possible. They inspire us to re-write our rules periodically. They describe moments of sudden change, when we decide it's time to stretch. To envision something new. They ask us to start over, and to do what we want to do this time. To forget the old rules and tap into The Dream.

The Outers as "Higher Octaves"

One more thing about The Outers. Each of them seems to correspond with one of The Inners, on a much larger scale. For example, Mercury is in charge of thoughts and communication—Uranus rules **futuristic** thoughts, computers, and Mass Communication. Venus rules personal love—Neptune rules **unconditional** love. Mars rules self-assertion and anger, the push of the ego over What's Out There—Pluto rules process, the destruction of old forms, the push of Inevitable Change—*en masse*—over What's Out There. Each Outer planet is called the Higher Octave of the Inner Planet, since it seems to magnify the energies of the Inner, to "reproduce" it on a grand scale, and make the energy accessible to all, rather than personally doled out to a select few.

Well. That's your warm-up for The Outer Planets. Now that you think you know what to expect, let's meet Uranus and change all that.

Uranus

Picture Uranus as an Ice-God with a mad, brilliant look frozen on his face. His robes crackle stiffly when he moves, like a sheet left out on the clothesline too long in February, and tiny icicles hang crookedly from the corners of his eyebrows. He's the Head of the Department of One Never Knows, and that's exactly what you can expect when he's around; the last thing you'd ever imagine. He's in charge of eccentricity and electricity, of lightning and tornadoes. He loves last-minute reversals and thrives on radical independence. He's the dude who sent Dorothy on that all-expense paid trip to Oz when things got too tight back at Auntie Em's place, the wild and crazy kid who talked you into your first cigarette when you were 15. Definitely not a boring planet.

Uranus challenges you to truly be You, to flaunt your oddities and eccentricities rather than trying to hide them. Uranus loves the odd, unusual, and off-beat, and his motto is "Personal Freedom at Any Cost." He never wears anything that Everyone Else is wearing, always has an idea that's jee-ust enough ahead of its time to be considered absolutely **mad**, and has been known to switch destinations after arriving at the airport. In a nutshell, he prides himself on being totally Unpredictable. A Wild Card. His energies transform the area of the chart he occupies into a place where—literally—Anything's Possible. And you've got one.

You can imagine what you're dealing with here. This is a spot where independence will be the order of the day. Individualism, too. There will be no "No's" here, because Uranus translates all "No's" into "I Dare You's," and all of **those** into invitations to Do Just That. So here's where Total and Complete Personal Freedom is the only way to go—regardless of the consequences. Uranus was discovered around the time of the French and American Revolutions, remember, and we never discover a planet until we're also ready to discover its principles inside ourselves. So Uranus in our charts shows us a place where we "tap in" to that need to be free, rebellious, and unfettered. We need to be Different here—at all costs. To shock and amaze the masses. And to Break Tradition. Because tradition reminds Uranus of a rut. And ruts are akin to death when you're into freedom like this guy is.

Now, speaking generationally, Uranus is the planet that's in charge of Science and Technology, of Space Stations and NASA, of new inventions, and of "Fads"—crazy stuff we mortals do, *en masse*, because it's temporarily Cool, that is. Purple hair, bungee-jumping, and pierced noses were all his idea to start with—but then, so were the Beatles. He's in charge of opening our collective eyes to what's new Out There, of getting us to wake up and smell the coffee.

Since he's a very airy kinda guy, Uranus is in charge of Mass Communications, and if he's really prominent in your chart, you may be involved in mass communication of some kind, too.

In the body, Uranus rules the involuntary nervous system, the "automatic" functions our bodies constantly perform. The beating of our hearts, for example, as well as digestion, breathing, and blinking all fall under Uranus' jurisdiction.

Neptune

See that pink smoke wisping out from under the door? That's Neptune. She makes her entrance just like that, a little bit at a time, ever so gradually, until, finally, she's infiltrated the room completely. Wherever she is in your chart, you, too, can infiltrate your environment easily, and you can be infiltrated, as well. See, her title is Head of the Department of Boundary-Dissolving and Alternate States, and she does it well. Picture her as a goddess in a long flowing gown, carrying a pink smoke machine with her wherever she goes, bewitching all who pass by. Her spot in your chart is a place where you'll always find your answers in Dreams, not reality.

Here's the side of you that's very soft, and very wistful. The piece of you who sighs and wishes. Who believes and daydreams. In fact, you may believe just about **anything** here—even what's not necessarily true—because this side of you always feels as if someone wonderful is rubbing your temples, singing you a lulla- by, and telling you that everything is already just exactly the way you want it to be. Magically. Forget reality. Neptune is your personal eraser, specially designed to remove all harsh lines and keep you happily enchanted in Never-Never Land. Temporarily, at least.

Neptune has long been associated with the concept of **glam- our**—what we think of today as artificial beauty. In The Olden Days, a "glamour" was a type of spell one would cast upon a per- son for the specific purpose of **changing their appearance**—on the surface, that is. It was a magical disguise, but only a tempo- rary condition. So when it "wore off," the person would return to their original physical form. The spell would be broken. And that's exactly how we operate our Neptunes when we've decided not to see the truth.

When you use your own Neptune to cast a spell, what you're really doing is reaching into the vault where you keep your magic pink dust—where your own personal power to cast A Glamour lives. You toss that sparkling pink stuff all over the object of your affections, be it Person or Situation, until it's coated in the stuff and completely unrecognizable in its present form. This magic dust has the ability to make The Object **appear** to be whatever you'd like it to be. Problem is, like I said, it doesn't last forever. Time passes, Things Happen, and reality inevitably arrives a lit- tle at a time as The Object moves around and the dust shakes off. When all the dust is gone and whoever or whatever was disguised in it has been returned to their original form, it can be like waking up from a great dream and finding reality a pretty disap- pointing place to be.

Now, Neptune can also be wonderful. If there's a good base coat of reality on The Object before the dust goes on, that is. In other words, your Neptune placement doesn't **have** to be a spot where you "lie" to yourself, or see things unrealistically and then become disappointed when reality rears its ugly little head. It can be a place where that urge to see things in a dreamy, romantic way makes you imaginative, sensitive, and caring. Where you use your magic to cast Special Moments into folk's memories. But it's a fine line.

See, Neptune's "real" job as Boundary-Dissolver is an important one—she's your respite, the place inside where you can go to wash away reality for a while—like a vacation resort. She can also erase the walls that separate us from each other and from our environments, and we need that, too. Neptune knows the truth—that we're all part of one world, that our world is part of one solar system, that our solar system is part of a heaven just Chock Full O' Other Solar Systems just like it, and that everything is really a part of The One. Neptune feels everything, then, since she is everything. It's not an easy job and you can see why she'd try to duck out the back door when she sees something especially hurtful coming. Reality? Uh uh. Take a hike, please. And take your data with you.

Generationally speaking, Neptune's sign reflects our opinions on What to Believe In—what we make Gods of, and what we outright **idolize**. Neptune also rules a generation's attitudes on drugs and alcohol—the ways it's currently hip to escape.

In the body, Neptune seems to co-rule fluids along with the Moon. She also has a connection with poisons, viruses and, consequently, with the body's immune system, which is how we keep our barriers intact.

Pluto

Here's the guy with the office in the basement, the guy who's in charge of Scary Stuff, who loves black, hates the spotlight, and always works Behind The Scenes. Here's Pluto, the Head of the Department of Death, Decay, Destruction, and other Unavoidables. A real fun kinda guy who looks a lot like Darth Vader. Now, Pluto's Favorite Topics don't make for what you'd call light dinner conversation: Death, for example. Sex. Reincarnation. No, Pluto isn't an easy planet, because he's not in charge of Maybe's. But he's not an Evil Demon Planet Bent on Your Destruction, either. He handles what absolutely **has** to happen. He disposes of situations that have gone past the point of no return, that absolutely must go.

He's a big, black, powerful figure. The dark side of The Force. Not necessarily the Bad side, you understand—the Dark Side.

It's often difficult to "own" your Pluto, however, because it means admitting to yourself that you **have** a Dark Side. That there really is a piece of your personality that would rather trash everything than just work it out. That's what Pluto's spot in our charts is like. It's an area of life where we'd just as soon toss everything and start all over. Where, as I said a couple pages back, we'll prefer to throw out the baby, the bath water, the tub the kid took the bath in, and the apartment where the bath took place.

The hardest—and most important—part to keep in mind is that this piece of you isn't **evil**, it's just intense. Power hungry, even. Ruthless, maybe. But certainly **not** evil. Pluto's into Power and Control. When something happens that puts you out of control, your Pluto steps in and starts figuring out what you might do to even things up a little. And you know, even when he's not enraged about something, he's still not an easy planet to handle because when he gets fixed on something, he just won't let it go. So here's where you're equal parts researcher, analyst and detective, where you tend to be extremely obsessive, and where you'll just love to dig.

In all, Pluto is an All-Or-Nothing kind of guy who's great at pushing stuff to the limit, at going to Extremes. He's not known for being especially sensitive to Humanity—but then, he has X-Ray Vision and can see the Master Plan, so it's difficult to fault his ends, even though his methods can be pretty tough to take.

The high side of Pluto is that this planet holds an amazing well of Concentrated, Transformative Energy. Your Pluto shows you a place where you are never, ever the same person from one moment to the next, where you're constantly in a state of evolution, where intense experiences are the order of the day because they're how you learn what "juice" is. Here's where you crave intensity. Most importantly, here's where you **understand** the importance of **process**.

The sign Pluto was in when you were born (and it spends, at the very least, 13 years in a sign), reflects your generation's attitudes about The Undiscussables—Sex and Death, for example, neither of which are quite so Undiscussable since Pluto hit Scorpio, its Home Turf, back in 1983. Recycling is also a Plutonian topic, however, as are Reincarnation, Regeneration, and Rejuvenation.

See, since Pluto rules **process**, birth, growth, death, and re-birth as a cycle are all under his jurisdiction. Pluto is also associated with the reproductive organs in the body and with sexual maturity. In fact, biological puberty is occurring much earlier since Pluto reached Scorpio, the "fast" end of the cycle.

Planetary Vital Statistics

No section on the planets would be complete without mentioning their "vitals," a few important facts about orbits, rotations, discoveries, and so forth. So for all of you out there who like Saturnine statistics, here goes:

SUN

Contrary to popular opinion, the Sun doesn't just sit there in the middle of the Universe—it moves. It rotates, matter of fact, and takes 28 days to do it. It's 870,331 miles in diameter and has an odd habit of periodically throwing out flares that disrupt radio waves here on earth. The Sun isn't really a planet, of course, it's a Star. Our star.

MOON

The Moon circles us in 27.32 days—everybody knows that, because it's where our modern "moonth" came from. But the Moon also rotates—at exactly the same speed as its orbit, too—27.32 days. Which means that the same side of the Moon always faces the Earth—hence the "Dark Side of the Moon" expression. The Moon is 2159.89 miles in diameter and "only" 252,698 miles away from us—which explains why it's the only Other Body Out There we've visited in person so far.

MERCURY

Mercury is just a bit larger than the Moon. It's all of 3031 miles across, with a rotation of 58.65 Earth Days, and an orbit of 88 days. Its retrograde period occurs every 3 months for about 3 weeks.

VENUS

The Lady Venus takes 224½ days to orbit the Sun. She is nearly the same size as Earth—7521 miles across, as compared to our 7926 mile waistline. Her rotational period is 243 Earth days and, just in case you weren't convinced about her connection to fuzzy Neptune, Venus has her very own cloud cover to hide behind, a shell that's jee-ust about 15 miles thick, that hovers 30 miles above the planet.

MARS
The Red Planet takes 687 days to orbit the Sun, and 24.62 hours to Do the Rotation. It's not terribly large—4212.28 miles in diameter—and yes, there really is a face on that planet that looks a lot like someone from this planet. Mars has two Moons of its very own. Phobos is about 15 miles in diameter, Deimos about 8 miles.

JUPITER
Just as the name suggests, this planet is, indeed, the "King." It's the largest planet in the heavens—appropriate enough for a planet whose job is exaggeration and Big Stuff. Jupiter is 88,650 miles in diameter, takes 12 years to do a loop about the Sun, and rotates at a breakneck speed of 9.84 hours. As the King of excess, it's not surprising to learn that Jupiter has 16 Moons of his very own.

SATURN
The Lord of the Rings is legendary, both for his amazing rings and for his 29½ year cycle that marks the rite of passage from childhood to adulthood. He also marks a point in the Universe where a line of sorts is drawn; he's the last planet that can be seen with the naked eye. Saturn is 74,565 miles in diameter, rotates in just 10.25 Earth hours, and has an elaborate collection of over 20 Moons to call his own.

URANUS
As enamored as he is with the concept of Personal Freedom, it stands to reason that Uranus would be Different than the other planets—physically, as well as symbolically. And well he is. First of all, he's the only planet that wears the name of a Greek God, rather than a Roman one. He's also got a rather odd habit of rotating backwards—on his side. His axial inclination, in fact, is 98 degrees. This wobbly rotation takes Uranus just 17.3 hours. His orbit amounts to 84 years. He's 32,116 miles across, and he's got at least 15 Moons. He was "discovered" in 1781 by William Herschel and actually went by that alias for a while.

NEPTUNE

Back in 1613, Galileo Galilei observed Neptune and recorded it. Neptune being who she is, however, Galileo was a bit confused about what it was he actually saw, and so he recorded it as a Fixed Star. Neptune remained Officially Invisible for a number of years, until 1846, when Heinrich Ludwig D'Arrest and Johann Galle decided they were observing the eighth planet. She is a lovely blue-green color, is 30,758 miles around, and has an orbit of 165 years. Her rotational period is 15.8 hours, and she has at least two Moons.

PLUTO

Pluto was identified by Clyde Tombaugh on February 18 of 1930. Long sought after by Percival Lowell, the man actually credited with its discovery, Pluto was actually photographed in 1915, and again in 1919, but apparently chose, as Neptune did, to remain anonymous for a while longer. A concentrated ball of energy, Pluto is tiny—just 1375 miles across—but takes 6.3 Earth days to rotate. Pluto's Moon is Charon, a body very close in size to Pluto whose rotation and orbit are also 6.3 Earth days.

CHAPTER THREE

YOUR CO STARS: CHIRON AND THE ASTEROIDS

In addition to the planets, there are a few other bodies you'll eventually want to add to your Astrological Repertoire, five personalities that will add a deeper, more complete dimension to your interpretations.

First, meet Chiron, who, at this writing, is officially a comet—a very big one—orbiting between Saturn and Uranus. He was discovered on November 1, 1977, and since that time has been demoted twice—from "planetoid" to "asteroid" and from "asteroid" to "comet." Admirably, Chiron's job performance didn't suffer in the least because of all this—in fact, he's our Metaphysical Chirurgeon General—and I'll tell you all about what happened to him in just a second.

The other four bodies astrologers work with are the four major asteroids: Ceres, Pallas Athena, Vesta, and Juno. Now, these asteroids have been used since January of 1973, when Eleanor Bach published the first asteroid ephemeris. Since that time, several books have been published on the asteroids, time has passed, and we've all had time to put them in our charts and get to know them better. They have a lot to do with different aspects of The Feminine and with women's issues.

Now, there are folks who are going to tell you to blow off anything but the traditional ten planets. They'll tell you that all the other bodies out there in the Solar System don't "work," and that you shouldn't waste your time with them. Well, fine, except we didn't even **find** Pluto until this century, so at one time there were only **nine** "traditional" planets and **Pluto** was on the "doesn't work" list. 'Course, as we know now, Old "Darth" is **far** from, um… "impotent," and nobody would even **think** of doing a chart without him. (Just in case he ever found out.) At any rate then, rather than tell you what you should and shouldn't believe in, I urge you to investigate **everything** and find your own truths. Really. Try everything.

What else is there? Well, we'll cover that in "Exclamation Points," Chapter Eleven. But it's wonderful that you asked.

End of lecture.

Okay. We'll start with Chiron—not because he's more important than the others, but simply because he's my personal favorite. When you write your own book, you can do this, too.

Chiron—First, The Vitals

So what **is** Chiron, anyway? And what's all the fuss about? Well, back in November of 1977, an astronomer named Charles Kowal spotted a rather large body cruising smoothly along between the orbits of Saturn and Uranus. Because of its color, Kowal believed the body to be either a "planetoid" or a wayward asteroid. He named the newcomer Chiron—and opened up a whole new door for astrologers.

Now, as recently as 1981, most researchers had Chiron filed safely away under "A" for asteroid, due mostly to the color he seemed to be. Although, to be honest, it certainly was odd to find a lone asteroid between Saturn and Uranus, especially since the path most of the other asteroids took around the Sun was the lane between Mars and Jupiter. Chiron was initially diagnosed as being "lost," a stray asteroid. Then, in 1988, a team of researchers at the University of Hawaii noticed that Chiron had nearly doubled in brightness since Kowal first spotted him. That type of torch-light couldn't belong to an asteroid; only comets were that bright. They began to search for a "tail"—the trademark of a comet.

Eventually, they found one. It was official; Chiron was, indeed, a comet. Not a planetoid, not an asteroid. Now, this Shape-Shifting is what made astronomers even more fascinated with

Chiron. Astrologers, however, took a step back, and crossed their arms. If Chiron was "only" a comet, was he really "worth" studying? There's no shortage of comets out there, after all, and it wasn't as if we didn't already have our hands full just trying to figure out what to do with our ten "traditional" planets. Did comets "count?"

Not to mention that, according to his myth, Chiron was a Centaur. We already **had** one Centaur, and we were pretty fond of him—even if he **did** tend to be a bit on the clumsy, pompous side. How was Sagittarius going to feel about this? Couldn't he sue if he really wanted to push it? And what were we supposed to give Chiron for keywords? All the good ones were gone. Pluto had Transformation, Saturn had Mastery, the Sun was The Hero, and Neptune was Sacrifice. How were we going to use Chiron if we couldn't describe him?

Well. The only thing to do was to go back to his myth, to take a little "history" on him and see what kind of guy he was. Here's his story.

Chiron—The Myth Behind The Man

Once upon a time, up on Mount Olympus, Saturn (of all Gods!) decided to be unfaithful to his wife. Seems he'd become smitten with a Sea-Nymph named Philyra, and, Saturn being Saturn, he intended to have her. The lady, however, didn't feel the same. We know this for a fact, because she changed herself into a horse to escape, and ran off. A pretty clear "No Thank You" in my mind.

Not to be put off, however, and since he is nothing if not persistent, Saturn chased Philyra down and "mated" with her anyway—at least, that's the word traditionally used for their encounter. Personally, I'm of the opinion that when only one person says "Yes, I'd like to mate," and the "mating" takes place anyway, it's not "mating" any longer, it's rape. So Philyra, for all intents and purposes, was raped by Saturn that day and became pregnant.

The child that was born was a true product of the "encounter," half human and half horse, divided at the waist. A Centaur. A wondrous oddity, but not an easy pill to swallow—especially since the child, no matter how "special," was the product of a rape. Needless to say, when she saw her child, Philyra was horrified. Regardless of the fact that she hadn't done anything wrong, she was positive that she was being punished and she implored the

Gods to change her into anything other than what she was to escape this monster child. They obliged. Philyra became a linden tree and Chiron became motherless. Of course, he was already fatherless, since Saturn had long since returned home to his wife, Rhea.

Now, this left our little hero all alone up there on top of Mount Pelion, wondering where his parents might be. Remember, at this point, he was just a colt. A wide-eyed baby. With no idea why everyone had rejected him before they'd even met him.

Well, it must have been awful for him. Illegitimate. Abandoned. Most kids would have gotten into trouble. But not this guy. He spent his time studying instead. He became an expert at lots of things, too. He played the lyre and learned the skills of healing and battle. He was said to be the first astrologer, as well. In time, his talents became the stuff legends are made of, and Chiron was sought after to foster the children of the Gods and Goddesses. Hercules, for example, was one of Chiron's pupils, as were Jason (of Golden Fleece fame), Achilles (of Achilles Heel fame), and Aesclepius (the Doctor). Regardless of how he was conceived, Chiron turned out to be a truly Special Kid—one who would've made any parent proud, given half a chance.

Chiron spent his life teaching, until one day when, as he handed an arrow to Hercules (an arrow dipped in a poison of his own invention), it fell from him and wounded him in the leg. The poison he had dipped Hercules' arrow into would have killed a mortal, but since his father was a God, Chiron was immortal and couldn't die.

He lived in agony with his wound for many years, trying to cure himself, still teaching when he could. Finally, Chiron gave up—he asked Zeus to free him, to allow him to die. Zeus agreed, and Chiron exchanged places with Prometheus. He was elevated to the heavens for all he'd done, however, and placed in the constellation Centaurus.

THE HEALER, THE WOUNDED ONE, AND THE ONE WHO WOUNDS

Now, his myth is just jam-packed with wonderful symbolism. First of all, Chiron was abandoned because of the **imperfection** of his physical form, and because of how that physical form came to be. So one of the strongest "themes" you'll find with Chiron is the issue of imperfection.   His spot is a place where we each feel "wounded" or "broken" or "handicapped" in some way. Where we feel **different**. Where we feel that people are automatically **prejudiced** against us because of our difference. As a result, his placement is also where we strive for perfection and feel driven to learn and understand.

Now, we experience all the urges or needs our charts describe— one way or the other. We either "do" the energy consciously, "do" it subconsciously, or hire the part out to another person and deny it completely.[3] One way or the other, however, life provides each of us with opportunities to see all three sides of every planet's motifs. And Chiron is no exception. The main theme in his myth is The Wound, so wherever he's placed in your chart, you'll find the triple face of that Wound[4]—The Healer, The Wounded One, and The One Who Wounds.

It works something like this: if you're aware of how you're hurt, of how you feel "different" from others, of your Sore Spot, that is, you'll be more likely to "use" it to heal others. It's similar to the way a recovering alcoholic "sponsors" someone who's just facing their own addiction. The conscious use of Chiron often shows through working with people, things, or situations that are "wounded" or "handicapped" or "broken" in some way.

If you're not aware of your Wound, however, you might become The One Who Wounds. This subconscious misuse of Chiron's energies is similar to an abused child who grows up to be an abusive parent. When we're in pain too great to handle, we often attack a helping hand. Remember, a wounded animal in pain will bite. If Chiron's energy is totally denied, we can become The Wounded One, attracting others to us who wound us in our sore spot. We may end up in abusive relationships, both physically and emotionally.

Now, I have Chiron right next to my Moon, so he's been Following Me Home for a very long time, in a variety of disguises. In fact, as long as I can remember—even **before** Chiron and I were formally introduced—I've had a thing for animals—Special Animals. "Wounded" ones, with Special needs. Three-legged dogs, one-eyed dogs, birds with one foot, cats with no tails. Animals that have **Ch-ironic** illnesses, too. I don't go after **them**, either—

---

3 Another jewel from Robert Hand's considerable collection.
4 Melanie Reinhart, *"Chiron and the Healing Journey,"* Arkana Publishing.

they just arrive with their collars and their bowls or That Look on their faces. Since my Moon is in pretty delicate shape to start with, I used to think that was all there was to that.

Then I noticed that Chiron was nestled just a few degrees away from that Moon, and I knew immediately that I had something here. Once I made the initial connection between Chiron/ Moon and my rather unusual "kids," I went to Jerry Lewis'[5] chart. I figured if Jerry didn't have a Moon/Chiron connection, I'd have to seriously question the way I was interpreting my own and Chiron's validity in general.

Well. It was In There, just like it had to be. Big Time, too. Another conjunction: Chiron at 26 Aries, Moon at 0 Taurus. Perfect for dealing with Special Kids. That's what I was looking for. Since then, I've found example after example of Chiron's potency in charts, and he's always, always right where you'd expect him to be.

CHIRON AND THE SYMBOL OF ACCESS

At any rate, one fine morning, en route to do a workshop on Chiron, matter of fact, I passed an amazing number of cars with the "Symbol of Access" displayed in the rear window.

At first, I didn't pay much attention. The Symbol has become a "normal" sight to us. But, after a while, I saw so many cars with it displayed that I began to feel a bit like Richard Dreyfuss must have felt about The Mountain in *Close Encounters*. A bit uneasy, you know? Like the symbol was "following" me. Of course, it **was**, but since I was on my way to do a distinctly Left-Brain thing, it took a while for The Message to infiltrate over there to the Right Side. I remember thinking that The Symbol of Access looked a lot like a Glyph just seconds before the light bulb **finally** went on,

5 Source for Jerry Lewis' birth data is *The Gauquelin Book of American Charts*, [o.p] by Michel and Francoise Gauquelin, ACS Publications, 1982.

when it finally hit me that the Symbol **was** a glyph. It was Chiron's glyph. Rearranged a little.

Just look at them. They're made of exactly the same shape and the same number of pen strokes. The only difference is that we've "humanized" the symbol by putting a head on it. We're also finally "humanizing" folks with special needs. We're even referring to them in a whole new way, no longer as "handicapped," but simply as "challenged."

Once I'd noticed the similarities between The Symbol and The Symbol, my Sagittarian Wondering Mechanism kicked in: Where did this "glyph" for challenged folks originate? How was it chosen? And, most importantly from an astrological viewpoint, **when** did it arrive? I called The President's Committee on Employment of the Handicapped and asked them to send me everything they had on it. And, as with astrology, the information I got was simultaneously amazing and not at all surprising.

The Symbol's purpose is officially defined like this: it tells a handicapped person (one who's using a wheelchair, in particular), that here is a place where they're **free** to conduct their business **independently**. Here's a place that's been specially designed with them in mind, a place they can use without fear of their movement being **blocked** by **architectural barriers** of any kind. A place where they can be free, despite their **physical limitations**.

Now, Chiron has also been thought of as The Bridge between Saturn and Uranus, so the concepts of "Freedom from Barriers," "Independence despite Physical Limitations," and "Integrating Unique Individuals into the Mainstream" all sound like Saturn/Uranus keywords strung together. So you might also call Chiron's placement in your chart a spot where "Necessity is the Mother of Invention," where you'll need to be ingenious to find a way around your limitations.

When I read that The Symbol was, in fact, "invented" in 1968, I was initially a bit disappointed. I **wanted** The Symbol's "debut" to have come about with Chiron's discovery, in 1977. When I checked, however, I realized that back in 1968, Chiron was, in fact, just crossing **0 degrees of Aries**, the very beginning of the Zodiac, the starting point which corresponds with the first day of Spring. The moment of "birth."

AND THAT'S NOT ALL

There are other "symptoms" to Chiron's placement. This is a spot where you'll feel burdened by a flaw of some kind, one that you have no choice but to live with. As a result, and since addictions are what we often use to escape our wounds, you'll need to watch carefully for that tendency here. Chiron's mother "walled herself up" inside a tree to escape the memory of what had happened to her—but then, that's what addictions do. They make us prisoners until we decide to deal openly and consciously with the wound we're trying to cover.

Now, as much as Chiron can be considered Your Tragic Flaw, he can also be considered Your Greatest Strength. This high side of Chiron is best explained by using the example of Rudolph the Red-Nosed Reindeer—and his very shiny nose—an example brought up by Dale O'Brien, another astrologer who has been strongly drawn to Chiron. Although Rudolph's nose was what originally ostracized him from the others, it was eventually this unique gift that made him a hero—once he stopped hiding it. So wherever Chiron lives in your chart, you're wounded, but you're also gifted, and there's a very particular set of circumstances that will allow you to share your gift and become a Healer.

One final note: when you poke here, poke gently. The deeper the wound, the more carefully it's been buried, and the more delicately it will need to be handled.

CHIRON AS METAPHYSICAL CHIRURGEON GENERAL

In a Mundane sense, that is, speaking through a wide-angle lens, Chiron is best thought of as our Metaphysical Chirurgeon General. Since, on an individual level, he shows where we are both wounded and able to heal, his position at the moment shows the Current Healing Rage, the piece of humanity's collective psyche we're interested in opening up and "fixing" right now. So the sign he wears shows our Health Fads, both positive and frivolous.

For example, when he passed through Cancer (July 1988-August 1991), holistic health practitioners everywhere began encouraging us to heal ourselves by dealing with our "roots"—quite the Cancerian topic. The phrase that paid in all the New Age Journals at that time was "Healing the Dysfunctional Family," and we all finally realized that just about **everybody's** family was "dysfunctional" in some way. Yellow "Baby on Board" signs began to appear in car windows, too. We even held a second Earth-Day, a symbolic way of making our peace with Our Collective Mom, the Earth, and bumper-stickers everywhere read "Love Your Mother."

When Chiron crossed over into Leo (August 1991-September 1993), our focus changed from the family to childhood, and the new phrase on every magazine cover and brochure was "Healing the Inner Child." Our attention also shifted to the part of the body Leo rules—the back—and wooden roller seat-covers showed up on every other car. Chiron's passage through Leo, the sign of Fatherhood, also corresponded with a tragic mass enactment of his tale; thousands of little Chirons were born in the former Yugoslavia, children born of rape. Their fathers, like Saturn, served only as biological vehicles, and their mothers abandoned them immediately.

Chiron's entry into Virgo (September, 1993-September, 1995), which may be his favorite sign or sign of **dignity,** brought Health-Care to the forefront of our minds. He had only been in Virgo a few days, in fact, when President Clinton announced to the country that America's Health-Care System was "badly broken" and had to be "fixed." Again, the holistic shift changed, as well: vitamins and herbal supplements began to face regulations on their distribution, and the FDA got stricter on its requirements that manufacturers list all ingredients on food packages. Warnings also began to appear on packaged meat.

Chiron's Orbit

Now, Chiron's 50.7-year orbit is as erratic as they come (see diagram). He spends about 8 years on the Pisces/Aries end of the loop, but only a year and a half each on the other side of his orbit, as he passes through Virgo and Libra. This, too, seems significant since, as we'll see in the next chapter on The Signs, Pisces has an awful lot to do with being wounded; Aries is Mars' agent, and so knows how to wield a weapon quite well; and Virgo and Libra are the two signs most con-

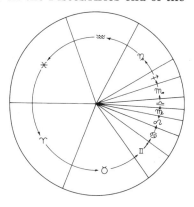

cerned with **perfection**—albeit for different reasons.

For more information on Chiron, see "Where To Find It," in the back of this book. Also, this book has an appendix (pages 221 - 242) giving the position of Chiron for the years 1920-2010 .

The Asteroids

ASTEROIDS IN GENERAL

As with everything else in our orderly universe, the planets are right where they "should" be—mathematically speaking, that is. In other words, planets appear exactly where we'd expect them to, given their physical "statistics" and the amount of space they need to accommodate their lifestyles. This whole theory is the heart of what's known as Bode's Law, a Scientific Rule that basically says what I just said in far more confusing language. So just trust me on this.

At any rate, right in between Mars and Jupiter there's an open lane—a spot just large enough and just far enough away from either of those two planets to stick another planet into. That open lane is called The Asteroid Belt, and although it doesn't have a full-size planet to call its own, it does contains thousands of asteroids—thousands of fragmented bits of rock.

One theory reasons that all of the asteroids used to be one planet—which makes sense, since they do tend to travel in "packs." The current preferred astronomical theory is that a planet **started** to form—with stony iron cores—but the combined gravitational pulls of the Sun on one side and Jupiter on the other were sufficient to keep the planet from coming together. Some asteroids are named for mythic figures, like the planets are. More recently, some have been given names that correspond to places, like California or Asia. Some even have given "ordinary" human names—like Franke and Kate, for example. Right now, there are computer programs available that will print out the positions of over four thousand of them. Although that certainly does sound overwhelming, I can't encourage you enthusiastically enough to track yours down and spend some time hooking them into your chart—because you'll be amazed where they'll turn up: attached to your Moon, wearing your Mom's first name; or sitting on your Venus, wearing your husband's name; maybe even on your Sun, wearing your name. Like I said, it's amazing. If you'd like more info on asteroids in general, see "Where to Find It," in the back.

A WARNING ABOUT TRYING
TOO MUCH TOO SOON

In all fairness, I've got to tell you that I was never much on asteroids when I first became interested in astrology. My excuse was that I had enough to do just trying to figure out what I ought to be doing with Saturn. Secretly, though, I think I always knew that if I opened the door a crack to the asteroids there'd be no going back, and I wasn't ready to learn four new principles.

One day I weakened. I put them in my own chart and they "worked." Real well, too—no stretching required. I began to watch them in the charts of Famous Others, too—and, well, they just kept right on "working." They did what they were supposed to, when and how they were supposed to. Ever since, there truly has been no way to do a chart without them.

There's also no doing a chart **with** them until you're ready to. So don't try to fake it, and don't be surprised if you Don't "Get" them at first. They're a layer deeper than the planets and a lot more specific. They add details to a picture and allow us to refine our descriptions of ourselves. The hard part is that to do all that, we've got to dig around In There—we've got to go down a couple more levels and get to know ourselves more intimately. We can only gain access to this next level by **looking** for it, in other words. So when you start to investigate the asteroids, it's going to be because you're ready to study your actions more Consciously than you have in the past.

Sure, it's complicated. All the best things are.

At any rate, be patient with yourself. Don't use them until you're ready. When you are ready, read on.

CERES, PALLAS ATHENA, VESTA, AND JUNO
THE GREAT GODDESSES

There are four asteroids that have been used in astrology for some time now, as I said earlier. They've come to represent Women's Issues in a very big way. Originally brought to light in 1973, when Eleanor Bach first published an ephemeris for them, these bodies are now used more and more frequently by astrologers.

The "big four" asteroids were named after four goddesses, Ceres, Pallas Athena, Vesta, and Juno, who were on absolutely equal footing with The Gods and considered every bit as powerful. Demetra George has written a wonderful book on the asteroids, *Asteroid Goddesses*[6], in which she relates each goddess to the various roles of women as mother (Ceres), daughter (Pallas), wife (Juno) and sister (Vesta).

Again, to really understand the symbolism of a body you've got to take a little history, so we'll go over each Goddess myth as I introduce them to you. Let's start with Ceres.

Ceres, The Great Earth Mother

In mythology, Ceres (who was also known as Demeter), was the goddess of the grain, of agriculture and the harvest. She had a lovely daughter, Persephone, and the two were so close that they hardly ever spent time apart. One day, however, Persephone was out with some friends, picking flowers in a meadow, when suddenly what seemed like a terrible earthquake occurred. The ground opened up and Pluto, the God of the Underworld, appeared in a fiery chariot pulled by huge black horses. Pluto kidnapped Persephone and took her to the Underworld, and afterwards, the ground repaired itself, leaving no trace of what had happened. Brokenhearted, Ceres searched for her daughter by night and day. When she was finally told what had happened, and when she found that Zeus, her brother, knew what had happened all along, she left Mt. Olympus and began to wander.

Now, Ceres was the goddess of the crops, and without her care, the Earth became cold, gray, and unproductive. Nothing grew, and what had already grown began to rot. The Gods and Goddesses got worried—who'd worship them if all the mortals died? Finally, Zeus arranged for Persephone's return. Unfortunately, before she left him, Pluto offered Persephone several pomegranate seeds, which she ate.

Since the pomegranate symbolizes Knowledge, and since she took the seeds willingly, Persephone was tricked into giving up her innocence. She was bound to Pluto. For half the year, then, Persephone was allowed to be with her mother, but for the other half, she had no choice but to return to her husband in the Underworld.

Now, this story raises several Issues. The delicacy—and exclusivity—of the Mother/Child bond, for example, and especially the bond between a mother and daughter. The myth also de-

6 *Asteroid Goddesses*, by Demetra George, with Douglas Bloch. ACS Publications, 1986.

scribes the struggle between the love of a mother and sexual love, so Ceres carries a Moon/Pluto "feeling," which for many women is the symbolic struggle between being "a good girl" and being fulfilled, not just sexually, but by taking charge of your life. Moon/Pluto is also the combination that produces Hospice care, which allows the dying to spend their last days in their own homes.

Food is also a Theme in this myth. It's used both as bribe and reward, and so Ceres in your chart can also show the tendency towards eating disorders. Loss of a child is mentioned, also. With Ceres' placement in our charts, then, we'll find experiences of parenting, being parented, and the loss of that relationship. She seems to work well as a secondary key to our mother figure, after the Moon. Ceres is where we feel obligated to **feed** what's around us, to care for it as if it were our child (or our garden). She represents how/where we tend to nurture others. Here we experience what it's like to let go, and grieve for what we loved. Here, too, we experience the joy of reunion.

Pallas Athena

Although Pallas Athena's myth isn't quite as involved as Ceres', it's equally important to her meaning—and quite a story. Pallas Athena was Zeus' child, and Zeus' alone—she had no mother. She was born out of Zeus' head, arriving full-grown and in full armor, and of all his children, was his favorite. She was known for her logic, her wit, and her diplomacy. She fought well, but always for a reason—never for the pure "enjoyment" of battle. In ancient times, she held the title of Goddess of Justice and Wisdom.

Inside each of us, then, where our Pallas is positioned, is a warrior-woman, a cool, airy strategist on duty who steps in and figures out how to win this one—no matter what the battle might involve. Pallas shows where you're all business, where you're not bothered by emotional concerns, where you judge strictly by what's fair. Here's where you'll be completely logical at all times. (If this sounds familiar, it ought to be—lots of us grew up with an excellent example of Pallas on television, a pointy-eared male version of the goddess known as "Mr. Spock").

Now, Pallas represents the father/daughter bond, so Pallas' spot in your chart is where you'll probably find the fingerprint of A Mentor, a father-figure you worshiped and wanted to impress with your intelligence. Regardless of whether you have a male mentor or not, however, here's where you'll feel that someone wise and wonderful taught you everything you know. If Pallas is extremely prominent in your chart, you may feel that your bond to your father is much stronger than what you feel towards your mother. Pallas also "dotes on her heroes," as Astro buddy Blain Bovee often says, so here's where you'll be prone to defend your very own hero, whoever that might be.

Pallas in your chart shows where you'll have both wisdom and intelligence, and if she's very involved with the rest of your chart, that combination will produce "common sense." Her position is where you **can** be completely fair because you're not attached to anyone or anything emotionally.

Vesta

Vesta (or Hestia, as she was called) is the Goddess of the hearth-fire, the child of Saturn (Chronos) and Rhea. Now, since Saturn had an awful habit of swallowing his children whole Hestia (as she was also called) spent a great deal of her life inside her father's stomach. When Zeus, the last-born of Chronos and Rhea, finally freed his brothers and sisters from their father's stomach, Hestia was the last to emerge. She chose to remain "single" throughout her life, refusing both Poseidon and Apollo's proposals. Zeus gave Vesta rulership of the sacred gift of fire. She protected all homes with her warmth, offered hospitality to strangers, and united communities by the fire in the town center. When the Romans renamed Hestia "Vesta," she was again given charge of fire, and her priestesses (the vestal virgins), tended the eternal fires in the temples.

Now, fire, of course, is what passion is all about, and passion has everything to do with sexuality. So Vesta relates to sexuality, but also to approaching all encounters with the intensity usually reserved for sexuality. The vestal virgins (who weren't virgins at all, in the traditional sense of the word), tended the temple fires, remaining chaste until called upon to give themselves physically in sacred rituals. If a virgin conceived during one of these rituals, the child was considered the child of The God. Other than for these times, however, the virgins had no choice but to remain untouched. The penalty for having sex otherwise was to be buried alive in an underground chamber.

Vesta's spot in your chart is a place where you'll guard your passions—where you'll guard **all** your feelings most carefully—

and where you'll serve as a vessel, both for holding and for pouring. Here's where every action carries a sacred, special tone, where you'll withhold your energy for long periods, use it up in one intense moment, then draw back and regroup. You'll need periods of isolation from the area of life where Vesta is found in your chart, time to focus, concentrate, and rest. To get a real "feel" for the sacred quality of Vesta, however, step inside a cathedral on a sunny afternoon and "listen" to the sound of "holy." Regardless of who or what you believe in, stepping on sacred ground of any kind brings with it a Vesta experience. Sedona's Vortices and the Mayan temples work too.

Juno

Juno (also known as Hera), was the sister and wife of Jupiter (also known as Zeus). In mythology, Jupiter was the King of the Gods, the dude in charge of the sky, and apparently, a pretty good King. He was not, however, a notoriously faithful kind of guy, and, in fact, had several children by other women after he married Hera. She, on the other hand, was known both for her beauty and her faithfulness to her husband. Although he did betray her several times, Hera was far worse on the women Zeus was with than she was to him. She killed them and cursed them, and gave them monsters for children—but she didn't betray her husband. Unfortunately, throughout their marriage, Zeus withheld from Hera what she really wanted from him: his fidelity, his sexuality, and his children. Yet he kept her as his wife, and she refused to break her vows. She became the Goddess of faithfulness in marriage, and served as a role model for young brides.

Zeus and Hera seem to have had a relationship much like Katherine Hepburn and Peter O'Toole in "The Lion in Winter." The Queen was kept prisoner for most of the year, allowed to emerge only for official events and holidays—for the sake of appearances. The King, however, confided in her, took her counsel, and seemed to care for her in an odd way. She remained faithful to him, yet became resentful and deceptive, and plotted against him whenever the opportunity arose. Still, the strength of her commitment held her to him even under the circumstances.

Juno in our chart represents that principle of absolute commitment, with all the fears and joys that accompany it, from fear of rejection, to jealousy, to the happiness and security of being bound to another. A strong Juno personality lives for the spouse, to be the perfect companion, consort, and homemaker/provider. As a result, Juno shows where we'll repress our own personalities, where we'll have a tendency to exist for An Other, and give up our power to another because of our commitment to them. She has rulership over women (and men) who stay in abusive relationships simply because they're married. Juno's spot may also show where you'll consider deception, manipulation, and mind games to try to take back a bit of control over The Other. That's Juno at her very worst. At her very best, Juno represents our ability to **keep** the promises we make to an other.

CHAPTER FOUR
SIGNS—THE WAY YOU DO
THE THINGS YOU DO

But First, A Note
to the Transient Reader

Okay. Everybody who's been here right from the Introduction, now's your chance to Take Five. I need to talk to these Other People for a minute. The New Folks, I mean—the ones who just walked in.

You know who You are—You're standing in the Metaphysics/ New Age aisle wondering how you got here, holding this book entirely by accident. You figure you'll get a quick "fix" of your own sign, maybe skim over your Significant Other's characteristics a little, too, and then be on your way. As soon as whoever you came with is finally ready to go, that is.

If that's you, and you're really **determined** to just read your Sun-sign and leave, well, I certainly can't stop you. You've got the right chapter, and they're in the usual order. Help yourself. And thanks for dropping by.

But if everything you've ever heard or read about your Sun-Sign's characteristics rang very true, I feel it only fair to warn you that there's a lot more to this than **just** your Sun-sign. There's eight other planets, a Moon, a bunch of asteroids and a sky-full of comets out there, and they all get a sign to call their own. And we

all get one of each of them to call our own. So you might actually
find information about You listed under **several** sign descriptions.
'Magine?

Now, if you really do only have time to read a Sun-sign or two,
keep in mind that there's a whole lot more to your Sun-sign than
can be captured in a few cute adjectives, and try to stop by again
sometime. But if your Significant Other hasn't shown any signs
of leaving the Photography section, well, then, assume a comfortable stance, settle in for just a minute longer than you thought
you might, and we'll talk. About what the signs are "made" of,
first of all. And then you'll get what you **really** came for—not
just a few words you'll forget as soon as you step back out into the
mall, but a little more insight into what makes people tick.

So Let's Get Busy

Okay. The first thing to remember is that signs aren't objects,
they're **attitudes**. They're not heavenly bodies, like the planets,
so they don't **represent** urges or needs, and they don't hold titles. Their job is to **interpret**—to describe **how**. See, each sign
is really a **style**—the style of the planet (or house) who's "wearing" it. They're screens, in a way—energy **fields**. They **filter**,
color, or **flavor** the way an urge or need is expressed. Here's
why.

ELEMENTS, QUALITIES, AND GENDER

Each sign is composed of an element, a quality, and a gender.
These three categories assemble to describe the sign's motivations. What it's "after," in terms of experiences, that is—and why
it's after it.

The elements—(fire, earth, air, and water)—represent the
ultimate goal of the sign—the types of situations it "specializes"
in, and the level of existence it represents—physical, emotional,
inspirational, or intellectual. The qualities (cardinal, fixed, and
mutable) show a sign's *modus operandi*—the general flow of its
energy. The genders (feminine or masculine) describe whether
the sign prefers to attract or pursue experiences, respectively.

Each sign gets to "pick" one from each category—and that
combination produces the sign's personality.

Now. You're wondering why you need to know all this.
Wouldn't it be easier to just make a list of keywords for each sign,

memorize them, and be done with it? Well no, actually, it wouldn't. See, learning the element, quality, and gender of each sign explains not just **how** a sign's presence describes a planet or a house—the symptoms—but why. And once you understand **why** signs inspire a planet to "do the thing it does," you'll understand a little more about human nature.

It's like getting a complete character profile instead of a snapshot.

Elements

So. Let's start by explaining the **elements**. And here's the best part: everything about the elements as you know them is absolutely the same when it's applied to signs. The four elements, then—fire, earth, air, and water—act the same way in human form as they do in their natural forms. We all know folks who can only be described as "fiery," "earthy," "airy," or "fluid." Each of those words describes the **general temperament** and **basic motivation** of the three signs that belong to its group.

For example: **Aries, Leo**, and **Sagittarius** are **fire**, and fire acts like fire is—uncontainable, ardent, enthusiastic, spontaneous, warm. Fire signs are bold. They're not afraid to act on impulse—they're afraid not to. Think of how quickly a match leaps to life when you strike it—that's how immediate fire is. The fire signs can even be a little too impulsive, matter of fact. Sometimes the fires they light are too big to handle. Still, they're fun, entertaining companions. They're the kids who drove when everyone skipped school and went to the beach. Fire represents the **spiritual** and **inspirational** level of existence. The real stuff—acting on impulse—on what you want to do.

Taurus, Virgo, and **Capricorn** are **earth**. The earth signs are solid and dependable, like the earth herself. They're practical, thorough, and conservative. They're concerned with the physical world, the matter at hand, and the body itself. They correspond to the physical plane, and to the duties and responsibilities associated with it. What binds us to the material plane? Well, there are our bodies, for starters, and their health and hygiene. Then there are money and possessions. Everything that's **tangible**, everything that's holdable, sellable, and marketable—and therefore **valuable**—all that falls under the jurisdiction of the Earth Kingdom. If you need it to live here on the planet, it belongs to the element of Earth. That goes for your job, too, for the work you're doing here. The earth signs root us to the planet, via our possessions, our function, and what we'd like to be known for contributing.

Gemini, Libra, and **Aquarius** are **air.** Air signs are concerned with words—with the intellect. They live for their ideas. They're logical, objective, and downright chatty. Invite folks with lots of air to a party (especially if one of them has a fair amount of Libra energy In There), and you'll never even have to turn the stereo on. Air signs are built-in entertainment committees. The air signs correspond to the **intellectual** side of life—to our built-in need to mingle. Like fire, they're uncontainable—and "interesting."

Cancer, Scorpio, and **Pisces** are the **water** signs. Their jurisdiction is the **emotional** realm. They feel everything, for better or worse, give the best hugs in the zodiac, and operate on their guts. In other words, they just **know** things. Cancer "knows" because its specialty is **instinct**. Scorpio understands through its detective-like powers of **perception**, and Pisces operates on **intuition.** They all gauge moods, feel the ripples in a room when they enter, and operate automatically on their sixth sense. Water likes to work alone, water always, always gets its way eventually, and water loves silence—there's nothing better when you're trying to concentrate.

These **elements** provide clues as to what each group of signs does, naturally—what each needs to function at optimum capacity. Oh, and here's those **Why's** I promised you:

Fire signs, with all that active energy, need to stay **free**, unencumbered, and spontaneous, so they can continue to be impulsive, to experience something new whenever an opportunity rears its head—instead of next weekend—and to provide the rest of us with models of How to Be A Kid Forever.

The earth signs need schedules, and regimens, and lists. They need to know what's theirs, and they love to Take Care Of Business. Just as the Earth supports us, our connection to our bodies and to our environments is **grounded** by the earth in our charts.

Air signs need to be able to mingle, communicate and verbalize their ideas with like-minded folks. They're the communicator signs. They collect data and give it back out. Planets "wearing" the air signs are more likely to distance themselves and observe a situation than to actually experience it.

The water signs need safe home bases or havens—nests, even—to be able to function happily. The issue here is How This Feels to me—always—and they need to have a lifestyle that allows them to be free enough to follow their senses, to chase the river downstream.

Qualities

The second way the signs are divided is by quality. Qualities show the sign's **energy flow** and describe the general M.O. of a sign—that is, whether it's more likely to lead, follow, or get out of the way.

The three qualities are **cardinal, fixed**, and **mutable**, and, like the elements, they also act the way they sound.

The **cardinal** signs are **Aries, Cancer, Libra**, and **Capricorn**. These are the signs (the piece of sky, that is) the Sun enters at the start of each new season. For example, Aries and Libra are the signs the Sun passes into at the beginning of spring and fall, respectively. Cancer and Capricorn mark the beginning of summer and winter, as well. Planets wearing cardinal signs are initiators. They provide the ideas and the impulse to begin new projects, and they're wonderful to have around to get a project off the ground—but they're not always so great at finishing them.

The **fixed** signs are the **finishers**. That's **Taurus, Leo, Scorpio,** and **Aquarius**. These are the signs that the Sun passes through during the second month of every season. The Sun is in Taurus in May when Spring is at its peak, and in Leo during August when Summer's really cookin', and so forth. Fixed signs are fixed in purpose. They tend to block change—unless it's on their own terms—and they prefer enduring 'till the end to switching horses in the middle of the stream any day.

The **mutable** signs are **Gemini, Virgo, Sagittarius**, and **Pisces**. These signs represent the end of a season—the Sun passes through Sagittarius during the last month of autumn, for example. Needless to say, since their job **is** preparation for change, mutable signs are flexible, adaptable, and versatile. They're also very easily distracted. They tend to become interested in several things at once and they love variety. Their function, in a nutshell, is to know when to hold up and know when to fold up.

Since these **qualities** really describe styles of expression, and techniques of **taking action**, it's important to recognize **your** own technique—the natural flow of your energy, whether it be constant, like the fixed signs, fluctuating, like the mutables, or just a sudden burst that's over as quickly as it started, as with the cardinal signs.

If you've got a cardinal Sun-sign, then, or an abundance of cardinality in your chart, you need to be allowed to start new projects on a regular basis—you need "newness" to stay interested. So your ideal situation is as an ideas person, not as follow-up. Find yourself a fixed person to actually take your projects to completion.

If you're toting around a tool-kit full of fixed signs, recognize that you need outlets for your steadiness, for your, um, **stubbornness**, you might say—and so you need to always be right in the middle of a long, time-consuming plan, and already sure of the next one.

That same prescription, on the other hand, feels like death to a chart full of mutable signs, who can't stand being put into circumstances that don't allow a "go with the flow" kind of attitude. Mutable signs need change on a steady basis.

Gender

The last way to divide the signs is by **gender**. It goes something like this: all the fire and air signs are **masculine**, and all the earth and water signs are **feminine**. Period. Now, this does not mean that you can't "do" your masculine energies if you happen to be a woman, or vice-versa. We are all multi-faceted creatures with both masculine and feminine energies inside us. We are all both **passive** and **aggressive** at times, and we all spend equal time **acting** and **reacting** to what the world tosses our way. In a nutshell, the genders simply describe whether a sign operates like a circle or a straight line.

Masculine signs are "linear" energies. They are outgoing and assertive. They push, pursue, and assert themselves. They go after what they want, speak their minds, and prefer offense to defense any day. The feminine signs, on the other hand, are receptive and magnetic. They're circular energies. They hold, absorb, and pull energy in. They attract, rather than pursue. They wait to see what will happen.

Read This Before You Go Any Further

This next section is a recap. Although all of you should read it, just to reinforce what you've learned in capsule form, it's specially designed for all you fire signs who didn't make it through the last section on elements, qualities, and genders because it looked too long and you wanted to just cut to the chase, as per usual. Caught ya. Before you go any further, read the next couple of paragraphs. And don't ever try that again.

THE SIGNS—AGAIN

Okay, gang, let's review. You're "built" of a whole pack of planets and signs. One of each, to be exact. So if it's Out There, it's got a place in your chart. The twelve signs decorate the "doors"—the house cusps of your chart—and each of your planets gets to "wear" one of the signs, too. Planets represent the **urges** or **needs** we all get the moment we step inside a body, and houses are where we keep the twelve different sides of our personalities. The style we use to present our planets and our houses is what the signs are all about. They're the "flavors" or "filters" that tell the How of the story.

Building Blocks For Signs—Again

Signs are "built" of an **element**, a **quality**, and a **gender**. The four elements are fire, earth, air, and water, and they act just the way you'd expect them to. Fire represents the spiritual side of life; earth, the physical; air, the intellectual; and water, the emotional. The three qualities are cardinal, fixed, and mutable. They correspond to the flow of an energy, and if you link them with the three months that are contained within every season, they work pretty well, too. Cardinal energy begins, fixed maintains, and mutable allows change to happen. The genders are masculine and feminine, and they either act or react, respectively. Again, each sign gets one element, one quality, and one gender to call its own.

There. Was that fast enough for you? Good. Oh, and here's a little something that will make it even faster for you next time—a chart.

Sign	Element	Quality	Gender
Aries ♈	Fire	Cardinal	Masculine
Taurus ♉	Earth	Fixed	Feminine
Gemini ♊	Air	Mutable	Masculine
Cancer ♋	Water	Cardinal	Feminine
Leo ♌	Fire	Fixed	Masculine
Virgo ♍	Earth	Mutable	Feminine
Libra ♎	Air	Cardinal	Masculine
Scorpio ♏	Water	Fixed	Feminine
Sagittarius ♐	Fire	Mutable	Masculine
Capricorn ♑	Earth	Cardinal	Feminine
Aquarius ♒	Air	Fixed	Masculine
Pisces ♓	Water	Mutable	Feminine

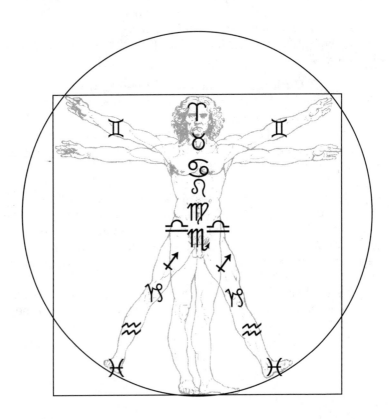

Now, keep this in mind: the descriptions that follow are not a list of Sun-Sign personality traits. They're not. They're general outlines of **how signs describe planets or houses** because of the "flavor" they add. So before you start bad-mouthing Scorpios or beating up on Virgos, remember that we've all got each sign In There somewhere. And nobody's perfect. Except maybe Leos.

All that said, let's grab our building blocks, and build us some signs.

Aries

The Sun's entry into Aries symbolically represents birth—it's the first day of spring in the Northern Hemisphere, the beginning of a brand new year. Which means that Aries always gets to go first in chapters like this one. Good thing, too, because this sign isn't world-renowned for its patience. Aries is infant energy—it wants what it wants yesterday. Failing **yesterday**, now will do—but it's got to be **right** now.

This is the fastest-acting, most impulsive sign around, made up of the three most volatile energies of all—the fire element, the cardinal impulse, and the masculine approach. Aries is action for its own sake. It turns your planet or house into a bullet, a red bullet that fires first and thinks later—maybe. It's concerned with You and You alone.

As a result, Aries refuses admission to obstacles, and doesn't have time to be deceitful. There's only Point A, where your Aries planet is, and Point B, where it wants to be. No speed is ever fast enough, and no challenge insurmountable. Now, that's absolutely wonderful when you need to be bold, brave, or pioneering. In fact, any time you need to Boldly Go Where No One Has Gone Before, you can count on an Aries planet to do just that; to take the front line and charge into battle, sword drawn, ready to roll. Aries wrote the book on Just Doing It. It blazes a path—sometimes quite literally—and it's very, very feisty. Think of how quickly that match we talked about flared up when you struck it. Well, these matches go out quickly, too. That describes the cardinal side of Aries. Its energy flow is one quick burst. It's not built for The Long Haul. It's a catalyst, an initiator. It's built for beginnings. So Aries planets or houses may show where you have a tendency to leave things undone or unfinished.

Mars oversees your Aries house or planet, and produces a tendency toward stressful situations and a craving for conflict. If there's none out there, you won't be above generating some, either. Make it easy on yourself—remember that this is where you're always going to need to be first, where you're always going to need to win, where you'll love competition.

In the body, Aries corresponds to the face and the head. It's literally **headstrong**, too, so if you've got this sign prominent in your chart, you may be famous for your broken nose collection. Or your scar collection. Aries is "ruled" by the planet Mars, after all, who, as we know, is quite fond of Action.

Taurus

It's amazing how two signs can be neighbors for so long and be so different. Taurus is every bit as solid, stable, and lasting as Aries is impulsive, impetuous, and spontaneous. Taurus is fixed, so it's solid. It's earth, and it's feminine, so it absorbs. Think about that. Solid earth that absorbs is **mud**. This could be where that reputation for "stubbornness" came from. Ever try to move a pile of damp earth?

This is the sign that's most connected with the earth plane. Which makes Taurus the most sensual of the signs, a walking Super-Receptor built specially to enjoy—and produce—the best physical experience possible for each sense. The right touch from the right person. The taste of a perfectly prepared, perfectly seasoned meal. Silence and symphonies. Roses and perfume. Watching an orange sunset dip slowly behind a mountain range. All earthly delights. All under the jurisdiction of Taurus. Your Taurus planet or house functions mainly on how things **feel** to it, physically. So pleasure is very important.

It's natural, then, that wherever you find Taurus in your chart is where you'll want nothing but the very best of **everything,** since you know exactly what that is—and what it isn't. You may also want to "own" what you love where your Taurus energy is found. This sign is into the concept of possession with a capital P, and needs to be on guard against identifying too much with its possessions.

Taurus' symbol, appropriately, is the bull, a heavy, grounded beast. Taurus is determined, thorough energy. It plows through—it continues until the job is done—once it finally gets the machinery started, that is. But then, it takes time to do something right. Taurus doesn't mind taking the time. Taurus acts with caution. It aims for stability and the long run.

Now, speaking of time, Taurus has charge of the thyroid gland in the physical body, which is what regulates our metabolisms. So your Taurus house or planet just loves a routine. Matter of fact, here's where you can get a little **too** fond of routine and never notice that you haven't done **anything** differently for a while. Taurus also rules the neck, the throat, and the vocal cords. Since we nourish ourselves through our throats, Taurus also rules food.

Venus is in charge of Taurus, and she's also in charge of money—so money is a priority to a Taurus planet, since it represents another type of "rootedness" on the physical plane—the kind that comes from Financial Security. Remember, one of Taurus' keywords is "appreciation," which means that an item is valued or "has weight."

All else aside, if you really want to get a feeling for what Taurus is all about, go outside after a spring rain, and take a deep breath. That good, fertile, green smell is The Real Taurus. It's solid, it's clean, and it's real.

Gemini

Well, now, here's Gemini, the sign that's head of the Department of Movement. Constant movement. The sign who taps, fidgets, and has an answer for everything; the sign you never want to challenge to a "quick" game of *Trivial Pursuit*. Life's a game-show to your Gemini planet, Chock Full O' Colors, Categories, and Special Prizes. Gemini, remember, is mutable air. Air is intellectual and mutable energy likes change. It's masculine, too, so it goes out and gets its information. That combination gives Gemini the ability to switch subjects at break-neck speed, to take a right in the middle of a sentence. Your Gemini house or planet has always, always Gotta Go.

And speaking of taking a right, there's no sign who can learn the short-cuts faster than Gemini. That applies to navigating through town as much as it does to conversation, by the way. Your Gemini house or planet is where you'll have no patience—not for stop-signs, red lights, or periods at the end of sentences. In short, here's where it's going to be tough to make you pause, where you'll develop a way of negotiating any maze—animal, vegetable, or mineral—in no time flat.

Now, the combination of the mutable impulse and the air element gives Gemini a gift for entertainment: for accents, and jokes, and Stories From College. No matter what else it does, your Gemini house or planet will not bore people. Not at all. Here, then, is a spot in your chart where you won't be able to stand being bored, either, where you'll always be restless, where you'll like nothing better than variety. Mercury's connection inspires a need for constant intellectual stimulation—Gemini's *Incredible Lightness of Being*. Gemini literally thinks on its feet, and does just about everything else on the run, too. It's free-wheeling, nimble air, perfectly capable of juggling two and three tasks at once, and of doing them right, too. Picture your Gemini planet or house as a place with a switchboard operator on duty 24 hours a day, taking information from Out There and passing it along the right lines to wherever you need it.

As a mutable sign, Gemini can be very easily distracted—so all that lightning-fast subject switching and versatility can turn to scattered thinking and an inability to focus and concentrate—the wires can get tangled, in other words. But, then, Gemini wasn't born for precision, or endurance. It was born to be a breeze. To pick up a bit of data here, and a bit there, and to send it back out into the world.

Now, Gemini is the sign of the twins, so in the physical body it rules pairs—eyes, ears, lungs, hands, feet, and so forth. It's in charge of any body part we use to speak, write, and get ourselves back and forth with, too. Gemini rules the nervous system since navigating short distances requires that all of your senses communicate with your environment.

Cancer

Okay, I'm going to break tradition here just for a second and talk first to all you Sun-sign Cancers out there, especially those of you who are sick and tired of being referred to as "moody." If that's you, if you've had it with being called "moody," raise your hand. Uh huh. Now, tell me you're not. Moody, that is. Because you'd better be. Cancer is in charge of personal emotions, so Cancer planets and houses are **supposed** to be pretty darned emotional places.

See, first of all, Cancer is a water sign and it's feminine. Water is emotional energy, and feminine signs react rather than act. Cancer is also cardinal—the type of energy that starts up and dies down quickly. It fluctuates and flows. Cancer **needs** to be moody to do its job. So let your Cancer planet or house be as moody as it wants. In other words, cry, if you feel like it. Here's where it's your **job** to feel.

'Course, Cancer's also in charge of instinct. Now, instinct is really nothing more than **collective memory.** It's how a new-born anything arrives knowing it needs to nurse. Your Cancer planet or house understands the need to protect the past, since everything that's stored there is geared towards safety, towards survival.

Cancer is ruled by the Moon, so also under Cancer's jurisdiction is the Moonly subject of **Mothering.** Your Cancer places are where you'll always stash a bit of your own Mom, where her fingerprint will show up well after you're grown—whether or not she was physically there for you. However, contrary to popular opinion, not all Cancer planets come in cheerfully equipped to **be** a Mommy—not at all. They do come in with a knack for knowing how to care for another's needs, however.

No other sign can soothe, comfort, and protect like Cancer. In fact, Cancer can get so wrapped up in caring for others that it forgets to care for **itself.** That's where the issue of Dependency comes in. Your Cancer planet or house is where you're so into caretaking, it's tough not to **become** what you're caring for. It's also where you'll be pulled into safe, family-like situations, and where you'll need to display **personal emotion.** Cancer rules the breasts, the womb and the stomach, the places where we provide physical and emotional nurturing to ourselves and to our loved ones.

Leo

Okay, let's admit it. It's true what they say about Leo—that it's the sign that's out for just one thing above all else—Attention. It's true. It's also true that Leo owns Center Stage even when it doesn't want it. So wherever this sign is in your chart, whether you're into it or not, realize that the spotlight is going to be on you at all times. Get used to it and enjoy it. Here's your stage, the house with a great big star on the door. Leo rules the **Pride.** And the **Ego**. This is a place where you need to show off, where you need to hear about how good you did. And what's wrong with that?

See, Leo is all about Creation. It shows what it's made of by pushing a little piece of itself out into that spotlight for all the world to see. So strut your stuff here. Create something that expresses You. The idea is to see yourself in your creations—the best part of you, the most imaginative side.

Leo wants to play, wants to enjoy life, and wants others to be entertained by its performance. After all, what would life be without fans? Consequently, the way to a Leo planet's heart is through an honest compliment. (I say honest, by the way, because they can tell when you're buttering them up—so don't think you can slide forever by telling folks with lots of Leo in them how great they look—although it **will** work like a charm for a while.)

See, Leo is fixed fire, and it's masculine—which adds up to one roaring bonfire. It's proud, all-encompassing, and can easily turn arrogant. It's ruled by The Sun (which makes sense, since the Sun is one nonstop, roaring bonfire), so it really needs to be The Star. Leo can't help but catch our attention, and since it's fixed, it wants to keep our attention. It's Leo's job to **Perform**, you see, to entertain us. In return, Leo asks only for our **Appreciation**. For our applause. And it will just about trip on its lower lip if it doesn't get it.

Leo rules the heart in the physical body, and just as the physical heart is the very core of our being, the need to know it's loved and appreciated is at the very heart of your Leo house or planet. Leo owns fun, and just adores Show Biz so you won't settle for anything less here. Leo also rules the back and the spine in the body. It holds us upright, in proud, regal posture.

Now, needing attention like it does, your Leo spots are where you'll have a strong predisposition to **Drama**, so don't be surprised if this is a place where you feel as if your life is a Docu-Drama. Remember also that Leo is the sign of Royalty, so here's where you'll always treat yourself to Nothing But The Very Best.

Virgo

Both Gemini and Virgo are "ruled" by the planet of the mind, Mercury, and, appropriately, both of those signs could easily be called "Mercurial." They both delight in word games, contests of wit, and puzzles. They both love to have the last word, too. The main difference between the two is that Gemini loves information—all information. Gemini takes in data indiscriminately, and considers every fact just as important as every other fact.

Virgo, however, is all **about** discrimination, and knows very well what's important and what's not. Virgo's half of the mental process was explained to me recently by Michael, a dear Virgo friend. Virgo, he said, **needed** to be "picky" (his word, not mine—honest), about what they became involved in "because not everything warrants our attention." Now, he was speaking strictly of his Sun-sign, but this one sentence did more to explain Virgo—to me, at least—than anything I'd ever read.

Virgo is mutable earth and it's feminine. It's adaptable, practical, and responsive. Yes, and picky—like **he** said. Because it has to be. Virgo can't waste time on the uninteresting—so it specializes in spotting the uninteresting fast. It's good at noticing **details**. The trees, rather than the forest. The fine print. The lint. And that run in your stocking.

It's this attitude that got Virgo into trouble in the first place. Now, I swear, I'm not going to use the word "critical." I'm not. But your Virgo planet or house certainly does arrive with an Automatic Fault-Finder built right in. It's Standard equipment. So, for better or worse, nobody can spot What's Wrong as fast as Virgo can. It's the sign that's best at analyzing, organizing, troubleshooting and critiquing—not always the most popular job to have. Virgo people criticize or fault find in order to identify problems which they can then **fix, enhance, repair and improve.** The goal is to function more efficiently. If applied to its proper areas—the job and one's physical health—the essence represented by Virgo is extremely valuable.

In the body, Virgo rules the intestines, and there's no better way to see just what Virgo is all about than to think about how important this organ is to the **functioning** of the human body. Here's the place where your body analyzes and discriminates between what to keep and what to toss away, where it selects what it needs from what you've provided, and sends it to the appropriate department.

Now. The key to running this sign without any snags is to turn down the volume on the Fault-Finder once in a while, and put aside the lists. This is a place where you'll be even tougher on you than you are on others, where you'll measure personal success or failure by how well you've handled The Problem. To be a little kinder to yourself in your Virgo spots, then, force yourself to see what you've already done, and done well.

Libra

What most folks don't understand about this sign is that just because Libra has always been connected to words like "Balance" and "Harmony" doesn't mean that Libra arrives that way. "Balance" and "Harmony" are two **very** difficult states to achieve, if you really think about it. Balance means that two sides of an issue must both **give** and **take** just enough so that neither is heavier or lighter than the other. **Harmony** means that **all** the components in a group, whether it's an orchestra or a committee, need to participate equally—no more and no less than any other factor. No easy task.

So rather than automatically providing a wonderful array of happy, balanced situations, your Libra planet or house will most often find itself in unbalanced situations. See, Libra's real job is to **Restore Balance**—to produce **equilibrium**. To see which side needs to give for total equality to take place, and to tap the scales down appropriately.

Libra is cardinal and it's air. It's masculine, too. So Libra wants to go out and start something, and it needs to be intellectual in nature. Which sounds like a conversation—one of Libra's specialties. No sign is better at wielding charm, at displaying Behavior That Is Pleasing To The Other, at knowing exactly what to say in any social situation.

And speaking of relationships, keep in mind that your Libra planet or house may be a place where you won't ever want to act alone. You might even want so desperately to be **with** somebody that you're willing to sell out your own needs to do it. In other words, if The Other won't compromise, Libra may **over**compromise—just to keep the peace. The real idea here, however, is to learn to juggle, to share and cooperate, to function as half of a partnership. An equal half.

In the physical body, Libra rules the kidneys and the adrenals, and all physical organs that keep the system in balance.

Scorpio

Scorpio is fixed water. It's feminine, too. Water is emotional in nature, so Scorpio cares. It feels. The fixed quality holds on, and feminine energy absorbs. So your Scorpio houses or planets feel everything—intensely and permanently. They operate on what they "sense" from the environment rather than what they learn—and no sign is more perceptive, either. Here's where you're equal parts detective, analyst and researcher, where you become **so** fixed on your subject that you're not able to see or think of anything else.

Here's where you may become a bit obsessive, in other words.

Now, don't you even try to look surprised. You know you've got an Obsessive Department in there—we all do. Find Scorpio in your chart and you'll find yours. And don't try to tell yourself it's not there. Just admit it and find positive uses for it. For example, the only way to really become skilled at something is by **becoming** it—by **absorbing** it. Scorpio knows that. So there's a method to its madness. When this sign wants to understand what makes something tick, it studies the subject—from the inside out, over and over. Your Scorpio planet or house and you will sit up long into many nights together, reviewing The Subject and The Situation, sifting for subtle clues, analyzing what they **really** meant by that.

Your Scorpio house or planet is just as good at sending those signals back out to the world, too. This sign is really, really good at imperceptibly altering the outcome of a situation with just the right phrase or just the right gesture. Here, then, is where you'll automatically know how to work the crowd and where your ability to persuade will be the stuff that legends are made of. Here, also, is where you'll be an expert at the delicate art of strategy. By the time your Scorpio planet or house actually acts, before it **does** anything, 90% of the footwork happens internally. Scorpio plans, plots, and spins busily, just below the surface. It waits. It's relentless—and it's jealous, too. Scorpio searches for **intimacy** above all else. For real sharing. Never mind polite conversation—Scorpio wants your soul.

In the physical body, Scorpio rules the reproductive organs and the sexual organs. It's the opposite sign from Taurus, and as much as Taurus is all about taking in, or accumulation, Scorpio is all about elimination, and so Scorpio also rules the eliminative organs.

Sagittarius

Jupiter is the Patron Saint of Sagittarius. Makes sense, too. Jupiter **is** the largest planet in the Solar System, after all, and he's in charge of expansion. And growth. And excess. And "waste." So the words "very" and "too" are the exclusive property of Sagittarius, as are "much," "more," and "many." Your Sagittarius house or planet won't be world-famous for its willpower. Or for its moderation. Or for having "just a sliver" of anything. Sag is an expert at overdoing—at overdoing everything. If one is good, Sag believes that two, then, must be better and, if two is good, well, how about ten? Shouldn't that be just excellent?

See, things have a tendency to snowball when Sagittarius is involved. It's fire, it's mutable, and it's masculine, so Sag is inspired—momentarily, at least—by many things, all of which the fire element wants to dash out and experience immediately. The mutable impulse allows Sag's fire to spread, and adds a changeability to Sag houses and planets, however, which often amounts to chronic Grass-Is-Greener Syndrome. That is, you'll be tough to satisfy here, always wondering if there's someone or something better out there. The best way to handle this condition is by providing plenty of intellectual stimulation in these areas of your chart. Of course, if you find that France is where you want to be stimulated, so much the better. Sag loves to hit the highway, too.

See, Sagittarius is after The Truth, The Whole Truth, and Nothing But The Truth. Sag needs to know Why. So there'll necessarily be lots of experimenting to do here to find The Truth. You'll need classes and field-trips, exposure to many cultures and religions, and stimulating conversations with people who know at least as much as you, and preferably **more**. You'll be hungry for knowledge here, too, and known as a philosopher, only too happy to Espouse at Length on what you do know. Sag planets are all little billboards, matter of fact, always advertising what they believe, promoting their way as the only way.

This is a fun place, where you'll be completely optimistic, where you'll know when to just laugh—and that means at yourself, too. Matter of fact, Sag's most important quality is the ability to laugh, to learn not to take life quite as seriously as you might have to in other places in your chart and at other times in your life.

Sag is equal parts human and animal—that's what the Centaur is all about. In the body, Sag rules the thighs.

Capricorn

Capricorn has a tendency to build. It's automatic. The cardinal part of the sign wants to begin action. The earth insists that something solid be the end result. So construction in any form is what Capricorn does naturally—and what it's best at. Laying down the groundwork. Putting up the Main Beams. All that calls for Capricorn's ability to set realistic boundaries and put plans into motion within those boundaries.

Initially, then, it's Capricorn's job to make the **rules**. To **assign tasks**. To be The Authority Figure here. Capricorn knows what The Guidelines are—and about how to keep to them, too. Your Capricorn house or planet has an attitude built in—so wherever it is in your chart is a spot where you'll automatically be the Honorary Principal. And the Honorary Business Executive, too, since this is where you know How To Run It, no matter what It is. Your Capricorn house or planet may wear business suits or other "uniforms" on a daily basis as part of the "job." You may also find that here "the job" is everything. There may be a tendency to start driving before you've been given the keys, that is—because you already know how to take charge.

One of the reasons Capricorn leads as well as it does is because it knows What Society Expects—it knows exactly what "normal" is, right now—and what it isn't. It also knows a lot about tradition, and ancestry, and patriotism. About doing things the Old-Fashioned way—because that's the way we've always done them, that's why. Expect tradition to be a strong influence on a Capricorn house or planet. Now, leading well means keeping your feelings at bay—so Capricorn may not **allow** itself to feel. Instead, it will march around silently, absolutely starved for emotion and affection.

Capricorn rules the structure of all things, so the skeleton and the skin fall under its jurisdiction.

Aquarius

Aquarius prides itself on being one of a kind. Absolutely unique. So needless to say, here's where you're the last true Individual alive. Where everybody knows it, too. They know it because you make **sure** they know it. Your Aquarius planet or house goes out of its way to show that uniqueness to the world. Symptoms are as striking as purple hair and safety pins through the nose—and as "normal" as working for Greenpeace. It's all in the interpretation. The point is that you need to make Serious Social Statements with every gesture wherever your Aquarius energies live.

Rules automatically provoke Aquarius to rebel. To be radical. To shock folks. See, more than anything, your Aquarian house or planet wants to be completely free. So here's where you will absolutely refuse to do anything everybody else does. No way. Too much like following The Rules. If the rest of your family does it, your Aquarian house or planet will deliberately not do it. This piece of you is out to change all that.

Aquarius adores change. Bring it on. Its ruling planet is Uranus, and you know how he gets when he sees something that's been in one spot for too long.... Like a lightning bolt, he changes direction—suddenly. Abruptly. Any time your Aquarius house or planet feels stifled in any way, it will do just that—turn, switch, and change—when even you least expect it.

Aquarius planets are androgynous. They view everyone in a rather detached fashion and sex is irrelevant. So is race. But are you **interesting**? That's what your Aquarius house or planet really cares about. Now, believe it or not, Aquarius is a fixed sign, so when you're committed here, you're really committed. 'Course, it's an air sign, so Aquarius is better at committing to an idea—to a Cause—than to a human. Friendships are the real specialty of an Aquarius planet or house—here's where you need to be with kindred spirits.

In the body, Aquarius rules the circulatory system, and the calves and ankles.

Pisces

Pisces is mutable and Pisces is water—so it's all about infiltrating the ranks. Pisces dissolves dividing lines. Subtly. It's a bit like pouring a glass of water on a table. There are no limits—nothing to separate Pisces from the rest of what's out there, so here's where you **feel** everything, good or bad, where you're a regular sponge. Here's where Pisces' reputation for compassion comes from, where you'll have a tendency to take in strays: animals, people, even plants on the reduced rack in the grocery store.

Here too, is where you'll be really good at the delicate art of sacrifice. You may be **so** good at sacrifice, in fact, that you feel emotionally victimized by others where Pisces falls in your chart. You may have a tendency to martyr yourself here, too.

Which brings me to the issue of Escape. When the world outside gets too unkind, your Pisces planet or house will feel around through the dark for the plug—for The Way Out. Might be sleep. Or television. Might be alcohol or drugs, too. Pisces gets so overwhelmed by the world at times that any Escape is better than nothing.

Well, fine. If you know you've got to draw back here and let your mutable little water energy recharge, then pick your method. Before you can get to the sand you'd like to stick your head into, jump into a pool, instead. Pray. Meditate. Chant, if you need to. Do whatever it takes, just so long as you don't try so hard to escape that it works. Your Pisces planet or house needs to be on the lookout for addictions.

In the body, Pisces rules the feet. It also has a tie with the immune system, the body's ability to keep its walls "fortified" against What's Out There.

The Difference Between
Inners and Outers in Signs

Divide 365 days by 12 and you'll get about 30.5. That's the number of days the Sun spends passing through each sign—about a month. Since there are 30 degrees in a sign, too, that translates into about one degree a day. And that, of course, is where Sun-Signs come from.

Divide 28 days—the length of the Moon's orbit—by 12 and you'll get 2.5. That's the number of days the Moon spends in a sign. That breaks down into approximately into 1 degree every 2-ish hours. Pretty fast travel. Since they're personal planets, the sign the Sun and Moon "wear" when you're born is pretty important—they describe something very **specific** about You, individually—something particular about the way you "do" You.

Now. Divide Uranus' 84 year orbit by 12. You'll arrive at 7. Seven **years**. So while the Sun spends a day covering one degree and a month passing through a sign, Uranus takes 7 years to pass through that same sign and covers less than 5 degrees of sky in a year. Which means that everybody on the face of the earth who's born over that 7-year stretch will have Uranus in the same sign, and everyone who's born that year will have it in roughly the same degree.

Well. What does this tell us?

It tells us that because they stay in a sign for so long, the sign an Outer Planet is wearing in our chart is more significant **generationally** than individually. When they pass through signs, they indicate "waves." It's like this: a whole **bunch** of humans arrive with an Outer Planet in the same sign. Those humans naturally hang around together, and as they become older, they start Trends—behavior patterns that belong specifically to their age group. These trends reflect one of the Collective Attitudes this group arrived with. So the sign an outer planet is in does say a lot that's **specific**, but what they're being specific about is the Generational Mind-Set you're a part of.

Now. If you're looking for **personal** information from the position of the Outer Planets in your chart, that's there, too. Just consider the house position, rather than the sign. For example, to find where you're going to be displaying a radical need for freedom, a la Uranus—look for where Uranus is by house—the sign will tell you the **style** of rebelliousness your generation is famous for. That goes, of course, for all the outer planets.

And Speaking of Trends

While you're at it, as a matter of fact, get yourself an **ephemeris**, if you don't already have one—and work with it every day. Start matching events in the news with what you see in your book. It's an excellent way to see how astrological symbolism really "works." For more info on this type of astrology, officially called the "Mundane" branch of the science, see Chapter Eight: Other Stuff.

The Concept of Rulerships: Dignities, Debilities, Exaltations, and Falls

Before we go any further, we need to talk about **dignities, debilities, exaltations**, and falls. Now, those are scary-sounding words, I know, and I know I promised you there'd be no tables in this book, but if you look closely, you'll notice that this table has no numbers—so come in off the ledge. You need to know dignities and debilities, because you'll run into them over and over in your study of astrology, and it's always better to learn them sooner than later, and I'd rather have you hear it first from me, okay?

Besides, they're easy. And kind of fun, too. Look at it this way. You've met all the planets, so you have a feeling for their personalities. You've met the signs, too. By now you can imagine how each planet might feel about having to do a stint wearing each sign. Well, dignities and debilities are all about just that—about a planet's "taste" in signs. Needless to say, a sign that one planet feels ultra-comfortable wearing is always going to be some other planet's least favorite sign—or "outfit."

The thing to keep in mind when you're studying this table is that all signs are workable with all planets. They are. Just think of how ingenious you can be at making a not-so-favorite outfit fit the occasion when none of your "preferred" clothes are ironed. It's like that with planets and signs, too. There are no "bad" signs, and no signs that any planet can't make do nicely with. Some relationships just take more work than others. And don't tell me you don't already know that.

TABLE OF DIGNITIES, DEBILITIES, EXALTATIONS, AND FALLS

Planet		Dignity		Debility		Exaltation		Fall	
Sun	☉	Leo	♌	Aquarius	♒	Aries	♈	Libra	♎
Moon	☽	Cancer	♋	Capricorn	♑	Taurus	♉	Scorpio	♏
Mercury	☿	Gemini	♊	Sagittarius	♐	Aquarius	♒	Leo	♌
		Virgo	♍	Pisces	♓				
Venus	♀	Taurus	♉	Scorpio	♏	Pisces	♓	Virgo	♍
		Libra	♎	Aries	♈				
Mars	♂	Aries	♈	Libra	♎	Capricorn	♑	Cancer	♋
Jupiter	♃	Sagittarius	♐	Gemini	♊	Cancer	♋	Capricorn	♑
Saturn	♄	Capricorn	♑	Cancer	♋	Libra	♎	Aries	♈
Uranus	♅	Aquarius	♒	Leo	♌				
Neptune	♆	Pisces	♓	Virgo	♍				
Pluto	♀ or ♇	Scorpio	♏	Taurus	♉				

A planet in the sign of its **dignity feels** dignified—like you do when you're dressed for work, you might say. This is the sign (or "outfit") that allows the planet to do its job best—its most **practical** ensemble. We say that a planet "rules" the sign of its dignity, because it's best able to perform its function in this sign.

Pay special attention to the planets that **rule** a sign, because when we get to Houses, you'll need to learn that again, and you might as well get the jump on it now.

When in **debility**, a planet is "wearing" the sign opposite to its dignity. It feels encumbered. It's like borrowing someone else's clothes—you can manage, and you'll probably manage just fine, too, but you may need to take in the waist, or take down the hem a bit, because the outfit isn't something you would have chosen for yourself. Consequently, rather than affecting the planet in a "bad" way, wearing the sign of its debility may encourage a planet to become more **conscious** about the way it expresses itself.

A planet wearing the sign of its **exaltation** is wearing its very favorite outfit—its **play clothes**, you might say. Although this outfit isn't at all **practical**, it's just fine for being comfortable. Similar to the way you feel in your favorite jeans and sweater. Now, since it's so comfortable, a planet in exaltation isn't feeling restrained at all—so you may notice that it expresses itself more freely and more **loudly**, even—than do the other planets.

In its **fall**, a planet is wearing an outfit that's several sizes too large or too small, and the wrong color, to boot. A planet in its fall feels the same way you do when you've stayed over a friend's house, and you have to grab their bathrobe to answer the door— you're dressed, but you had no choice about what you've got on, and it shows. You'll probably try to stand behind the door. A planet in its fall, then, finds ways of hiding without really hiding, of "doing" its job without **appearing** to be acting.

Again, remember that any sign can be adjusted to fit the needs of any planet or house, and there are no "bad" or "good" signs. Using the clothing analogy again, think of how the look of a whole outfit changes when we add a piece of clothing that's the "right" color. It becomes workable. Even comfortable. That's how we make all our energies "work." We add new experiences that prompt us to reach for the higher end of a sign, or we bring in outside influences that add just the right touch. We work at it till we feel "balanced." Think of how being in the right job or being with another person alters our outlook.

CHAPTER FIVE

THE HOUSES—
PIECES OF YOUR PERSONALITY

All right, then. Let's review. Yes, again. Because I know you fire signs keep skipping ahead when I'm not looking, that's why, and all you (I mean, um, **us**) Sags can't even be **forced** to read unless it's from the back of the book forward—to get The Big Picture first. But mostly because it's good to review. It is. How do you think you learned your numbers?

Anyway. There are, as I told you way back when in Chapter One, **Four Astrological Food Groups** to learn en route to understanding astrology. The first Food Group is made up of the **planets** which each symbolize an **urge** or **need** that automatically comes with the package when you sign up for a human body. (Chiron and the four Asteroid Goddesses fall under the category of "Planets" since they also represent inner urges and needs of more specific kinds.) Group Number Two consists of the **signs,** the "outfits" your planets "wear," the **flavors** or **filters** that describe the **style** of behavior you'll use when you're acting on one of your urges or needs.

You remember all that, right?

Great. Because that brings us to Food Group Number Three— The **houses**—and they're up next. Now, houses are different from planets and signs. Planets represent **what** you need to do, and signs describe **how** or **why** you need to do it. Houses, however, reflect the actual life circumstances we create around us as we toddle merrily about our business here on Earth. They tell us where to find the **side of our selves**, or the "piece" of our personality, we bring out when we're participating in each of those particular Life Circumstances.

For example, the second house is where the "piece" of you lives that's in charge of What's Dear to You: money, possessions, and so forth. So your second house describes The Shopper side of you, the "slice" of you that comes out when you walk into a store, any store, whether it's your favorite boutique or your basic A&P. You know how it sometimes feels like that side of your personality has a mind of its own? You're right. It does—at times. Matter of fact, there are 12 houses in your chart—12 "pieces" of your personality, that is—and they've **all** got minds of their own—at times.

It's like this: we humans are complicated critters—that's no secret. Our personalities are made up of **many** personalities. Think of how you feel—and **act**—when you're drinking wine with your best friend at your kitchen table in your jeans and your favorite ancient sweat-shirt. Now think of another "you," the you that you "do" when you're in your best pin-stripes, politely sipping coffee in front of a prospective employer's desk. It's you in both situations, of course. You're even **doing**, basically, the same thing—having something to drink with another person. But that's where the similarity ends. Everything else about the way you act in those two situations is dramatically different. You won't tell your prospective employer any of the secrets you'll tell your Best Buddy—not if you want to appear "professional," at least. Likewise, you won't bore your best friend with endless details on how well you organized the mayor's last campaign.

The point is that different life situations call for different behaviors. Houses describe the twelve primary life Situations and, through the signs and planets involved, show your **view** or **perspective** on those matters which, in turn, shapes your behavior in those situations.

Houses as Rooms

Think of the houses as 12 rooms in one big house. The house is You and the rooms are "pieces" or "sides" of your personality. In the example above, for instance, you were using your seventh-house personality with your best friend, because the seventh house refers to the you that emerges when you're in the presence of **just one Other**—and especially An Other that you're committed to in some way. Sipping coffee at your interview, however, you were using both your seventh house (relating One-To-One), **and** your tenth house side, since the tenth house is where we keep our "business only" persona, the side of us that acts in what we consider the "proper" way when we're in the presence of **authority figures**. ('Course, this is also the side of you that emerges when you **become** The Authority Figure Here, but that's another story.)

And Then There Are House Cusps

The lines that separate your houses are the "doors" that open onto "rooms" in a house—so it makes sense that the line **preceding** a house is its cusp. The **sign** on a house cusp shows how you've decorated your particular room's door—the style of the way you act, in other words, when those particular life circumstances come up. House cusps represent your attitude—what you expect from life—at those times. **Planets** in your houses are symbolically like **people** who **live** in your rooms. (We'll talk more about them in a minute.)

FEELING THE HOUSES

If you really want to "feel" the different sides of you that you keep inside each of your houses, think of how you react when you've got to **mix** them. Not like the prospective employer example above, which you were prepared for, but when you're "doing" one house and someone who belongs to the part of your life **another** house handles arrives on the scene. This type of situation puts you in the position of combining "pieces" of you—and depending on which pieces it is that you've got to get out simultaneously, you may or may not be a happy camper.

For example, you're out to dinner with your Brand New Baby, the guy/gal you've been worshipping from afar for weeks. Since the fifth house is where we stash the piece of ourselves that specializes in Love Affairs, your fifth house side is currently "driving." So here you are, all dressed up in a brand new outfit you bought specially for the occasion. You're "on," in other words. Your head is cocked at **just** the right angle, and you're listening attentively to every word your new Other utters. The two of you are probably even holding hands across the table. You're having a nice night. A very nice night. You're thinking it may get even nicer.

All of a sudden, along comes your Dad. He kisses you on the top of your head/punches you in the arm, scowls at the neckline on your dress/asks you where you got that hideous tie, and pulls up a chair. Before you can recover from the shock, he scolds you for not calling your Mom lately, asks the waiter for a menu, and starts talking baseball/baseball to your date. Talk about a good time, huh? All of a sudden, you can feel a shift happening inside. You are now in the extremely awkward position of trying to be both Daughter/Son and Lover—of operating two sides of you at the same time. They're sides of you that don't normally get to work together, so it's a tricky situation. To make things, as the Chinese say, **really** interesting, let's bring in Glenda from Accounting. She saw you from outside and she's alone—is it all right if she joins you?

Well. Due to circumstances beyond your control, there are now three "doors" open inside you. Three of your houses are competing for control of the wheel. In human terms, that means that three sides of your personality normally reserved for three very different situations are trying to work through the same body—at the same time. It's a challenge, to say the least. Should you be your Daughter side, your Lover side, or your Co-Worker side? If your bowling team showed up, you'd be hard-pressed to avoid a social overload.

You get the picture. Houses are Departments, too. They're where you stash the 12 sides of your personality that you only use in particular life situations. Now, it's not **always** uncomfortable to mix and match Multi-House Life Situations. If you're out shopping with your Mom and your best friend happens along, for example, that can be fun—and so can other mixtures. The point is that when you find yourself in the company of people from a particular "department" of your life, you immediately "shift" to the side of you that's appropriate to that situation. You become the persona you've decided is appropriate behavior in that instance. When folks from **several** "departments" appear all at once, you have to either choose—make a behavioral decision, that is—or keep shifting, depending on who you're relating with directly at each moment. Either way, it's exhausting.

Okay. Everybody huddle in this corner for a minute—it's time for a Meeting. We've touched lightly on a couple of the houses through examples in the overview you just finished. Hopefully, now you understand that the houses in your chart are like "rooms" in a house, that the house really represents You, and that the rooms symbolize the different "sides" of You—different "pieces" of your personality.

You've got all that, right?

If you don't, go read it again, and think about how different you are at work, at play, with your Mom, and when you're alone. Better still, **call** your Mom, your honey, and a co-worker, and pay attention to the "You" that emerges with each call. (Try not to get involved in anything lengthy, 'though—we've got work to do here.) When you're ready—when you can **feel** it, Brothas and-a-Sistas— continue reading. We're going to talk next about the structure of your house, and specifically about the "Main Beams" that you've built to keep You together.

The Ascendant and the Midheaven
The Angles: The "Main Beams"
in Your House

LOCATING THE MIDHEAVEN, IC, ASCENDANT, AND DESCENDANT

All house cusps were not created equal. In fact, of all the **house cusps** on your wheel, there are a couple that you'll hear about over and over again as you continue to study. Although each of the twelve cusps is a "door" and an "opening" in its own right, the "doors" we're going to open first are especially significant. They're referred to as **"The Angles,"** and they're the primary "entryways" in your chart. They function like "openings" between You and Out There, and point to where You slip out to interact with your environment and your environment comes in to touch base with You.

The first place we're going to talk about is the spot on your chart that corresponds to where "12" would be on a clock. It's called the **Midheaven**. This "door" opens onto the "Roof" of your chart, the highest, most exposed degree in the chart. The Midheaven is your personal bulletin board. It's where you put all your accomplishments, and all the things you want the world to know about You. This degree is calculated from **The Moment** you were born—your planetary debut. It says an awful lot about what you see as your **purpose** here on Planet #3, and about the way you handle your public life and the formation of your reputation, too.

The second place you'll hear a lot about is the **Ascendant**, or the **Rising Sign**. That's the door found right where "9" would be on a clock. The Ascendant corresponds, in part, to your physical appearance and to the type of first impression you make on others. It's like the "Front Door" of the chart, and although it may not say much about what the rest of the house looks like, if it doesn't look friendly, the kids won't come there for Halloween. If it looks too friendly, on the other hand, there'll be a constant flow of traffic through that door. You'll be exhausted—as tired as you would be if you had live-in guests at your home all the time. This degree corresponds with **The Location** of your birth, so it's a symbolic description of how you like **your** location—your immediate environment, that is—to look and feel.

Now, neither of these two points exist separately. They're attached to an axis—a "hallway," you might say. At the opposite end of each hallway is another "door" which (since each axis divides the chart in half), will always, always be wearing the same degree and minute as its counterpart—in the opposite sign. These house cusps are where you keep opposite sides of your personality, sides of you reserved for very different situations. Opposite to the Roof, then, at the other end of that "Hallway," is the Imum Coeli, affectionately called the "I.C." here in Astrology-Land. Tucked safely away at the very bottom of your chart, the I.C. is the door to the fourth house, where the part of you who's into "nesting" lives. It's similar to the "Cellar" in a house, so it represents a side of you that's every bit as private as your "Roof" persona is public. The piece of you that handles privacy, home and family operates out of this spot.

At the other end of the "hallway" from the **Ascendant** is the **Descendant** ('Magine?), and as much as the Ascendant is like your Front Door, and the face you present to the world on first impressions, the Descendant is like a "Back Door," the spot that corresponds with the side of you that handles One-To-One relationships. This side of your personality is more casual than the Ascendant and less concerned with "appearances." It's here that we each keep the side of us that wants to really **share** ourselves with An Other person. The sign on this door represents the qualities you look for in An Other, and, more importantly, the qualities you like to be able to exhibit when you're with An Other.

Basically, these two axes form the Main Beams in your house. They represent the rules you set up to live by, and the style you display as you make your way through your world, interacting with others. You rely on these "doors," polish them up for company, and reinforce or adjust them periodically to better suit the weather "Out There." When circumstances change and you need to re-vamp your way of **relating** to the world, you symbolically renovate your Main Beams—by changing or altering your **style** of interaction. These Main Beams are the framework the rest of the house depends upon, just as your ability to have successful encounters with others and your environment, both personally and socially, forms the framework of your life.

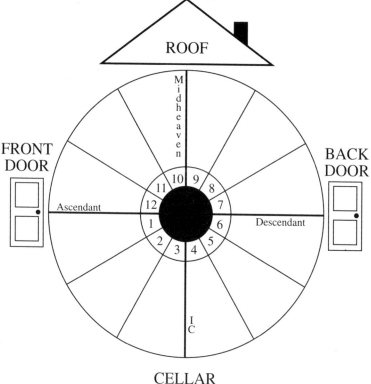

HOW BIRTH TIME FIGURES IN

By the way, getting the houses right is the reason we astrologers are such sticklers for accurate birth times. Here's why: I've already told you that the Midheaven is where the 12 would be on a clock. Well, that point represents Noon on the chart's wheel, the time of day when the Sun's rays are the strongest. Makes sense when you consider that your Midheaven is the most Public spot in your chart. Across the board, at the IC, is Midnight—where you keep things private. Your "rising" sign, appropriately enough, is at 6 AM—and even if you **don't** "rise" that early, most of us do spend our early mornings tending to our physical selves and readying them to meet the world properly: bathing, dressing, exercising, too. Your Descendant is 6 PM, the time of day when you're finally able to kick back and just "be yourself" with An Other. The house cusps in between those "Main Beams" divide the wheel further, into approximately 2-hour segments. Since the houses are the **framework** for the rest of your chart, we need to know what time of day you were born to know where to start "building" your "house"—and which signs to put on which "doors."

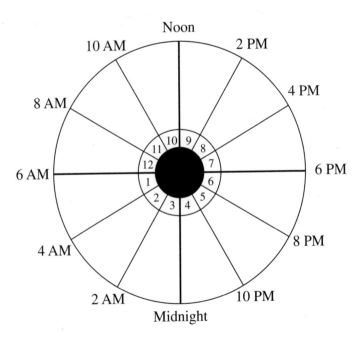

For example, say you were born at midnight and you're a Cancer. Well, that means that your Sun is going to appear somewhere around the IC of your chart. Since the order of the signs **never** changes, and since there are 12 signs to match the 12 houses, if you've got Cancer on your fourth-house (IC) cusp, you'll have Leo on your fifth, and Virgo on your sixth, and Libra on your Descendant. (Unless, of course, you're "missing" two signs. In which case you've got what's known as an "Interception" and, if you hang on for just two more paragraphs, I'll tell you all about them.) If Libra is on your seventh house, well, then, since the opposite sign from Libra is Aries, **that** would be your Ascendant—your Rising Sign. Which would explain why you don't think you "act" at **all** like a Cancer. See? So please don't let anybody give you any guff when you ask them for a **time**. Matter of fact, when you start doing charts on your own, make it a practice to absolutely **hound** whoever you need to for the most exact birth time it's humanly possible to get.

Remember—each chart shows the exact position of every heavenly body Up There, at the moment and from the perspective of your birth. The more exact the time, the more accurate the chart you'll be reading.

All right. The tirade about Accurate Birth Data is officially over. If you think that was bad, just get Lois Rodden going. Now we can talk to all of you out there with the "missing signs."

Interceptions—
Not As Awful As They Sound

About the "Missing Signs." First of all, they're not missing. Second, you are going to live—and you're not living out a "Karmic Lesson" because you were "bad" last lifetime, either. Honest. See, you still **have** those signs in your chart, even though you can't "see" them on any house cusps. As I said, these are Intercepted Signs, which really just means that you've got one pair of houses that are much larger than the others. Period. Intercepted houses are sometimes even **double** the size of other houses, matter of fact, because they've got all 30 degrees of those "missing signs" **inside** them, along with a couple of degrees from the sign before and the sign after. This type of house distortion happens more (and becomes more drastic) the farther North—or South—you go, since the angle at which we view the Sun is more "slanted" the farther we get from the Equator.

Now, since **intercepted houses** are so large, it's not uncommon to find several planets, perhaps even in different signs, "living" in those houses—"sharing a room," you might say. When you're reading intercepted houses, then, remember that your behavior is going to be as varied as the selection of archetypes you've got printed on the page in front of you. "Varied," however, is not "bad." It can even be exciting—ask any Gemini if you don't believe me.

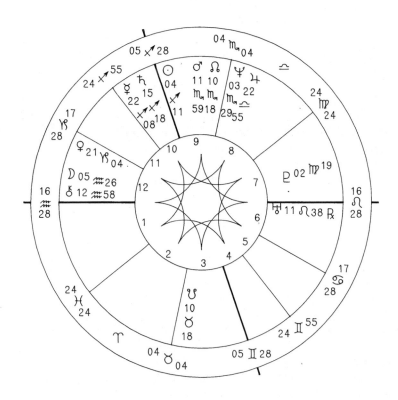

Kim Rogers-Gallagher

No Planets—Or Many,
Many Planets—in Houses

While we're discussing particulars, let's talk about another condition you might initially think is terminal—Empty Houses. If you've got one—or a whole bunch, even—don't panic. You don't need to call anyone. Some houses contain planets and others don't. That's all there is to it. There's nothing wrong with you or your chart; **nobody** has a planet in every house. It's impossible. There are ten planets and twelve houses. Even if you're already using Chiron and the asteroids, you'll still probably end up with one "vacant" room. Planets, you see, tend to cluster—for company, maybe. Again, don't panic. Regardless of whether or not they're inhabited by planets, each of your twelve houses is very real and very active.

Think of it this way, there are several rooms in your apartment or home where no one "lives"—the kitchen, for one. The bathroom, for another. That doesn't mean these rooms are nonexistent, and it certainly doesn't mean they're not useful. The same goes for empty houses in your chart—you've still **got** every house In There—you just won't be as concerned with those areas of life as you will be with others. As a **very** general rule, then, empty houses are "rooms" you've got—areas of life you do participate in and do have some interchange with—but not as obviously as those areas of life with planets involved.

Without a planet "living" in it, a house may be a little quieter—at least, until a Transiting Planet or two moves in and calls your attention to ordinarily "empty" rooms. (More about that in Chapter Eight under "Transits.")

Stellia—Hands Across the Water

We've just talked about how quiet a room in a home or apartment is when no one lives there—and we've seen how that "quiet" works on a symbolic level when a house in your chart is empty. But what about when the opposite situation is true—that is, when several planets share a room? Well, you'll have the opposite problem. It may get so noisy in there that you'll have to go in every so often and ask them to **please** turn the stereo down. Think of planets in groups like **people** in groups—the bigger the crowd, the louder the volume. If they're all in the same sign, they're "dressed" the same, so they'll be speaking the same language, to boot. Planets in groups are called **stellia**—they show areas of life in which you have special interest and, probably, talents.

In a nutshell, a **stellium** is a group of three planets or more, clustered together. To get a really clear image of how a stellium "works" symbolically, picture the characters we described in Chapter Two holding hands, forming a planetary chain. They can hold hands across both house and sign boundaries. If they're stretched out across house cusps, the "door" separating the houses "disappears." In other words, you automatically blend those two **areas of your life**, those two "sides" of your personality, because "pieces" of you are passing notes back and forth and chatting as if there were no door there at all, no separation between one "side" of you and the next. A stellium involving planets in two signs is like characters dressed in different outfits that nonetheless are working on the same project. Since the planets in our charts represent our individual human **urges** and **needs**, bundles like these show urges and needs we've **combined**. These "group situations" show where you, literally, have bundles of energy. Stellia are dramatic and exciting.

Emphasis by Quadrant and Hemisphere

Now, sometimes we have more than just a simple Group Situation in our charts. Sometimes we have all our planets clustered together in four or five neighboring houses. Makes the rest of the chart look like a ghost-town, but it makes you a specialist—even more so than just having regular stellia. Here's the story.

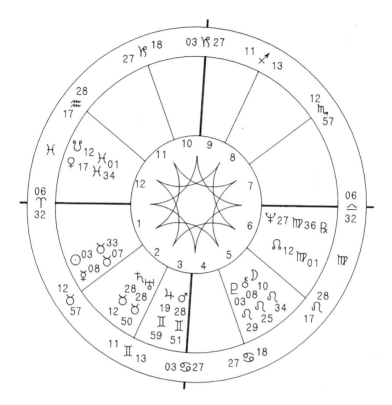

Barbra Streisand

Whole books have been written about "Bowls," "Buckets," and "See-saws," all of which are basically names for shapes the planets form in the heavens at any particular time. A "Bowl," for example, is a collection of all of the planets over one half of the chart. It's said that Bowls show where we tend to collect experiences—the occupied half of the chart.

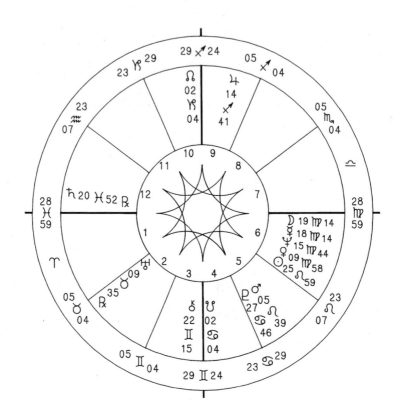

Robert Redford

"Buckets" are bowls with one planet more or less at a 90-degree angle to the other planets at either end of the bowl. Bucket charts are often interpreted by first examining the planet that looks like the "handle," since it's all by its lonesome in one half of your chart, "opposed" to everybody else, and symbolically "carrying the weight" of the rest of the chart.

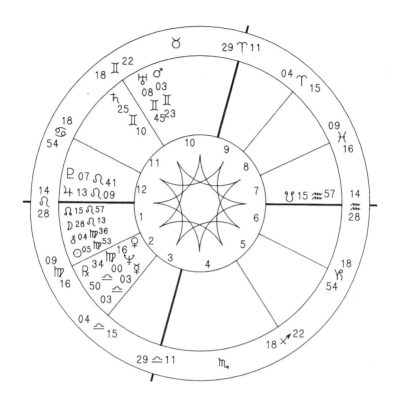

Jean-Claude Killy

"Bundles" are just what you'd expect—chart with all the planets clustered together (over less than 120 degrees, traditionally). Bundle charts are like super-stellia—so the chart owner may be super-focused on the areas of life covered by the occupied houses.

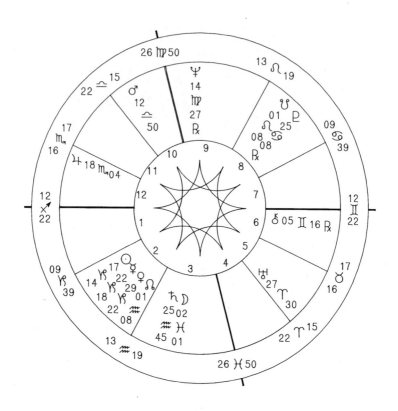

Elvis Presley

"See-saws" are charts with two distinct bundles of planets and, just as you'd expect, they indicate a personality that's constantly seeking balance in life situations.

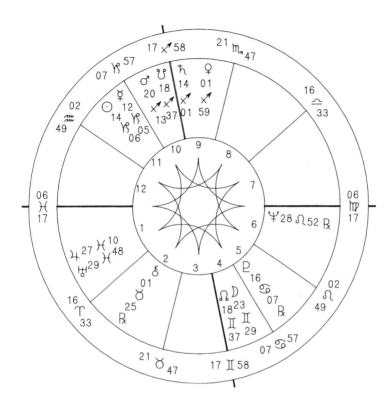

Walter Mondale

"Splashes" are charts whose planets—and, therefore, whose owner's interests—spread out, and "Splays" are more of the same.

All of these chart shapes usually (but not **always**) reflect just those qualities in the lives of their owners, and it's important to teach yourself to notice them.

Now, while we're on the subject of planets in Group Living Situations, let's talk about what happens when all—or most of—the planets live together in a particular "wing" of the chart. In one quarter—or **quadrant**—or in one half—**hemisphere**. Once again, I want you to **use what you already know** to understand how this "works." What's above the earth's horizon is what we can literally see without the aid of a telescope or other device. What's below is "hidden." Naturally, then, individuals with all their planets above the 1st/7th axis are said to be here to experience life with others, to deal with relationships, to live a public life in which Others will be actively involved. Conversely, folks with most of their stuff packed below the horizon are traditionally more private, more "self-involved," and less liable to require Others for their own development. People with all their planets on the left side of the chart are considered "go-getters," theoretically because these are the houses the Sun covers as it climbs up, up, and away from the peak of night—midnight—to the peak of day—noon. When all the planets are on the right side of the chart, individuals seem to "re-act" to life, rather than act. Again, traditionally, because the Sun is on its way down, from noon to midnight.

Now, as with everything else in life, exceptions to these rules abound. If, for example, you were born with all of your planets above the horizon, but packed in the shadows of the 8th and 12th houses, you're not going to see yourself as a "public" person. If you're born with all the planets below the horizon, but half of them are in your first house of personality, you certainly won't think of yourself as a "private" personality. That's where the Quadrants come in.

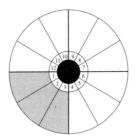

First Quadrant emphasis (houses 1, 2, 3) shows a personality symbolically working on the issues of Personal Presentation: Physical Appearance, Possessions, and Communication Skills.

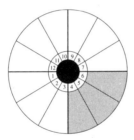

Second Quadrant emphasis (houses 4, 5, 6) points to a personality that's centered in The Basics of life on the planet: Home, Children, and Work.

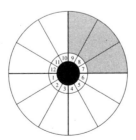

Third Quadrant emphasis (houses 7, 8, 9) may be primarily concerned with Interpersonal Presentation: One-to-One Relationships, Sharing Resources, and Social Functions.

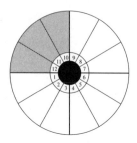

Fourth Quadrant (houses 10, 11, 12) folks may be working on Extrapersonal Issues: Life Purpose through Career, Group Affiliations, and Mass Consciousness.

There's a lot of good data to be gleaned from this type of analysis, and lots of folks get much more specific about it—like about the actual number of degrees that make up a "true" Bucket or Bundle, or what actually constitutes "emphasis" by quadrant or hemisphere. Personally, I look at it this way—consider **everything**. Everything. And, more importantly, before you start to analyze anything, Look At The Chart. Just **look** at it. Allowing yourself to "see" the planetary emphasis in a person's chart will help you to really **feel** the way the symbolism may be acting in their lives.

Singletons

One more thing: whether you're looking at a "Bucket" or a "Bundle" with one planet all by its lonesome, you've got what's called a Singleton. The technical definition of a Singleton is that it's a planet that's operating solo in one half of the chart. However, when you're looking at a planet that's all by itself—whether it's in the middle of six houses, or three, or even just a large chunk of space, consider what you already know. Think about **people** that tend to stay on their own, and you'll understand all there is to know about singletons. They're independent and/or lonely, self-sufficient and/or reclusive, self-contained and/or "shy." Now, of course, it's not all **that** simple. If the plant is not aspecting the rest of the gang in your chart—if it's not "mingling" with everybody else, that is—you may have a truer "loner" planet than you will if it's trining half of the other planets in your chart and sextiling the rest. Check the sign and house placement too. The Sun in Aries in the tenth house as a singleton, for example, will be much different than the Moon in Pisces in the twelfth. Again, just use what you already know about life to interpret astrology and you'll be hard-pressed to go wrong.

Behind the Twelve Doors— Which Side of You Lives Here?

So, let's see now—we've established that houses divide the chart's circle into twelve **places**, twelve "arenas" or **glimpses of life**, each of which represents a **piece of your personality** that emerges when you're dealing with that situation. We took you out to dinner with your honey, paid your Dad and a co-worker to show up so you'd understand what each house feels like, then talked about planets in your houses. We've established that both empty houses and stellia are perfectly all right to own, and definitely nothing to be scared of. You know all about the main beams in your "house," too, how the sign on each "door" gets there, and about the supreme importance of accurate birthdata.

Well. Now it's time to take a look at each house individually and meet the side of you that lives behind each door. Kindly keep in mind, as always, that I'm painting cartoons for you here because I want you to have fun reading my book. That way, I figure you'll learn this stuff without even realizing it, probably have some fun in the process, and maybe even be able to tell all your friends how great astrology is...

THE ASCENDANT AND DOOR NUMBER ONE— FIRST IMPRESSIONS

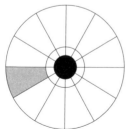

Ever watch yourself on videotape? No? Well, how about when you get stuck in the front of the aerobic class, right in front of the mirror? You know this one—you end up staring at yourself in the mirror for a whole self-conscious hour. In either case, you're seeing how you "look." The you others see, the **outside** of you—your personal "**front door**." That's what the Ascendant and the first house are all about—your surface. Now, "appearance," is just that—the way something "appears" to be on the surface—but not necessarily what it is. So, here's the "piece" of your personality that handles the initial impression you make on others, the way you "come off" to folks who've just met you and the general "style" of your **physical appearance**.

What's included in "appearance?" Anything that contributes to it. Anything, from the body size and shape you were born with, to the way you choose to dress it. Whether or not you decorate yourself with jewelry, cosmetics, or other "special effects" is in there, too, as are your gestures, movements, and posture. They're all part of The Big Picture—along with anything else that composes your **surface**. Of course, the condition of your body also affects the way you "look," so the general state of your health is also under your first house persona's jurisdiction.

Now, I know everybody's Mom taught them never to judge books by their covers, or people by the way they appear, but in reality, it's just about impossible for appearances **not** to affect how we react to someone—or something—when we first see them. We form opinions based on what we know of someone, so our opinions of folks quite naturally mature along with our knowledge of them. Initially, however, the Ascendant is all you get, so if the way a person seems to be doesn't "feel" right to you, you may hesitate to make contact with them, or you may not try to "break the ice" at all. Needless to say, then, it's very important to keep your first house working. It's the symbolic "Front Door" of your house, remember. If it's scary-looking, the kids won't come there for Halloween, and **no one** else will bother to see what's going on **behind** the door, either.

Now, since it only describes the outside of you, your Ascendant can be changed easily. Clothing, hair styles, and other "accessories" can make you **appear** to be an awful lot different than you really are. Which brings me to the subject of disguises and the Ascendant. See, there are groups of people who necessarily pay a lot more attention to their **appearance** and **surface demeanor** than most of us do. Actors and actresses, for example, need to be able to shape-shift, to make their Ascendant and their first house suit their current role, to convince us they really are someone they're not. Politicians do something similar every fourth November with their Ascendants, too—and that's all I'm going to say.

DOOR NUMBER TWO—YOUR STUFF— WHAT YOU "HOLD DEAR"

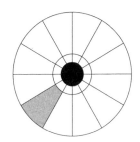

When it's time to talk about possessions— about what you've "got"—this is the "slice" of You that steps up to the mike. This includes the **selection** of new possessions as well as **tending** to the possessions you've already got. So here's where you'll find both The Shopper side of you and The Owner, too. How do you take care of Your Stuff? Do you abuse it, break it, lose it, and buy more? Do you hoard all kinds of things, from rubber bands to used aluminum foil? And what type of Stuff do you like, anyway? Do you set out deliberately to own only One-Of-A-Kind items—absolutely unique objects? Or do you just love picking through Consignment Shops and antique stores? Maybe you pride yourself on not owning much of anything. These choices are second house variations, just a couple of the attitudes different folks have about Their Stuff.

This second house side of you decides **what's dear** to you— what your priorities are, that is. So when you hear someone say that they're "getting their priorities in order," they're symbolically redoing their second house. See, your possessions are earthly representatives of qualities you **value** enough to surround yourself with. As your **value system** changes, then, so does your choice of objects.

'Course, there's no time quite like Moving Time to **really** get in touch with your second house persona. When you move, you find yourself in the exhausting position of actually, physically touching **every single thing you own**—all in a few day's time. You have to pick it up, decide if it still has **value** to you, and then either pack it, discard it, or find it a suitable home. You may laugh, cry, and think of things you haven't in a long while as you sort through your possessions, remembering what each of them meant to you at the time they were bought or received. Whatever you keep after this process, you keep because you still **identify** with it, because it still has "worth" of some kind in your life. Whatever you toss doesn't. Not any more. You're no longer interested enough in those qualities to keep physical representatives around. It's the second house side of you that handles that decision, and all the other aspects of moving, too—from packing to unpacking to deciding where to put things in the new location.

Now, the money that you trade for those objects you just brought to your new place came at a "dear" price—hours of your life. So this house also describes **what** you're willing to do for money, the piece of you you're willing to trade for food, objects, and admission to experiences, like movies and travel. Here, then, is where you'll find a description of How You Make Your Money, of the skills and resources you **own** that you're willing to exchange for what you **don't** own.

'Course, money is part of your Stuff, too. How are you with money? Do you balance your check book? If you've got Virgo here, you probably will, and you may even know, to the penny, how much is in your account. With Sag here, on the other hand, you might round off your account to the nearest hundred dollars and count on luck to get You to the bank before the check you just wrote. (Don't ask how I know.)

In a nutshell, gang, this side of your personality is the side of you that represents what you think you're worth and what you think you deserve. Keep your second house standards high—or get yourself to an Abundance Workshop and renovate the room.

DOOR NUMBER THREE—
IT'S A SMALL WORLD, AFTER ALL

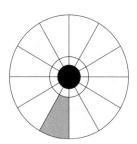

Draw an imaginary circle around Your World, the world you travel through every day, the places that are so familiar you could walk through them with your eyes closed. Include your neighbor and his dog, whom he walks at 6:20 every evening, the jogger who runs past your car as you turn left out of your driveway in the morning, and the woman with the long, long hair who drops the stacks of newspapers off on the corner next to the traffic light you always, always catch. This is your third house world—on a physical level.

The third house side of your personality is what you reach for when it's time to **perform automatically**. To walk. Turn on a light switch. Or drive to work past all the usual "landmarks" we just talked about. You don't consciously **think** out each of those actions—not any more. So this side of you is the "Auto Pilot" slice—it's driven by habit, routine, and What I Always Do.

Now, you didn't always know how to write your name, or flip that light switch—or even walk, let alone drive. You really did have to learn how, once, long, long ago. So there's a stage of life that relates to the third house. This Auto Pilot stage is made up of your early years. Toddlerhood, grammar school, and so forth—the years you spent learning everything you know how to do now without thinking about it consciously, the years you spent learning to **communicate** your needs to your environment. You learned the importance of communication when you were still hanging on to coffee tables to get around, when you said "Mom," and she responded. Brothers and sisters are traditionally included under the affairs of this house since (if you had any), they were a part of your world during this growing stage and presumably "taught" you something about how to relate.

Since this "piece" of you handled your way of tackling **the learning process** way back when, you naturally turn here whenever it's time to learn something new, no matter how old you happen to be when you take on the project. This side of you, then, describes your personal style of **assimilation**, how you set about acquiring a new skill or body of knowledge. If Sag is on the door, you learn by having The Big Picture explained first. If Virgo's there, you learn by perfecting and assembling details, one at a time. This house shows your **memory** and your reasoning process, too. It's your inner switchboard, where you receive stimulus from your environment, process it, and relay it to the appropriate department for consideration.

Since this is, in effect, your Communication Department, it's where you keep the part of you that writes letters, makes phone calls, and gets you to your appointments. Think of this side of you as a combination Scriptwriter, Secretary, and Scribe.

THE IC AND DOOR NUMBER FOUR— ## THE CELLAR

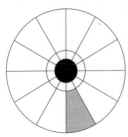

Think about what you keep in your cellar, about what's "buried" way down deep at the bottom of those stairs. There are boxes of memorabilia down there—newspaper clippings, diaries and yearbooks, old scrapbooks and letters—stuff that reminds you of Your Past. Now, you don't go through these boxes every day. In fact, you probably don't even touch them once a year. Still, you hold on to what's in them because you "feel" better knowing they're down there. The IC of your chart is very similar. It's your emotional "cellar," the place where you keep your memories—all of them. See, everything that's ever happened to you has had some type of emotional effect on you, and contributed in some way to the person you are right now. All those memories weave together in a tapestry that makes up your **foundation**, the emotional **roots** of your being—and that's what the fourth house is all about.

Pretend that at the foot of your stairs lives a tiny, older woman with rectangular reading glasses perched on the tip of her nose. She's your personal Librarian. It's her job to keep track of all those memories on the shelves and in the file cabinets, and how you react to them on a daily basis. She knows better than anybody what's "good" for you—and what's not. I hired this tiny lady to act out your IC, to give you a picture of the internal "mother" we've each got inside us, but you can think of her as a meditation exercise—whenever you want to get in touch with your "roots," imagine going to visit her.

This fourth house personality is the side of ourselves we turn to when we're put into situations that are unfamiliar and "scary" in some way. In other words, when you're trying to decide if what you're about to do is a "good" idea or a "bad" idea—based only on Past Experience—this is where you'll look for the answer. This is the side of you who keeps track of How That Felt last time you tried it. How **everything** felt, that is—from the first time your Mom held you, to the last time someone yelled at you. Whenever you make a decision based on your "gut" feelings, you come here for the answer. Remember, the IC is the lowest point in the chart, the most private place of all. It's the spot in each of us where our

instinct lives, the instinct that's at the root of every move we make.

A primary part of that same instinct is a sense of Personal Security, of what "feels" safe to us and what doesn't. Our homes are the places we create here on the planet to keep ourselves safe and comfortable—our "nests." Your fourth house side decides what your "nest" ought to look like and what it ought to be lined with, too, to make you feel secure. Traditionally, this house is assigned to A Parent, and usually to The Mother, but since more and more of us are being reared in homes that are no longer "traditional," a better way to look at the fourth house is as the **time in your life** when you were nurtured, the way you were nurtured, and the ongoing **effect** it has on your life. See Donna Cunningham's great explanation in "Moon Signs."

DOOR NUMBER FIVE—THE LOVE BOAT

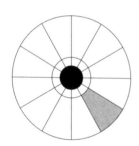 Behind Door Number Five lurks the side of you that only comes out to play. Here's the You that emerges when you're doing what you **choose** to do, as opposed to what you feel obligated to do. This is the lighthearted, fun side of you, the part that decides what you'll do when you've got an unexpected day "off"—and it's not a boring side of you, either... Your fifth house persona is the You who you become when you're out to have a Rully Good Time—no work involved, no Hafta's allowed.

Needless to say, this side of you is jee-ust wonderful. Sparklin', even. Here's where you're as creative as a Cruise Director, and just as charming. This is where The Lover in you lives, the part of your personality you save For Special Occasions. Ever notice when you put on your tux and/or gown, the brilliant smile that automatically goes on with the clothes? Your posture even changes. You know what I'm talking about. All of a sudden, Every Moment Counts, Every Second is special, and a whole darned **evening** is just too wonderful for words. When you find yourself in that situation, when you're positively high on what you're doing, you're using the brightest, lightest, most imaginative side of you. This is it. This is the "room" where you keep that side.

Sounds like a great place to take a date, huh? Well, it is, and you do take your dates here—your "love affairs," as they say. Think of how imaginative you are when you're deciding where to take a brand new beau. A cruise on the river, maybe? How about a quick flight into The City for dinner and a show? When you find yourself tipping a waiter to give your request to the band and bring the rose over on a tray, your fifth house side is currently at the helm.

So what do you **enjoy**? What do you just **love** to do? This side of you chooses the hobbies you'll pursue and the recreational activities you'll fill your spare time with. If you don't ever **give** yourself spare time, that's in here, too. But it's a shame. That expression "all work and no play makes Jack a dull boy"? This is the house it was written about. Allowing yourself to play brings out the creative side of you that work and responsibility often beat into submission. If you don't play, you don't let this side of you out, and this, friends, is the house where the fresh "juice" lives. This is where your creative ideas originate, where the side of you that's free enough to imagine lives away from duties, responsibilities, and commitments. In short, it's You at your most playful.

Since you're already feeling so wonderful, this is one of the places where you'll find the part of you that believes in "luck." It's the part of you that's willing to bet because you feel like a winner—and you can't win if you don't play, after all. But what are you willing to gamble? What new enterprises are you willing to undertake? This house shows the side of you that feels so good, it'll try anything once...and so the fifth house refers to our attitude about gambling, whether that happens to be on a riverboat or in an office.

Now, my first teacher used to say that this house is where we get to "See ourselves through our creations." And it's true. See, it doesn't matter **what** we've created—whether it's a work of art, a magazine article, or a child. Any creation is a little piece of Us—just standing there shining. The **pride** we feel when we look at our creations is a very distinctly fifth house kind of feeling—as is the woundedness we experience when someone we love rejects us—or when our creative efforts are criticized.

Children, as I said, are also created by us (hence the word "procreation" I s'pose), and the way that we raise them has everything to do with how we were raised, which is another part of our fifth house side.

Wedged in as it is between the houses of Home and Work, it's easy to dash through this room without really allowing yourself to set a spell and play—without allowing your mind to wander. Don't—okay? Just plain old feelin' groovy is important for everybody, once in a while.

Pets... And Where They Belong

Here's another one for the Top Ten list I keep telling you about, another item on the "Most Argued-Over Astrological Topics" List. It's like this: traditional astrology assigns the sixth house to animals—small ones, like domestic pets, that we "tend" to. (The twelfth house is traditionally given to large animals—like horses and goats—that "serve" us in some way.) Those who put pets in the sixth house assert that these critters are in our lives to "serve" also, to kill the mice in the barn, keep the sheep in line, and protect us from intruders. The hired help, you might say. Since the sixth was the "House of Slavery" in Ye Olde Time Astrology, some folks assign cats and dogs to the sixth house.

I personally find that concept hysterical. Not the idea of "slavery" and "pets," you understand. **That,** I believe, makes **perfect** sense. We certainly do drop whatever we're doing and obediently go to the door when Benji or Fluffy get That Look on their fuzzy little faces, we certainly do go out and work to bring home the Magic Cans, and we do have occipital thumbs to open the above-mentioned cans **with** (which, I'm sure, is why they keep us). No, although I can definitely see the connection between slavery and pets (to some extent), it's not because **they're** the slaves...at least, not around here. It's because we tend to them, I suppose, the way we tend to lots of sixth-house duties. They become part of our Daily Gig. Not to mention the fact that they are "domestic" or "tamed" animals.

However. **Some** of us treat our animals like lovers—or children. We kiss, cuddle, spoil and pamper them. We take them for rides and promise them fast-food hamburgs after The Doctor. They even sleep with us. And they're fun to play with, too—like living teddy bears. Since most modern-day domestic **pets** serve no "purpose" but to be "petted," then, they can justifiably be connected to the fifth-house, where all our **other** children, lovers, and playmates are found. My Mighty Editress also mentioned that pets are **family** for many people—so you could also include them in the fourth house. I suggest applying the house you feel is most appropriate to your relationship with your beast(s). Personally, I'm torn. I mentioned the whole thing because I know you're going to be at an astrological cocktail party one day soon when the subject comes up, and I don't want you to be caught unprepared.

DOOR NUMBER SIX—WHAT DO YOU "DO"?

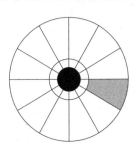

What do you "do" with your time? Do you get into the shower every day at 7:32, get out at 7:43, pour the coffee that's set to automatically begin perking at 7:40, and head out the door **precisely** at 8:15? Is that you? Or do you work nights, get up somewhere between 7:30 and 8:45, exercise at some point—maybe—and have lunch—sometimes—before you go in at 3? Choose the scenario that best describes your attitude about what the rhythm of a day ought to be like, and you'll find yourself describing your own sixth house.

Yes, this "piece" of you decides how you like things to go along over the course of a day—predictably, as in Scenario #One, or unpredictably, as in #Two. It's the activities you perform over the course of a day, and the part of you that you take out when there's work to be done. For that matter, it's the side of you that talks the rest of you into **going** to work at all. Period. It's your need to have a "function," and the persona you assume when you're **at** work, **in** work, or **with** people from work, "functioning." This house really ought to describe what you "do" all day long at work, too—since your skills and abilities are here.

And speaking of work, and speaking of slavery, again—well, most of us have no trouble making **that** connection. Even if you do like what you "do," when you're doing it on a gorgeous, sunny day in mid-July, it sure **feels** like slavery. It takes the truly dutiful side of you to talk the rest of you into staying there and working just because it's got to be done.

Now, you're also a slave to your body. You have no choice but to take care of it—if you want it to perform for you. You've got to wash it, feed it, and keep it healthy the best you can. How well you do at that is reflected in the condition of your health. If you don't "take care of yourself," in other words, you'll be sick and unable to work—you won't be "functioning" up to par. Likewise, if you're really involved with a project, you're less liable to **allow** yourself to be sick.

But back to the Health and Hygiene You. This is the side of you with the thermometer and the yellow rubber gloves, the piece of you who's There To Help, a real Girl Scout/Boy Scout type. This side of you delights in doing tasks well and feels satisfaction from finishing a job. In short, here's where you're a combination nurse, worker-bee, exercise trainer, dietitian, and Good Doobee. Frequently, then, if this house in your chart is especially "packed" with planets, you'll find yourself exhausted. All the time. (In which case, you might want to make your way over to the twelfth-house "room," turn out the lights, and put your feet up.)

THE BACK DOOR AND DOOR NUMBER SEVEN

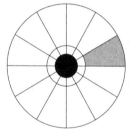 Across the chart from your Ascendant is your seventh house, or Descendant. Just as the Ascendant represents your personal **front door**, the **Descendant** represents your **back door**. This is the person you become when you're Relating to just one other person who is also, hopefully, Relating directly to **you**. Your seventh house side opens up after the Initial Screening and Formal Introduction process takes place, after you've checked out each other's first houses (or "front doors," that is). When you've been left alone at the hors d'oeuvres table and you're poking around for common ground, once it's just You and Them, the seventh house side of you is running the show. This is the side of you that comes out when you are in the company of just one other person.

Now. Since it's the room where you stash the One-on-One Expert inside you, you swing your seventh house door open **especially** wide for people you'll be relating to on a long-term basis, i.e., Committed Relationships. A marriage, for example. Or a business partnership. A scuba-diving "buddy" or work-out partner, too. Any time you use the word "My" to describe another person, it's because You and They need one other as **partners**, to fulfill a specific purpose, and in your mind, they're a member of your seventh house club. "My," you see, denotes **ownership**, which means that you identify with this person so much you consider them as part of you. My Spouse. My Partner. My Wife. My Husband. My Best Friend. When you start using one of those words, the seventh house "piece" of you has spoken.

Another way of looking at the seventh house is to think of it as the side of you that relates to folks that you consider equals. So while we're on the subject, let's not forget about enemies— "open" enemies, as they say, as opposed to "secret enemies," which we'll cover in the twelfth house. Why enemies here, you say? Well, because they're **your** enemy—they **belong** to you, in much the same way that your partner does. You also **choose** your enemies because they allow you to "do" a side of You that no one else does. Unfortunately, it's not usually a side of You that you **like** seeing, and that's why you don't like the person. You also really do consider your enemies your **equal**—at least—whether you're willing to admit it or not. (That's why they scare you.)

But you've also developed relationships with the fifth house side of you, you say. Well, yes, except that in the fifth, you're **playing**—there're no strings attached. So these can be temporary relationships, with folks that you only share one particular thing—a sport, a game, or a place, for example. Fifth house relationships aren't notoriously good at holding up through Tough Times and that's okay—you don't choose them for Tough Times, you **choose** them for Fun Times. Now, the seventh house side of you wants more than a playmate, more than someone to giggle with. The seventh house wants An Other. A Significant Other, you might say, rather than **in**significant Other(s). See the difference? Here in the seventh house, You and They come together to create a We that will be a We for a while. (Got all that?) And here's the final test, when you find yourself wearing sweat pants and glasses instead of lipstick or a tie, trust me—the transferal is complete. You've officially switched The Other over from the fifth house to the seventh house. Because you've switched your **behavior** style when you're around them.

Since we only use our seventh house persona when we're in the company of just one Other, after we haven't been with An Other for awhile, we begin to feel "lonely." There's a piece of us that isn't used. When this "room" hasn't been inhabited for a while, then we go out looking for tenants. For company. For An Other.

The hardest thing to do with this "piece" of your personality is the most important. In order to operate this side of you successfully, you've got to resist the urge to project your seventh-house qualities onto someone else and, instead, find someone who makes **you** feel comfortable **being** that side of you.

DOOR NUMBER EIGHT—
THE CRISIS EXPERT IN YOU

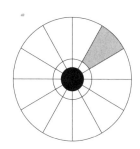

Picture Door Number Eight as a dark, heavy one with an iron ring for a handle. It's such a heavy door, in fact, that when you want to "be" this side of you, you've got to back up and use all your weight to pull it open. Yes, here's the piece of you that comes out when The Situation is not for the faint of heart. In fact, any time you find yourself in a situation where you're experiencing either "agony or ecstasy," (as Michael Lutin puts it), it's this "slice" of your personality that's driving.

Yes, this is the side of you that's tough enough to handle the Peaks and Valleys of both Major Crises and Peak Experiences. Or should I say Peaks and Black **Holes**—because when you're down, in an eighth-house way, you're **really** down. Big Time. And when you're up, you're really up, too. This is where the Deep, Heavy, Intense side of you lives, the part of you that craves Life or Death situations, that knows it's by experiencing "death" that we find out how good life really is.

Now, while we're in the neighborhood, we're going to talk about "death"—just a little—because death certainly does fall under the category of "crisis," and handling crisis is one of the reasons your eighth house side exists. First of all, there are many **types** of "deaths." Only **one** has anything to do with an actual, physical ending of a life. We deal with deaths every day, in all shapes and sizes; we just call them "endings" so they're easier to take. Divorce, for example, is a death of sorts; it's the end of a marriage. Leaving a job situation is a death, too, as is moving from one home to another. Basically, any time you find yourself in situations where you have to tear down one whole part of your life and start all over again, your eighth house Crisis Expert does the tearing—

and the rebuilding, too. See, "crisis" is nothing more than the loss we feel when something or someone we were attached to is no longer available to us. Doesn't matter whether we initiated the ending, either. When we're forced to **let go**, what we're "left" with is what we really **are**, not anything or anyone but.

Now, the time following a crisis is just as crucial as the process itself. So this eighth-house "room" also describes how you **rejuvenate** yourself when It's All Over, what you do to regenerate yourself after a loss of any kind.

I also mentioned "ecstasy" earlier—that's one of the job duties this side of you has that we certainly don't want to forget. Ecstasy—especially in the sexual sense—is very much about letting go—so it's a "loss" of sorts. When we experience ecstasy via another person, we've allowed the loss of our ego. We've let An Other infiltrate our physical, spiritual, intellectual, and emotional ranks in a very profound and private manner. Sex is really all about merging, after all. It's about letting down your walls and giving up **control.**

So what happens when you give up control? You get to touch the deep hidden side of you, where your real **power** lives. This eighth house "room" holds the Priest or Priestess, the You who's curious about The Mysteries, who wants to know all about them. And speaking of mysteries—any kind—it's your eighth-house persona that describes your Attitude about them. This is the side of you who peeks through your fingers and curls your toes at "the good parts" in movies. Yes, we've all got an eighth house side...but we don't have to talk about it any more.

DOOR NUMBER NINE—
WORLD NEWS TONIGHT

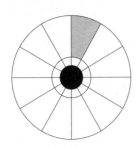

When was the last time you went Away? Away somewhere you've never been before, I mean. Doesn't matter whether it was by plane, train, *National Geographic*, or philosophy class, either. If it took you away from your routine, away from everything you know so well you don't have to even think to navigate it, it was a ninth-house adventure. Yes, behind Door Number Nine is the You who emerges when it's time to **travel**, learn new things, meet people with accents, and grow. Matter of fact, any time you leave your tiny third-house world and go far, far away, this is the piece of you who goes. You can tell this side of you is ready to take the wheel when you start hearing yourself say things like, "I really need a vacation," or "I've got to get away for awhile," or "I'm so bored..."

See, you can only "do" your daily life for so long before you feel cramped—like you're in a rut. Then you've just got to break away for awhile and "feed" this ninth-house side of you, to get a fresh perspective. Sometimes a movie will do it—a brief vacation from your routine. Since higher education is another "piece" of this ninth-house persona's job, taking a class often works, too; this side of you wants to hear something it's never heard before, see something it's never seen before, and **understand** how everything fits with everything else, too. This is the "piece" of you that gets a hankerin' for a course on world history or poli-sci.

Then there're times when nothing less than a month-long picture-taking safari to Africa will perk you up. Regardless of whether you do it from a plane or a movie theater, however, any kind of travel makes you realize what an awful lot of experiences there are to have on this wonderful planet we call home.

Now, once you're back, once you're home and unpacked, you'll notice that you feel different—like you've just "grown" a little, and you've got a broader perspective on Things than you did before you left. Well, you're right. You've opened yourself up to new experiences, and made yourself a regular wide-angle lens. Once you've grown in that way, once your **frame of reference** is widened, you can never go back. Each "trip" makes your view of the world a little wider. It's where the expression "being open-minded" came from. The more you see of What's Out There, the harder it is to be prejudiced in any way, against anyone. As your experiences widen so does your tolerance of the differences of others.

Of course, the more you see of The World, the more you'll consider yourself an expert on how Things ought to be managed—so it's here that you also formulate your opinions—with a capital "O." That includes your views on religion, politics, and The Current Mindset. Think of this side of you as the overseas anchor of the "World News Tonight" department of your life. When you're ready for adventure, look here to your ninth-house "room" for the side of you who'll pack the bags, buy the tickets, and travel. Here's the philosopher and the gypsy in you, the side of you that's hungry for experience. Whenever you feel that it's time to broaden your horizons, your ninth-house side is kicking up.

[By the way—speaking from the point of view of a Sagittarius with the Sun (the Executive Director, remember) in this ninth house—when you get the urge to go somewhere, go. Just go. Send me a postcard. Your contract on this planet is only a maximum of 120 years long, and there's an awful lot of planet out there. Find a way and go. Pretend you have to. It's good to treat your spirit to faraway lands. After all, you can only stay one size for so long...]

THE MIDHEAVEN AND DOOR NUMBER TEN

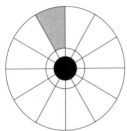

Pretend that just a minute ago, your boss walked in the room. At that time, you were leaning over your best friend's desk, telling him or her about Last Night. As you saw your boss approach you with That Look on her face, however, you stiffened up considerably and brought your conversation to a rather speedy conclusion. Matter of fact, everything about you changed the moment you spotted her. Everything—including your posture. You immediately shifted from The Co-Worker side of you to the Person You Are In The Presence Of The Chief. Maybe you became ultra-polite, efficient, and courteous. But then, maybe you didn't—maybe you became sullen, angry, and resentful. Either way, you pulled out the part of You that reacts to Authority Figures.

Know why? Well, see, we all have "bosses" at one time or another—folks in positions of authority "over" us. We learn early on that the more **respectful** we are of their position "above" us, the better Things work out for us. Matter of fact, it's our whole attitude towards our "superiors" that gets their attention, either positively or negatively, and makes them decide if they'd like us to be an Authority Figure, too. By the way, if this sounds familiar, it's probably because we learned all about how to deal with people who had control over our lives way back when, in our own homes. However we reacted to our parent's rules is a good indication of how we'll react to our supervisor's rules at work. Matter of fact, our opinion of the proper way to act around Authority Figures, in general, is right here, handled by the You whom you keep behind—or should I say "beneath"—Door Number Ten.

Oh, and that's another thing—notice the words I used to describe Authority Figures? I referred to them as those who were "over" you, "above" you—your "superiors." Well, think back to the first analogy we used to describe this house—as your "Roof," the **least hidden spot** of all in your life, the place where what you do is Public Knowledge, for better or worse. The way you react to your boss describes the way you act when you know that your **reputation** is at stake. And what's a reputation? Well, it's what you're **reputed** to have done, what you're **said** to be like. In a nutshell, it's what you're famous for. This highest spot on the chart is your personal bulletin board where you post all your accomplishments, where you parade Your Stuff for all the world to see. This is the side of you who worries what the neighbors think, the side who's into accomplishments, and Making A Name for Yourself. Think of this "piece" of you as a Publicity Agent, constantly thinking of What's Best For Your Future.

Now, we all get the chance to be authority figures now and then, to be "over" others—even if it's only because we're babysitting for our sister's kids for the evening. Matter of fact, you'd be hard pressed to find a life situation where there **aren't** Folks In Charge, and Folks Who Aren't. How often this happens to you depends on how much you like taking out this tenth-house side of you and being In Charge. (And the planets you **have** in here will tell us which of your urges or needs you'll express when you get to be The Authority Figure—or **with** The Authority Figure. You know that bumper sticker, "Question Authority"? That was written for folks with Uranus in this house.)

There's a Mantle of Authority that's standard equipment with this room, an imaginary cloak folks slip on when they're In Charge Here. If you want to catch a glimpse of it, watch an incumbent President. They wear it rather boldly just before they take office, and more respectfully just after—when the shock sets in.

DOOR NUMBER ELEVEN—KINDRED SPIRITS

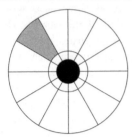 Remember back in high school, when your parents gave you a hard time about those kids you wanted to hang with, the ones that used to stand around up at the corner and smoke cigarettes? Remember how they said if you associated with those kids that you'd "end up just like them?" Well, gang, much as I hate to tell you this, your parents were probably right. At the very least, they were on to something. The **type** of group we chose as peers back then set the tone for all the groups we'd belong to after that—and I don't have to tell you **now** that we certainly are judged, at least in part, "by the company we keep" throughout our lives—not just in high school.

It makes sense, too. When we nestle inside a group, we're Choosing Sides. We're selecting a **category**, a **classification** for ourselves. Those categories are awfully hard to change, once they're In There. That's what your Mom and Dad were worried about, more than anything; they didn't want you to choose the "wrong" category before you were old enough to spot the warning signs. Now that you're all grown up and free to pick your own affiliations, it's this eleventh-house side of you who'll make that decision—without getting grounded.

Here, then, behind the eleventh-house door, is the "piece" of you who Joins Up—the Team Player in you, the person with the Pom-Poms and the lapel buttons—and maybe even the placards, depending on how radical your leanings are... This is the You who decides which team is your team. And speaking of teams, by the way, how do you act when you're on one? Or when you're in a group? Your eleventh house is the "room" where the "piece" of you lives that only comes out for Group Situations—for "meetings."

Now, since folks also band together to achieve a common goal, here, too, is the person inside you who feels strongly enough about A Cause or An Issue to surround yourself with others who believe in it, too. Which organizations do you belong to? Greenpeace, maybe? Mensa? The NRA? Think of how differently folks will think of you when you tell them you're a proud member of any of those groups. Think, too, of how it would feel to be in a room filled with members of a group you **didn't** belong to. See, there's a particular feeling we get from being tucked safely in the middle of a room full of folks we consider Kindred Spirits. It's reassuring. It validates what we believe, and how we see ourselves. We all feel stronger when we're with our group, when we're with others who are "like" us in some way. You've heard that expression "there's safety in numbers"? Now you know why it's true.

Now, once we sign up with a **peer group** we want to be a member of, we're making a statement about what we expect from our future. So who do you consider your peers to be, anyway? What's the common denominator that links your particular group of friends? Are you all aspiring attorneys? Or do you want to be astrologers when you grow up? Either way, the connections you form within that group will help you along in a particular life direction—or hinder you. Just like Mom and Dad said.

DOOR NUMBER TWELVE— ALONE AGAIN, NATURALLY

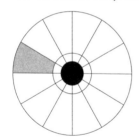

See that last room on the right? The one with the pink smoke leaking out from under the door? That's the last stop on our tour—the twelfth house. Now, don't be scared. This house isn't nearly as bad as it's been cracked up to be. It's just quiet here—and secret, too. Although traditionally saddled with labels like "the house of self-undoing," and "the house of secret enemies," this is really more like The Secret Garden of your chart, a special place where no one can go except you. When it's time to "get away from it all," to rest, recharge, draw back and regroup, this is the side of you who does, indeed, withdraw. This is the room where you keep the side of you who's in charge of retreat.

So it only makes sense that this house would describe your feelings about the concept of **sanctuaries** and "safe places"—like churches, convents, and hospitals. Since folks also draw back and regroup in places that aren't nearly as pleasant to think about—hospitals, asylums, and so forth—your attitude about those places is covered here, too. The idea is that behind this twelfth-house door is the side of you who needs **solitude**—Quality Time alone—just You with You.

Any place can be a twelfth-house place. All you're looking for is somewhere where you can be alone—completely alone—and undisturbed. That's the important part of a sanctuary, you see. It's a place where you won't be disturbed, where your privacy is "safe," where you don't have to worry about being "caught." And that can happen anywhere from a closet to a one-room cottage on the ocean. Even a steam room or a tanning booth can be a twelfth-house place, if you're going there with retreat on your mind.

Since the twelfth-house is just another "slice" of your personality, think of it as the "piece" of you who has access to The Force, the side of you who knows the code word for getting into The Great Subconscious. After all, when we set out to spend time alone, that's why—because we need to **regain** strength, to tap into The Big Soup and download...

Yes, this is the You who you become when there's only You there, and it's okay to do all those things you're afraid to do in front of anyone else. Like what? Well, I don't know. What do you do when you're alone? Eat? Cry? Whatever it is, it's usually a behavior we feel we were "taught"—very early—not to take out. We keep these feelings safe, all wrapped up in lavender tissue paper in the box on the top shelf of the hall closet. We all have secrets in our "closets" too—skeletons, you might say—and that's another good way to think of the twelfth house—as our "closet." This side of you is the person who keeps those secrets safe, the one nobody ever meets—not completely, at least. It's tender, imaginative, and completely in love with perfect beauty. It sighs at sunsets, sniffles at sad movies, and believes there's A Purpose to All This.

Now, sometimes we don't allow ourselves time to be alone. Sometimes life doesn't give us a chance to just Be. That doesn't mean our twelfth-house side will just go away, however. When we aren't "doing" our twelfth-house side consciously, sometimes we let the door swing open anyway, **subconsciously**, you might say, and some of that pink smoke leaks out. When we notice it, we wave it away and make excuses for it, instead of owning it—because we tried that and our memories of those attempts aren't good. Sometimes we fan that pink smoke away with such gusto and deny our twelfth-house stuff so emphatically that what's in there is only a "secret" to us. Everybody around us knows exactly what we're hiding, what we're protecting by denying that it exists. I like to call this "The Lady Doth Protest Too Much" syndrome—we spend so much time telling everyone about what we don't need, not at all, that what they begin to see is how badly we do need it. This door is, after all, right next to The Front Door of the chart. So, although our methods may not be direct, whatever's in here does trickle out, albeit in very subtle ways, into the first house—our appearance. People's faces often "say" what they deny.

Okay. Break time. We've covered planets, signs, and houses, gang. That's three out of four. Let the dog back in, pour yourself another cup of coffee, and stretch a little. If you're reading in bed, and about to turn out the light—see ya. Rest up, because tomorrow we hit the next piece of the astrological puzzle—Aspects.

Before you go anywhere, however, here's a little something else, a description of whom you'll be entertaining in each of those "rooms" we just talked about.

Houses and The Folks Who Visit
The People You'll Meet When...

Much as houses tell us where and when we'll act, they also say quite a bit about who we'll be interacting **with**. Each house represents the side of us we "use" in a particular life circumstance, and circumstances just about always come with people attached. So, in addition to mentioning where we'll act out a certain "slice" of our personality, houses also tell us with whom, who the lucky folks will be to see that "slice" of us. Each house "owns" a particular group, or type of person, then—and here they are:

First House   You. Period.

Second House   Merchants. Folks you pay for a product or service.

Third House   Brothers and sisters, neighbors, cousins, those you encounter in your immediate environment on a regular basis.

Fourth House   Whomever you live with, the parent who nurtured you emotionally. Pets?

Fifth House   Lovers, playmates, your children. Pets?

Sixth House   Co-workers, employees, health-care professionals, customers. Pets?

Seventh House	Committed one-to-one relationships—the word "My"—open enemies.
Eighth House	Sexual partners, joint financial partners.
Ninth House	Teachers, politicians, travel companions, clergy, judges, lawyers.
Tenth House	Superiors, principals, managers, authority figures in general and especially The President.
Eleventh House	Groups you belong to, peers, friends, churches, political parties, teams, organizations.
Twelfth House	Secret people—those you hide with and those who hide from you—hospital patients or secluded folks.

The Subject of House Systems and Which One is The "Right" One...

There are several ways to divide a chart into the twelve amazing wedges we just talked about. The difference between most **house systems** affects only the intermediate house cusps, however, and not the angles—the two main beams. But there's quite a selection of house systems to choose from—Placidus, Koch, Campanus, and Regiomontanus, to name just a few. All astrologers have their own favorite house system, and "proof" that it works, as well. I'm no exception. I like Koch. That, however, does not mean that you must use the Koch house system. Lots of folks use Placidus, the other of the Top-Two Favorites, or Campanus, or Regiomontanus—"Reggie," as some call it. You can even construct your houses by the Equal House System, which basically involves repeating the degree of the Midheaven on every cusp, with each sign, in order, all the way around, or repeating the degree of the Ascendant all the way around.

The subject of "house systems," by the way, is one of the top ten subjects that you'll learn quickly should **never** be brought up at an astrological cocktail party—not if you want to have a nice evening. We'll look at that list later, maybe even in its entirety, at the end of the book... if you're good and you read every chapter. Think of it as dessert.

CHAPTER SIX

ASPECTS

Before we get started, I'd like to reiterate that there will be no math involved here. Uh uh. None at all. I wouldn't do that to you. There will, however, be some counting. Nothing fancy, just 1 to 60. I didn't think you'd mind, as long as it wasn't anything you'd have to buy a calculator to do. Basically, if you can count, you can handle this chapter, so sit back down and don't look so worried. I have all the faith in the world in you.

Why Should You Care About Aspects, Anyway?

At this point you're wondering why you should bother to go any further. You've already mastered the planets since you're quite familiar with the urges and needs you have that they represent. You've recognized that the "disguises" your planets wear, a.k.a. signs, are really just ways you do the things you do, "styles" that you use when you "do" your urges and needs. You also understand that houses are situations—ordinary life circumstances we happen upon as we go through life here on the planet, and the piece of our personality which we call upon in different life situations. Great. Super. You figure it's time for your diploma. Forget this "aspect" stuff—you don't do numbers. Besides, we had a deal. Hasta la vista, baby.

Well, not so fast, gang. If you leave now, you'll be missing out on one of the finer points of chart interpretation, the fourth piece of the astrological puzzle, the part that separates the grown-ups from the youngsta's. Aspects add details, and details are what will make your chart readings great—and accurate. You want to amaze your friends and scare the hell out of your enemies? Then read this next chapter.

Look at it this way: you've already made it through the Sun and Moon, 8 planets, 1 comet, 4 or 5 thousand asteroids, a dozen signs, and a dozen houses. There're only 7 things left to learn— the aspects. You gonna let them scare you? You're almost done. Besides, aspects are easy. Important, too. They create direct pathways between your planets. Once you get to know them, you'll see how all of what's on that circle in front of you—every planet, sign, and house—is intricately woven into the tapestry of feelings and urges known as You.

Aspects in a Nutshell

Since your birth chart is really just a "map" of the sky when you were born, you've got 10 planets in your chart, just like everybody else. Each planet was in a particular degree of sky at the time of your birth, and some of these planets happened to be in angular relationships to one another. For example, if two planets are 90 degrees apart, they form a square—just like you learned in high school geometry. There are other angles, too: 60 degrees, 120 degrees, 180 degrees. When planets form these angles in the sky, we say they are "in aspect" to one another. Planets "in aspect" have a 24-hour hotline, a two-way intercom that's always on. They're "wired" together, so they're "up" on what's happening with each other at all times. Whenever one of those planets is stimu- lated, any planet(s) in aspect to it is also stimulated. When you own planets that are aspected to one another, it means that the urges and needs they represent in you also come out together.

The Major Aspects

Let's start from scratch. Basically, as I said, aspects are angles, and angles are nothing more than different ways to divide the 360 degrees of a circle. The major aspects are the **opposition, trine, square, sextile, and conjunction**.

If you slice a circle in half, you'll end up with two 180-degree angles. Planets that are 180 degrees apart are opposite to one another—so this aspect, quite naturally, is known as the **opposi- tion**.

(See? I tried to tell you this was easy...)

Okay. If we divide the circle by three, we get 120 degrees. That's known as a **trine**. Divide a circle by four and you'll end up with 90 degrees; that's a **square**. Divide by six and you get 60 degrees—a **sextile**. If you divide the circle by one, you end up where you started—0 degrees away. That's known as a **conjunction**.

Those five aspects are the traditional major aspects, or Ptolemaic aspects.

There are a couple more angles we use here in Astrology-Land that can't be found by dividing the circle equally. There's the **semi-sextile**, which is 30 degrees, and the **quincunx** or inconjunct, which is 150 degrees. Basically, all the angles we'll be concentrating on come in multiples of 30 degrees. If you learn the signs in order, you'll be able to "see" aspects in no time flat. Three doors down from Aries is Cancer—three doors up is Capricorn. Since there's 30 degrees in one sign, three signs adds up to a total of 90 degrees. That's a square. And that's it. Really. That's all there is to it.

I told you you'd be able to handle it...

These are the most commonly used aspects:

Aspect Name	Number of Degrees	Keywords	Orb and Glyph		Between Planets
Conjunction	0	Fusion, Union, Bond	8°	☌	0 signs
Semi-Sextile	30	"Testy"	2-3°	⊻	1 sign
Sextile	60	Excitement, Stimulation, Potential	5°	⚹	2 signs
Square	90	Action, Friction, Conflict	6°	□	3 signs
Trine	120	Ease, Harmony, Laziness	7°	△	4 signs
Quincunx	150	Adjustment, Discomfort, Alteration	2-3°	⚻	5 signs
Opposition	180	Awareness, Tension	8°	☍	6 signs

As I said, all planets in your chart will not be "in aspect" to one another, but the ones that are connected in this way have a very Special Relationship. The **type** of aspect between the two creates their relationship, so each aspect has keywords that describe what it represents to the planets involved. Get to know these aspects and you'll know everything you could possibly need to read any chart.

Okay. There're two steps involved in understanding aspects. First, you've got to find them. Then you need to know how they "work." We'll talk about the different ways to find aspects first.

Finding Aspects

OPTION ONE: THE ASPECTARIAN

The easiest way to find aspects is to use an "aspectarian," a 360 degree wheel divided into 12 signs of 30 degrees each. Check this one out:

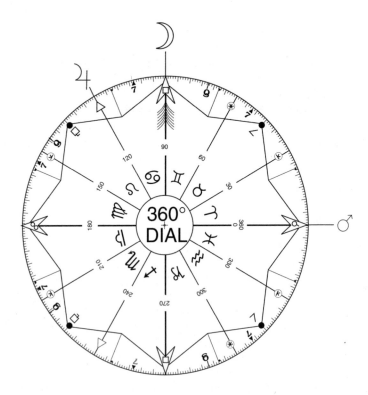

When you're using an aspectarian, you just plot the planets on the wheel next to the corresponding sign and degree, and look for planets in the same (or close to the same) degree in other signs. Count the number of signs that separate the two planets or points, multiply by 30, and look up the aspect on the chart. Works out well.

OPTION TWO: COUNT SIGNS

If you don't have an aspectarian, or if you prefer to just count the number of degrees between planets, remember that major aspects come in 30-degree increments, so it's easy to find them if, again, you just count signs. There are 360 degrees in a circle, and 12 signs in the zodiac. Dividing 360 by 12 gives each sign 30 degrees to call its own. So if you have a planet at 4 degrees of Sag, and another one at 4 Degrees of Aries, well, moving from 4 Sag to 4 Capricorn is moving up one full sign, from 4 Capricorn to 4 Aquarius is another sign, from 4 Aquarius to 4 Pisces is another sign, and from 4 Pisces to 4 Aries is another sign. Four signs that each contain 30 degrees add up to 120 degrees, which, as you can see from your handy-dandy little chart, here, is a trine. That's all there is to it. Piece of cake.

OPTION THREE: NOTICE ELEMENTS, QUALITIES, AND GENDER

Now, if you'd rather not count at all, go back to Chapter Four on Signs and look at the chart on page 64. You'll notice that there's a pattern to the elements, signs, and qualities. Familiarize yourself with the order of each category and you'll see that those patterns will help you to quickly "spot" signs in aspect. For example, the **fire** signs are all **four signs apart**, which is 120 degrees, which is a **trine**. Same thing goes for all the **earth** signs, all the **air** signs, and all the **water** signs. The **qualities** appear every **three signs**, which means that the signs they own are either 90, 180, or 270 degrees apart. **Oppositions** (180 degrees), are found between signs of the **same quality and same gender**—only their **elements are different**. **Squares** (90, 270 degrees) are found between signs of the **same quality whose elements and genders are different**. **Sextiles** are two signs apart (60 degrees), and those are found between signs of the **same gender**.

The Signs and the Building Blocks
They're Made From
BY ELEMENT
(SIGNS OF SAME ELEMENT TRINE EACH OTHER)

FIRE	EARTH	AIR	WATER
Aries ♈	Taurus ♉	Gemini ♊	Cancer ♋
Leo ♌	Virgo ♍	Libra ♎	Scorpio ♏
Sagittarius ♐	Capricorn ♑	Aquarius ♒	Pisces ♓

BY QUALITY
(SIGNS OF SAME QUALITY SQUARE AND OPPOSE EACH OTHER)

CARDINAL	FIXED	MUTABLE
Aries ♈	Taurus ♉	Gemini ♊
Cancer ♋	Leo ♌	Virgo ♍
Libra ♎	Scorpio ♏	Sagittarius ♐
Capricorn ♑	Aquarius ♒	Pisces ♓

BY GENDER
(SIGNS OF SAME GENDER SEXTILE AND OPPOSE EACH OTHER)

MASCULINE	FEMININE
Aries ♈	Taurus ♉
Gemini ♊	Cancer ♋
Leo ♌	Virgo ♍
Libra ♎	Scorpio ♏
Sagittarius ♐	Capricorn ♑
Aquarius ♒	Pisces ♓

ORBS—ANOTHER ONE
FOR THE TOP TEN LIST

What if that planet at 4 Aries was at 7 Aries, instead? What then, huh? Does every aspect between two planets have to be exact? Well, no. They don't. Take a look at your aspect chart again—at the last column on the right, in particular—and you'll see the word "Orb." "Orbs" are "extra" degrees. They tell you how wide you can stretch an aspect—and still consider it an aspect.

(I like to think of them as "point spreads," personally.) The largest allowable orb for a trine (according to our chart) is 7 degrees—so as long as you don't "stretch" any farther than 7 degrees on either side of the original 120, you're within the allowable distance—and you're golden. It's still a trine because it's still "in orb." So the Acceptable Degree Range—the allowable "orb" for a trine—is from 113-127 degrees. In my opinion, that is.

Got all that? Good.

"Wide" Angles

Now. You want to know if an exact aspect "feels" the same way that a "wide" one does, and that's a good question. The best way to explain how aspects "feel" is to think of how you feel when you're in a room with a wood-stove. If you're right on top of the stove, you're feeling pretty hot. If you're a couple of feet away, you're feeling warm. If you're across the room, you can just barely feel the stove at all. That's how orbs work. A good rule of thumb is to remember that the "tighter" (closer) the aspect is between two of your planets, the easier it will be for those two urges or needs to "feel" each other's presence.

You'll notice that some aspects have Allowable Orbs much wider than others. That's because the size of an orb varies with the size of the aspect involved—generally. When it comes to the quincunx, however, the rules change. Quincunxes (150 degrees) are close to the degrees of some other minor aspects I won't bother you with right now, so you've got to be a little more precise with them than with the others.

What If It's Seven and a Half Degrees—
And It "Feels" Like It's Working?

In a word—if it "feels" right, use it. In actual practice, astrologers use all kinds of orbs. Some folks go ten and twelve degrees if the Sun and Moon are involved. Some refuse to use orbs at all, and won't look at any aspect that's not exact. As you continue on in astrology, you may find that tighter orbs are more potent—or the opposite, that keeping your orbs too tight robs a chart of aspects that are really quite "active" in the chart owner's life. At any rate, keep in mind that the list of Allowable Orbs I've provided for you is only a guideline, a little something to get you started. Don't be afraid to modify it. (Within reason. Stretching an orb 15 degrees is pushing your luck—especially if you're a Sagittarius.)

The Difference Between "Applying"
and "Separating" Aspects

To modify your readings even further, you might want to think about applying, separating, and exact aspects. An aspect is exact when a faster-moving planet arrives at the exact degree and minute of a slower-moving planet. For example, if Mars is at 21 Capricorn 05, and Saturn is at 21 Virgo 05, we would say that Mars was exactly trine to Saturn, since Mars is the faster-moving planet of the two. From the time that Mars comes within "orb" and starts sidling up to Saturn, however, before he "makes" the aspect exact, the aspect is still potent—it's called "applying." After the contact is made, the aspect is "separating." So if Uranus is at 23 Sagittarius 15, and Venus is at 20 Libra 05, this is an applying sextile.

What's the difference between "applying," "exact" and "separating" aspects for the owner/operator? Well, think of it this way: An exact aspect is like an event that's happening right now—it's In Progress. A bride and groom exchanging their vows at the altar, for example. All events "happen" in stages, however, and that wedding took an awful lot of preparation—which is what applying aspects are all about. A date and location were chosen, the bridesmaids and ushers invited, and flowers, gowns, and tuxes had to be selected. That's how aspects work, too. Applying aspects are preparation aspects—the faster planet is approaching the slower—it has a meeting on its mind. When the aspect is exact, the event between the two planets occurs—they say "I do," that is. Once the event itself is over, the aspect is separating—which means the wedding is over, but the honeymoon is just beginning. The ceremony will live on, too. It will be right at the front of the minds of everyone who was involved in it for quite a while. There'll be conversation about it at work, pictures shown, and so forth. The assimilation stage, then, lasts well after the aspect is exact.

In your own chart, then, applying aspects between your planets are pieces of You that have a rather "breathless" quality to them. These urges or needs inside you feel—literally—as if they're "preparing" for something. Your exact aspects will be especially "lively." In other words, you'll want to be right in the middle of an "event" involving these two "pieces" of you at all times. Your separating aspects will feel to you as if the urges or needs associated with the planets involved are winding down, talking about what just happened. Basically, what we're dealing with here is the **feeling** you get when you're preparing for something in the future, the **feeling** you have when you're participating in an event that's, as I said, in progress—the present—and the **feeling** you have when the event is over—the past.

Yes, I know, you'd like an example, please. I don't blame you. Look at it this way, if Venus is approaching a square to Uranus, it's rather like she's anticipating a meeting with an exciting, electric Other. In human terms, that can translate into a person who's always looking over the shoulder of the person they're dancing with, wondering when the real Significant Other will show up, no matter how satisfying their present relationship is. If Venus is exactly square to Uranus, there may be an ongoing electricity to the person's relationships—so instead of the anticipation of the approaching square, the exact square's owner might always be In the Process of changing partners. With the separating square, Venus may be a bit leery of becoming involved at all, since it's experiences from the Past she's dealing with and what's she's assimilated about relationships is that they are erratic and unstable. The common denominator behind all three types of Venus/Uranus square is an unconventionality or unsteadiness in relationships and a real need for freedom and individuality. (Which might also mean you like dating astrologers, by the way...)

On Ignoring Houses

Now, there's one more thing you really ought to remember when you're looking for aspects. This is it:

IGNORE HOUSES WHEN YOU'RE LOOKING FOR ASPECTS.

IGNORE HOUSES WHEN YOU'RE LOOKING FOR ASPECTS.

IGNORE HOUSES WHEN YOU'RE LOOKING FOR ASPECTS.

That's not a typo. I wrote that three times because even though I know you're not going to do it, I'm here to tell you the best thing you can do when you're trying to learn to find aspects is to just ignore the houses, and count the signs. Why? Well, houses aren't always exactly 30 degrees in size—remember? They vary, according to where on the planet you are and they become extreeemely distorted as you go farther from the equator. So even though two planets are three houses apart, they aren't automatically in square. When you're measuring the distance between two planets, you're counting degrees. So just **count signs**. Trust me on this. Signs are reliable. They're always, always 30 degrees.

Well, that pretty much covers the mechanics of Aspects. Before we get into the interpretation end of this chapter, give yourself a reward for getting this far with a smile on your face. A cookie, maybe. Just one. Cigarettes don't count.

Interpreting Aspects

THE BUSINESS OF CHART DELINEATION

Here's another astrological term I thought you ought to know about—"delineation." Makes you sound as if you've been in the Astrology Biz for years. Basically, delineating a chart is the same as doing a chart interpretation; it just sounds more official. Now, "interpretation" is a very respectable-sounding word in its own right, but all The Best Astrologers "delineate." Then again, some of us just "do" charts—that's the fire-sign alternative.

INTERPRETING ASPECTS

Anyway. With aspects, as with all else in astrology, keep this in mind: if it sounds like a mongoose, smells like a mongoose, and looks like a mongoose, it's a mongoose. In other words, if I tell you that Saturn and Mars are in "conjunction" in your chart, please, please use everything else you already know about the word "conjunction" to help you understand an astrological conjunction. You know that if two (or three, or ten) things are working "in conjunction" with one another, it means that these things are bound in some way. They operate together. Same thing with your Saturn/Mars Situation. Those two planets are "bound together," too—so the urges or needs each represents are also bound together in your life. Get it?

Okay. That was just a warm-up. Now that you can see how easy this is, we'll get right to the heart of the matter, one aspect at a time. Feel free to stop and take a break when you need to—and please do refer to your own chart to "feel" your aspects.

Basically, what we're doing here is playing Cosmic Scrabble—combining planetary keywords to form sentences that describe personality traits you're familiar with, whether it's because you own them or you know someone who does.

The Conjunction

As we said earlier, two planets (or three, or five, or even seven) that are in conjunction in your chart are co-workers. They're a team. They never act alone, ever. Conjunctions are potent little bundles, too. Think of it this way: each planet is the head of one of your Inner Departments—Venus heads your Department of Other-Pleasing Behavior, for example, and Mercury runs the switchboard—he's Head of Communication Central. If they're "conjunct" in your chart, well, then, something about the way you talk, walk, or write (all represented by your Mercury) will need to be "Venusian"—beautiful, melodic, balanced, etc. You might write poetry or sing, since both of those activities require you to fire up both your Mercury and your Venus at the same time in order to create "beautiful words." If Mars and Saturn are conjunct in your chart, any time you decide to jump up assertively and take action—the function your Mars represents—you will also want to Wait, Stop, and Just Think About It A While More—as per the function your Saturn represents. You'll probably use your Mars/Saturn conjunction to trouble-shoot, then, since you need both those planets to Act Cautiously or to Plan Actions.

Needless to say, some planets pair up more easily than others—Venus and the Moon, for example, since both are feminine and receptive. Or the Sun and Mars, both masculine and rather feisty by nature. Regardless of how well their job descriptions mesh, however, planets in conjunction are sharing the same office—for better or worse. The best use for these bundles is to give them projects to work on together.

The Sextile

If you look back at the list of the signs on page 64, and at their elements and qualities, in particular, you'll notice that two doors down from a fire sign is always an air sign, and two doors down from an earth sign is always a water sign. Two doors is 60 degrees, and that's a sextile. Planets wearing signs that are in sextile aspect to one another are in compatible elements. Air fans fire's flames higher, for example, and water makes earth even more fruitful. These planets, then, represent parts of you that are inspired just by being together—so much so that they often show up as gifts or knacks. The keyword for the sextile is excitement. Steven Forrest says this aspect makes the two planets feel like "teenagers in love," and it's true. The sextile encourages an active exchange between the planets involved. Here are two inner impulses that you'll find are anxious to work together, two "pieces of you" that just can't wait to get started on an activity.

The Square

When you rub two sticks together at right angles, you're practicing the age-old technique of conjuring fire. The friction caused by the two sticks rubbing against each other causes sparks, and the sparks create flames. Flames, in turn, become a fire, and fire is volatile. That's how squares work. Planets wearing signs that are three doors down are "in square" to one another and, again, to understand how astrological squares "work," use what you already know. Think of how it feels when you "square off" with someone—or when you "rub someone the wrong way." There's a friction that's implied in those phrases, something that exists between the two of you that makes you feel like you have to be on your toes at all times when they're in the room. Although this can be an unpleasant experience, it can also be inspirational. Squares are action-oriented. The planets involved tend to keep moving, to shift and change constantly. The urges or needs they represent in you are very action-oriented, too, and without a proper outlet, the friction they create will turn to an inner unease.

It's like this: when you've been sitting in one position for too long, you need to uncross and re-cross your legs. If you don't, you become really uncomfortable; think of how it feels to be unable to move on a long plane trip, for example. When you don't move around for very long periods, your muscles atrophy and you can't move. Squares, then, are the inner discomfort you feel that inspires you to try a new position for more comfort. Of course, no position is comfortable forever—and neither are your squares. They require constant movement to keep them oiled. Movement creates actions, and actions are what a life is made of. Much as they can be irritating, then, look at it this way, your squares will never be boring. Give them projects that will keep both sides happy. For example, a Scorpio/Aquarius square can find happiness together if you supply them with astrological (♒) research (♏) projects and an Aries/Cancer square would work teaching children (♋) defense (♈).

The Trine

The trine has been the darling of the astrological crowd for centuries. Much as we try to deny it, all of us just love to see trines turn up on a day we're planning something, or better still, between our own Venus and the Venus of the person we've recently become interested in. Trines are formed by traveling four doors down—120 degrees—which puts you in the back-yard of a sign that's from the same element. Take Aries, Leo, and Sag, for example: they live four doors from one another, they're all fire, and they're all signs that are "in trine" to one another. Trines are famous for the inner ease they represent between the planets wearing those signs. "Ease," in fact, is one of the keywords for the trine—"harmony," too. Ever hear someone say they were "in their element"? I rest my case.

Now, as with all else, trines have a definite downside to them, a teeny little problem that's really tough to consider a problem. See, what with things going along so darned nicely all the time, trines can get lazy. Really lazy. There's no need to jump up and act—that's the squares' job. Trines don't need to do much to see results, so they can get spoiled. Sometimes they get so spoiled they don't "do" anything at all. They're so darned happy to be around each other that they can be boring. Planets you've got in trine to one another, then, show the inner urges or needs you've got that get along swimmingly, that automatically support each other. The catch is that you've got to make a conscious effort to get them up, dressed, and off the couch.

The Opposition

Know how it feels to oppose someone? Know how they say that "opposites attract"? Then you know all about oppositions. Planets in opposite signs have the same mission—the same goal—but their techniques are very, very different. Take a look at the signs that oppose each other, and you'll understand oppositions even better.

Take Gemini and Sag, for example—they're both concerned with communicating, and with understanding what's going around them. They both like to be free to move around, too. The difference is that Sag is into the Macroscopic View; it's interested in The Big Picture, in The World, and with how what's happening all over the globe affects each of us, right here in River City. Gemini, on the other hand, sees the Microscopic View—it cares about

Our Town, about the local scene, and the neighborhood. Sag and Gemini come together beautifully, however, in the phrase "Think Globally—Act Locally." The idea is that opposites do attract—in fact, they need each other. Sag wouldn't be able to get to Europe if Gemini didn't know which roads to take to the airport. With oppositions, the two planets need to compromise, to become aware that the other is out there and that they can do a lot for each other. Just as squares typically symbolize inner tension, oppositions seem to play out in our relationships. The opposition is the least difficult of the traditionally difficult aspects because it's above-board. The two planets may be pulling at opposite ends of an issue, but they can see each other quite clearly from across the room. Awareness is the most important thing to keep in mind with oppositions—awareness of The Other, but they aren't automatically aware. It's rather common for people to identify with one end of an opposition and project the opposite. "I'm not like that. My brother/lover/parent/boss (fill in the blank) is like that—but not ME!" If you've got oppositions, then, your job from this point on is to **look** at The Other, and **look** at yourself—honestly.

The Semi-Sextile

Folks have called this aspect a slightly favorable one for a long, long time—but, personally, I'm skeptical. First of all, aspects are created, in part, at least, by sign relationships, and this one is created by blending signs that are next-door neighbors. Now, Aries and Taurus have about as much in common as a soldier and a farmer. Same with Sag and Capricorn—you've got a world-traveler living next door to a businessperson. Still, we all have neighbors, and we certainly do tolerate their behaviors, so if you think of planets in semi-sextile as neighbors who have to work together because they share a wall, you'll have a good idea of how the semi-sextile works. They need to co-habitate, so although they live entirely different lifestyles, they also need to be tolerant and considerate of one another.

In human terms, this means that there are urges or needs inside you that affect each other indirectly. If your Mercury and your Venus are semi-sextile, for example, you may find that you have an unnoticed or very subtle need for Beautiful Words. Try singing, just for the heck of it. Making planets in semi-sextile aware of one another gives you even more behavioral options—and that's what it's all about.

The Quincunx or Inconjunct

This aspect is found by traveling five doors down—between the trine and the opposition. Now, whether you call it an inconjunct or a quincunx, this aspect sounds like it is—uncomfortable. Most astrologers see the quincunx as signifying a need for adjustment in the owner's life, as per the matters represented by the two planets involved. Take Aries and Virgo, for example: Aries is cardinal fire, and Virgo is mutable earth, so neither their techniques—the qualities—or their motives—the elements—match. Not to mention that Aries is masculine and Virgo is feminine. Basically, there's not much to talk to each other about. Since these two sides of you have nothing at all in common, but are still linked by aspect, quincunxes can signify feeling pushed, forced, or obligated to perform. Just about everybody agrees that they can also correspond with health matters, since the cause of disease is just that—dis-ease.

The "adjustments" being called for by a quincunx often have to do with analysis, discrimination, and figuring out how to improve or enhance existing circumstances. Sure, you may have to change some details to make things work better. And you may have to figure out what is no longer healthy and needs to be released. But figuring out what is dead and should be buried and what is buried treasure and should be dug out, refurbished, shined up and used with glee is the best, most productive way to "solve" a quincunx.

ASTROLOGICAL SENTENCE STRUCTURE EXPLAINED

There. Now those are the seven aspects. That wasn't so bad, was it? How about some practice, then? Just for the heck of it, get out your own chart, sit down with a cup of tea, and try to find your aspects. Start with the Moon, since it's the fastest moving planet in the chart, and compare its position to all of the other planets.

Then work with Mercury, Venus, the Sun, Mars, Jupiter, and so forth—in that order. Keep a column for the Moon, a column for Mercury, for Venus, and so forth. Remember to count signs, not houses. Make a list of the signs, if you aren't going to use the Aspectarian. After not nearly as long as you think, you won't need either. You'll automatically know which signs square which signs, which are sextiles, and so forth. You can see conjunctions, trines are in the same element, and oppositions are directly across from one another. So you're already halfway there.

As you find your aspects, write them all out. Put the faster moving planet's symbol first. That's the planet that's arranged the meeting. Next, write the symbol for the aspect. Then write the planet that's being aspected. Then pat yourself on the back. You've just constructed a series of phrases that can only be read by a very select group of folks—the same people who know what "delineating" means. After you've congratulated yourself on learning this whole new language, look at your astrological sentences and think about how they describe your personality traits. You may discover the technology that inspires you to count squares on the ceiling when you're bored is your Mercury/Mars square, keeping itself busy when you're not feeling sufficiently challenged. And how about that sweet-tooth? Might be You spoiling You with your Venus/Jupiter conjunction.

Of course, after you've gotten over the shock of seeing your traits appear via these amazing little sentences, you'll want to practice on Other Folks. Ask first. Otherwise, it's like astrologically invading their privacy. Then go right ahead. You won't believe how much astrology you'll learn from the charts of others. Especially fifth-house folks—Prospective Significant Others, that is. Makes you think that it might be true, after all—about how people come into our lives to teach us something.

"EASY" AND "DIFFICULT" ASPECTS

Way back in Ye Olde Days, when ordinary folks like you and me stood a good chance of being beheaded, blinded, or dying of The Plague, there were "malefic" and "benefic" planets, signs, houses, and aspects in astrology. I don't have to tell you what would have been considered "good" and what would have been considered "bad"—just imagine which planets, signs, houses, and aspects might collaborate to produce any one of those unhappy events.

At any rate, back then, it was very helpful to know which aspects showed up most often under less than pleasant circumstances. It might even have added a few years to your life. Nowadays, however, our astrology is a lot less fatalistic—mainly because folks do all kinds of wonderful things with aspects traditionally known as "difficult." Still, some "planetary arrangements" are easier to operate than others, so although I'm not going to label the aspects individually "good" and "bad," you should know that in general, trines and sextiles are "kinder, gentler" aspects, and oppositions, squares, and quincunxes are "tough but productive." Conjunctions can go either way, depending on the nature of the two planets involved, and the signs they're wearing, too.

Let me put it like this: you know how it feels to be pulled in two different directions over a decision—like one half of you really, really wants to try something, but the other side of you just won't budge? No matter what you do, there's one side of you that's going to be ticked off at another side of you. That's what a "tough but productive" aspect often feels like. The end result of that pull is that you'll need to integrate both sides, which means getting to know yourself better. In the process of deciding which side of you will "win" a particular battle, you'll learn moderation, or to take turns and alternate—so that **you** can win the war. Either way, you'll grow—and that's good—but the process itself can be less than pleasant, in human terms, mainly because, as I said earlier, we carbon-based creatures are remarkably resistant to change.

Those are the tough aspects. Now, on the other hand, think of how it feels to just know how to do something—whether it's Mozart's ability to write concertos at age five, or your own ability to spell any word, whether you've ever actually seen it written or not. That's what "kinder, gentler" aspects feel like.

Turning a "tough but productive" aspect into a "kinder gentler" one is quite possible, and quite exhilarating. Learning a talent others may have been born with, for example, makes that gift all the more precious. That's the blessing inherent in your difficult aspects, and that, too, is nothing you didn't already know.

In all, the very best way I've ever heard the "difficult" aspects explained was by David Pond, an astrologer/word-wizard from the Seattle area. When asked whether squares were always "bad," he responded that he had never seen a "bad" aspect that someone hadn't done a great job with. And that's the truth.

MINOR ASPECTS

Yes, I know, I said there were only seven aspects—and there are. There are seven major aspects, all of which we've just covered, all of which are plenty of work as is. But there are a couple more aspects I'd like to toss your way, since you're doing so well with the first seven. These aspects, traditionally known as "minor," sometimes seem to play out in pretty darned "major" ways. You don't have to bother with them at first, and some folks don't bother with them at all, but I feel obligated to mention them to you because I have Mercury in Sagittarius and I want to tell you absolutely everything.

Bear with me—I'm in therapy.

The Semi-Square and The Sesqui-quadrate

Anyway. These are the "minor" aspects most often used. Matter of fact, one of my first teachers, Nancy Hastings, used to use these two religiously. She always referred to semi-squares and sesqui-quadrates as "sneaky squares" because although they seem to "work" the same as squares, it's just a little harder to find them. See, if you slice a square in half, you get 45 degrees, and if you subtract 45 degrees from 180, you get 135—so the two are really opposite sides of the same coin. I'd like to add a little something to Nancy's definition, however—just as squares are action-oriented, not necessarily "bad," these two minor aspects are also more "action-oriented" than "bad." (Semi-squares are also called "octiles" from the Latin root as they are 1/8 of a circle. Sesqui-quadrates are also called sesqui-squares or tri-octiles—3/8 of the circle.)

Oh, and here's a trick she taught me for finding them in a chart: add 15 degrees to the faster-moving planet, and go up one quality. Any planets in close proximity to those degrees in those qualities are either semi-square or sesqui-quadrate. Here's an example: Mars is at 4 Libra 47 in your chart. Libra is cardinal, and fixed is the quality after cardinal. Add 15 degrees and one quality to 4 Libra 47 and you arrive at 19 degrees 47 of fixed signs—so any planet around 19:47 of Taurus, Leo, Aquarius, or Scorpio, is either semi-square or sesqui-quadrate to your planet at 4 Libra 47. This, too, takes time, and you shouldn't stress out about it initially—but it's a good, fast way to find those "sneaky" aspects.

There are lots of other aspects—quintiles, biquintiles, tre-deciles, and noviles, for example—all of which "work" when you find them. I encourage you wholeheartedly to pursue these "minor" aspects as your time and interest permit. We're going to stop here with our investigation, however, since I've already pushed my luck with you on the Math thing and we've still got miles to go before I let you turn out the light...Besides, I've got to save something for another book.

OUT-OF-SIGN ASPECTS

Okay. Speaking of "sneaky" stuff, let's look at aspects that are formed by signs that "hide out" at the tail end or very beginning of a sign. Turn back to your aspectarian for a second, keep your finger in the page, and consider this: since the signs are an ongoing circle, if you have a planet at 29 degrees of Pisces and another at 0 degrees of Aries, the two are only separated by 1 degree. That means they're conjunct—even though they're not in the same sign.

Here's another example: if you've got a planet at 3 degrees of Aries, and another at 29 degrees of Cancer, they're separated by 116 degrees, and that's a trine.

See, conjunctions—and all aspects, really—are formed because of the degree relationship. Usually those degree relationships work out so that all conjunctions are in the same sign, all trines are in kindred elements, and so forth, but sometimes planets at the very beginning or very end of a sign "spill over" and end up relationships that aren't quite what they seem to be.

For example, take Mercury in Scorpio conjunct Neptune. Now, ordinarily, that's a conjunction that might describe someone with a detective-like ability to operate just about invisibly. If Mercury is at 29 Scorpio, and Neptune at 1 Sag, however, the plot thickens. Mercury in Scorpio often points to someone who loves secrets, who loves operating from behind the scenes. Neptune in Sag, however, would tend to foil even the best-laid plans of Mercury, since Sag isn't notoriously good at either secrets or details, and Neptune's closeness to Mercury would describe a rather idealistic way of thinking and a tendency to believe what the owner would like to believe rather than what is.

In general, then, when you're dealing with what we call "out-of-sign" aspects, consider them more carefully than other aspects.

MAJOR ASPECT CONFIGURATIONS

We've all got aspects in our chart. Some of us have lots of them—two or three trines, or several oppositions. Sometimes all those aspects link up and create patterns—shapes we're already familiar with. When that happens in an astrology chart, it's called a "major aspect configuration," and depending on just exactly what type of major aspect configuration it is, there are "special" ways of delineating that chart. (Aren't you glad I taught you that word?)

Of the major configurations, the most common are listed below, with general rules on how to read them. Again, please modify what you know to help you understand these patterns.

The Grand Trine—If one trine is "good," well, then, two trines must be just great—right? Well, not exactly, but grand trines certainly do bring the personality traits of the element involved to the forefront of the owner's life.
Grand trines are sooooo easy to operate; you don't even need a license. If you own a grand trine, you'll find that matters concerning this element flow along quite smoothly—there's not an awful lot of effort needed to make things happen. As a result, grand trines can point to planets that aren't used much by their owners, since

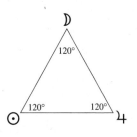

things come easily to them even without any ooomph. A grand trine in the intellectual air signs, for example, can describe a personality that's capable of rationalizing anything—so why bother learning anything? A grand trine in earth can describe a personality that's worn a groove right into the earth—a rut, you might say—so why bother changing your habits? Grand trines hold a wealth of talents—the challenge is getting up the energy to use them.

The T-Square—These are formed when two planets are found in opposition to one another, and a third comes along and stands in square to both of them. Needless to say, T-Squares are dynamic aspects. If you've got one, you need constant change to keep

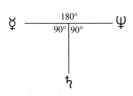

yourself occupied. Your T-Squares mean that you insist on movement. Tight ones mean that you'll insist on **constant** movement. These angles represent sides of us that shift and grind and push inside us—remember, they create both **friction** and **tension**, which tend to show up as drastic occurrences—Big Events. They're commonly found in the charts of people who get an awful lot done—because you need this type of ooomph to accomplish major tasks.

The **quality** the t-square is in also provides clues as to how it will be used by its owner. Fixed T-Squares are resistant to change that they don't induce. Cardinal ones are resistant to stagnation. Mutable T's are resistant to any type of structure.

The Grand Cross—Here's a push-pull situation—Big Time. Grand Crosses put four pieces of your life in what amounts to a constant struggle—or a constant need for creative work. Again, they show up in a particular element, so the element must be considered in order to understand the technology that's operating the Cross. Go back to "The Square" for advice on how to make your T-Squares and Grand Crosses happy.

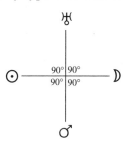

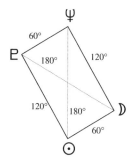

The Mystic Rectangle—Here's one that combines the best of all worlds—the ease of two trines, the excitement of two sextiles, and the tension of two oppositions. The rectangle has oomph and ease operating at all times and it seems to turn up in the charts of highly productive individuals. Ever meet someone that's blessed with luck, timing, and skill? Check their chart for a Mystic Rectangle.

The Yod—Often called the "Finger of God," the Yod is known for carrying a tone that's linked with "destiny." You've got two quincunxes, back to back, joined by a sextile—that basically produces a smooth effect on one side, via the sextile, and an "irritation" or necessary adjustment whenever the third planet is used. Since the quincunx often refers to health, the Yod may describe health issues in the life of the owner. Health only becomes an issue if the person cannot **constructively** integrate the quincunxes. Using either the single planet, or the sextile often helps. Making room for seemingly "incompatible" drives (al-

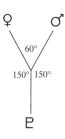

lowing them both equal air time) keeps the owner healthy and happy.

So It's A Wrap, Then

Well, now. I told you it wasn't going to be that bad, and you shook your head. Did I lie? No, I didn't. You sailed through aspects, and now you've got all four of the Astrological Food Groups tucked securely under your belt. Congratulations. You're now an Advanced Beginner. Practice a lot, every chance you get. And turn the page, because we're far from done—you won't believe what else you can do with this stuff.

CHAPTER SEVEN

PUTTING IT ALL TOGETHER—
WITH JACK NICHOLSON

Okay, you say. You've had all the data entry your brain can stand. You Get It. Enough with the facts, enough with the data—just cut to the chase. How does one actually "do" a chart?

Good question. Rully good question.

Unfortunately, I can't give you an answer—not one answer, anyway—because there's no shortage of ways to "do" a chart. Some folks dive right in and go for The Big Three—Sun, Moon, and Ascendant—and then look at the rest of the planets for a person's style. Some start at the Ascendant, as if it really were the Front Door of a house, and wind their way around, touring one "room" at a time with the owner. Still others start with Saturn, since he's the guy who lays the bricks for the foundation, and see what the "house" is made of. After doing a fair amount of charts, I find that when I'm with a client, we tend to start with the most immediate transit, and work backwards—but then, I'm a Sag, and we like to work backwards.

At any rate, you can see from all this that it really would be impossible for me to tell you how to "do" a chart. But I understand what you're looking for. You need a blueprint of some kind—a check-list. Fine. I can do that. The catch is that it's my battle-plan I'm handing over, not yours. So keep that in mind, and use this one only until your own arrives—which, I promise, won't be too long. Feel free to re-arrange the steps, with the exception of Step One, which I really think everyone ought to do automatically. Most importantly, don't ever get so caught up in following anybody's "rules" that you don't allow your intuition to help you.

Enough with the lecture. Here's your cheat-sheet:

Step One: Look at the chart. Forget what you're looking at, and just look around. Where are the planets primarily clustered? Are they clustered—or spread out all over the chart? (In other words, are you looking at the chart of a "specialist" or a "well-rounded" personality?)

Step Two: Check out The Big Three—The Sun, The Executive Director. The creative purpose, the *"raison d'etre."* The Moon, Head of the Security Department, the person on the inside who runs the show through moods, feelings, and emotional needs. The Ascendant, The "Front Door" through which the Sun, Moon, and everybody else In There enters and exits. Check for aspects these three make, too—especially to each other and to outer planets.

Step Three: Look at the angles—the "Main Beams" the "house" is built of. Are they fixed? Are these "doorways" made of only fire and air, only earth and water, or one of each? Are there planets attached to the angles? (This will give you some idea of how the person goes about the business of "mingling" with the environment.)

Step Four: Check for an emphasis by element and/or quality. (Think of it as taking a poll from the planets who are "residents" in the house. You're looking for a symbolic lifestyle.) A Cancer Sun with seven out of ten planets in fire won't be at all the same as one whose "cabinet" of planets is predominantly also made up of water signs.

Step Five: Be on the lookout for "themes"—similar set-ups that will symbolically "strengthen" a behavioral quality. For example, the Sun in Pisces, the Moon in the twelfth house (Pisces territory), and Neptune in some type of aspect to the Ascendant might all have a tendency toward rich fantasy or escapism—two sides of one coin. Two, three, or more of those placements is a more insistent "statement" of a Style.

Step Six: Practice, practice, practice. Read every book and magazine article that you can. Listen to tapes from conferences—go to conferences. Take classes. Talk to other astrologers. Teach your friends.

Step Seven: Try to practice on celebrities first, rather than folks you know. Why? Well, mainly because it's an easy way to look at lots of charts of people you're somewhat "familiar" with, but also because celebrities aren't immediately reachable, and therefore won't have to suffer through your Expert Astrologer Stage. This phase typically hits somewhere between the second and third weeks of your astrological education, and goes something like this: A) You begin to Understand things—in fact, you believe that, through astrology, you've discovered the answers to the Big Questions. All of a sudden, everything just makes sense. B) You're so excited, you can hardly sleep. You read, look at charts, and pencil in transits around the edge of every chart you've got—every day. C) You want to Share what you know with everyone—especially the people you care about. So, D) you start doling out free advice. To everyone. You'll decide that your Mom should take up writing, your best friend ought to dump his or her latest Other, and your Other definitely shouldn't board a plane this month.

I know, I know—you're sure it won't happen to you. It will. Just trust me on this. And before you hang out your Free Astrological Advice shingle, get a collection of celebrity charts, and look up all your favorite folks—and all your least favorites. (See "Where To Find It," under Chart Collections.)

Heeeere's Jack...

In the meantime, let's try one out together. Let's do an interesting one—Mr. Jack Nicholson. Now, Jack wasn't easy to choose, because he's not a "simple" type of person. He's the kind of guy who defies explanation, who, I think we can all agree, is either one of the most talented people on the planet, or right out of his ever-lovin' mind—and probably both. I mean, the man is Certifiable. He's also outrageous, totally unpredictable, and eminently entertaining. So what's the technology behind a personality like his? What exactly has he got in that tool-kit, anyway?

Well, first of all, let's follow our first step and Look At The Chart. To see where it's—visually—the busiest. That brings us up to the Midheaven—around which several of Jack's planets are having a nonstop meeting. Five out of ten planets in Jack's kit live up there in the vicinity of The Roof, matter of fact. Now, according to what we've learned so far, that ought to mean that

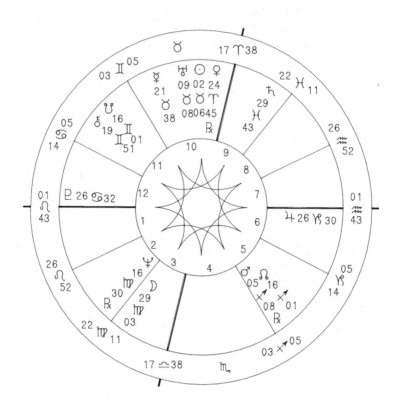

As published in Astro Data II, "from Jack to Mark Johnson," April 22, 1937,
11 AM, Neptune [Can you stand it?], New Jersey, 40N13, 74W01.

we're dealing with a pretty darned public person here, someone
who spends quite a lot of time in the spotlight.

So far, so good, I'd say.

Okay. Next, let's check out The Big Three, the Sun, Moon,
and Ascendant. Let's see—we've got a Taurus Sun, a Virgo Moon,
and Leo rising. First off, I've got to tell you, gang, I'm not particularly shocked to see that Jack's got Leo on his Front Door, and
I'll bet you're not, either. Leo is, after all, the sign of the performer and Jack certainly does "act" like a performer. Leo is also not

notoriously shy, doesn't exactly shun the spotlight, and is nothing if not "eminently entertaining."

But let's get back to that Sun. In Taurus. Nice, solid, respectable Taurus, the most practical, conservative, hard-working sign in star-biz—right? Um, well…yes, it is. And, um, well,…Jack certainly is a hard worker. It's just about impossible to think of a year when he hasn't been nominated for an Academy Award. He's also known to put in what he calls "an unavoidable 20-hour day—for three or four months" while filming.

Now, remember that Taurus isn't just dutiful, practical, and earth-bound. It's also a very sensual sign that loves nothing better than its earthly delights—like wine, chocolate, music, and Picassos. Being made of earth, Taurus is also realistic—plenty realistic enough to understand that the best things in life are not always free, so planets dressed in Taurus garb are usually pretty darned good at making money—to trade for their favorite pleasures. And that, too, suits Jack to a tee. He's now reportedly pulling in $7 million plus, per picture, some of which this Taurus has traded for art. He has a collection that includes Matisse, among others, and, yes, no kidding, Picasso, as well.

Okay. So he likes beautiful things—a very Taurean quality. But what about the rest of Taurus's keywords? Like "Practical"—and "Conservative"? Neither of those describe a guy who calls himself "an Irish left-wing unionist," who was photographed for a Vanity Fair article wearing zebra-striped socks, sunglasses, and a bathrobe. (Complete with a cigarette hanging out of his mouth and a golf-club in his hand.) 'Conservative' is hardly the word that leaps to mind to describe that scene, or the picture that graced the cover of the same issue, of Jack grinnin' That Jack-like Grin, arms full of the last thing you'd ever expect to see him holding—children. So what's the deal with that?

Well, Jack doesn't own just any Taurus Sun, you see. His Taurus Sun comes with Uranus attached. Now, as you know, Uranus is the dude who rotates backwards, refuses to stand up straight like everybody else, and is the only planet with a Greek God's name, rather than a Roman one. Uranus, as you also know, likes nothing better than Shock Effect. He's the Head of the Outrageous Department—and he just happens to be sitting 7 degrees from Jack's Taurus Sun—conjunct to it, even. Now, the Sun is the Executive Director of the chart. With his office adjoining Uranus', it's not surprising to find that Nicholson's Basic, Core Personality also seems to orbit a little on the wobbly side. Uranus is a rebel, too—Big Time—and it's well-known that Jack's favorite spot at Laker's games, Home or Away, is behind the enemy team's bench, where he heckles, produces all kinds of amazing, "unique" facial expressions, and makes a regular spectacle of himself.

Hard to believe, hmmmmmmmm?

To make an interesting chart even more interesting, let's look at The Lady Venus, who's also just 7 degrees away from Jack's Sun, but on the back side. Venus owns Taurus, so her presence next to the Sun symbolizes a double-dose of all those Taurus qualities we just talked about. (Jack also refers to himself as "an artist," by the way.) The Sun, then, is sandwiched between two planets—Venus, representing love, beauty, art, and relationship, and Uranus, the rebel, the radical, the guy that promises you absolute freedom or your money back. Who demands the same for himself—or he's history.

Now, those are very different energies bundled together. Love. Freedom. Ego. Eccentricity. How do you get them to mesh? Well, you might buy your significant other a home for her and the kids, and stay in your own place, across town—if you could find a lady who liked the freedom that arrangement allowed. Which is just what he did. Jack doesn't live 'with' Rebecca—he still lives in the same house where he's kept his stash of masterpieces for more than 20 years. Rebecca lives nearby with their two children. It's a neat trick, and it keeps both Venus and Uranus happy—no easy task. Of the situation, Nicholson says, "It's an unusual arrangement, granted, but the last 25 years have shown me that I'm not really good at cohabitation."

Which brings us to the Moon, not just in particular Virgo (who knows exactly how she likes her home to be), but also seated directly opposite to Saturn, the planet who just loves to do things alone. That Moon is involved in one of those "Mystic Rectangles" we talked about back in the Aspects chapter—the aspect that seems to provide the "best of both worlds" by combining the symbolic tension of the oppositions along with the ease and harmony trines and sextiles represent. This, too, sounds like someone who might invent a "creative" living situation.

Jack's angles are pretty darned interesting, too—fire and air on both Main Beams. Sounds like a spontaneous, intellectual personality—a volatile one, too. Not to mention the fact that he's certainly got a fair share of angular planets crouched by the red exit signs, ready to rock any time a door gets opened. Pluto's hiding just behind the Ascendant, for starters—which not only doesn't diminish the power of the urge he represents, but actually adds to it. Remember, Pluto symbolizes where we want to be The Force, where we're The Keeper of The Ultimate Power. He's the nuclear reactor inside each of us and he lives close enough to the Ascendant to be "feelable" in Nicholson. All his best roles are characters who seem to suppress their rage temporarily, then Uranianly blow. His is nothing if not a Plutonian face, too—when he squints up those eyes and turns them on you...it's absolutely terrifying. Even if he's not playing a werewolf, or The Devil.

Now, Jupiter, too, is angular—just a few degrees away from the 7th house, in Capricorn. Which describes someone who'd be either the giver or the receiver of support in relationships—a "good provider," that is. Using his Venus on the Midheaven also seems to have contributed to the popularity he's achieved with audiences, as well as to the financially successful career he's created.

There's an abundance of Earth in his chart—six planets out of ten are in earth-colored garb—which backs up the Venus stuff about being fond of material/earthy pleasures even further. The qualities are pretty evenly balanced—3 Cardinal, 3 Fixed, 4 Mutable. If there's a "theme" present, it's Lights (Prepare—Earth), Camera (Angular planets, get ready...), and Action—especially the Action part—through the fact that six of the planets Jack owns are in similar degrees and tangled up together in all kinds of major aspects—so when he gets one of them going, the whole darned crew gets involved.

I mean, check out this list of Major Aspect Configurations he owns, none of which is "common," all of which indicate an exemplary personality:

1) a Cardinal T-Square, between Venus, Pluto, and Jupiter,

2) a "Mystic Rectangle," involving the Moon, Saturn, Jupiter, and Pluto, and

3) a Grand Trine in Earth (a little wide, but certainly In There), involving Mercury, the Moon, and Jupiter.

Keep in mind, too, that an actor or actress can't play a role they don't already "own"—in other words, they have to have the planetary potential to become a character, or they won't be able to pull off the part. (This is why some actors and actresses become "typecast.") So let's take a look at the internal "characters" in this chart that have conspired so well to bring us all kinds of external characters. Both The Joker and the ax-wielding maniac from *The Shining* sound like somebody Mars in grinning Sagittarius might enjoy pretending to be. Devils and Werewolves are both shape-shifters, too—Pluto/Ascendant types, you might say. And for someone with as much moola as he's accumulated, he sure plays destitute well—via the hobo in *Ironwood*—with his second house Neptune. He created the ne'er-do-well drifter in *The Postman Always Rings Twice* from his Venus/Pluto/Jupiter T-Square, and used the Sun/Uranus conjunction to become an astronaut in *Terms of Endearment*.

I could go on and on with Jack's chart—I mean, this is the guy about whom Robin Williams said, "Here in Hollywood, there's two groups of people: there's us, and there's Jack." But it's not just Jack—you can go on and on about any chart. There's so much information contained in one of these babies, you can study one for a lifetime and still be surprised at what you'll discover. As a matter of fact, I can personally guarantee you that your own chart will continue to amaze and astound you, year after year.

Anyway. That's Jack. Now that you've got his "blueprint," think of how much you'll enjoy his next film. And speaking of interesting, check out these unbelievable tidbits about other Famous Folks:

***Saddam Hussein was born 3 days after Jack—yes, the same year. Amazing, isn't it—how differently both have acted out their ability to be "the devil"?

***Imelda Marcos, the Shoe-Queen, just happens to be a Sun-sign Pisces—of course. Pisces rules the feet.

***Madonna, the last person in the world you'd ever want to label a "virgin," at least by the modern definition of the term, has the Moon in Virgo, which translates, literally, into Virgin Mother—or The Madonna.

***Out of his ten planet tool-kit, Bill Clinton owns 4 planets in Leo, and 4 planets in Libra. Which certainly sounds like a President who plays the saxophone, hangs out with Celebs, and has been charged with "waffling" to "people-pleasing."

*** Hillary Rodham Clinton, on the other hand, is a Sun-sign Scorpio—and she's continually accused of operating a "Shadow Agenda."

***George Bush, a Sun-Sign Gemini, the sign of the twins, was given *Time Magazine*'s yearly Person of the Year Award—but not for Man of the year, for Men of the Year. The cover photo was two-faced—literally—and featured two photos of Bush, joined at the cheek. What's even better is that the accompanying article was entitled, "A Tale of Two Bushes."

The list goes on and on. But see for yourself. Get a collection of Famous Folk's charts and check them out. Think of them as Volunteers From the Audience, sent down to astrologically educate us.

The Inner Planets Through The Signs— A "Cookbook" Section

Okay. Welcome to the "cookbook" section. If you've just cut in from the "Signs" Chapter, I want you to know that I know what you're doing, and this is cheating. Besides, if you're here to look up each of the planets in your Significant Other's chart—to see why they act like that—good luck. Significant Others' Charts rarely explain anything you don't already know. They usually are, however, just Chock Full O' things you aren't quite ready to "see."

Anyway. Whether or not you're here legitimately, before you get started, I want to issue yet another disclaimer, about the "delineations" to follow. Because these, kids, are not going to be like Rob Hand's delineations, or Liz Greene's delineations, or any other delineations by any other delineator you've ever read. There will be no heavy psychological discussion on the motivations of each planet in its sign, and no explanation of Childhood Issues that may have brought this type of behavior about. There will be no flower remedies or affirmations offered, and I'm not going to try to get you to Creatively Visualize anything. This book is called *Astrology for the Light Side of the Brain*, so I've made these examples "light-hearted" ones. As you know by now, I like to think of planets as actors and actresses who act out our little human agendas for us, and of signs as costumes those actors and/or actresses wear. Consequently, many of these planetary descriptions will be just that—stories of planets "dressed" in costumes. There're some plain old ramblings here, as well—bits and pieces I've accumulated over time from seeing a fair share of charts with friends, clients, and celebrities attached.

Another thing: I've opted to discuss only the Personal Planets in the signs here, just because I know you need a little "kick" to get going. As far as the Outer Planets go, like I've told you in earlier chapters, they're generational symbols—"urges" that mass quantities of folks are born wanting to act out. As I also told you, they seem to show up as Trends, Fads, and generational beliefs, rather than personal traits. Whole books could easily be written on each planet in each sign, and how We act Down Here when That Planet shows up in That Sign. (See, for example, *The Book of Jupiter* and *The Book of Neptune* by Marilyn Waram and *The Book of Pluto* by Steven Forrest.)

Now, just because these are "playful" examples doesn't mean they're going to be any less accurate than other less playful books. Just make sure you read these descriptions in the spirit they were intended—to give you a light-hearted peek into a particular planet in a particular sign.

Anyway. If you can settle for thumbnail sketches of the Personal Planets, well, then, get out your chart collection, look everybody up, and remember—in astrology, just about everything is qualitative. That is, Mars in Aries won't be quite so much like Mars in Aries if it's got Saturn attached, and the Moon in Gemini won't seem so Geminian if it's hiding in the 12th house. In other words, I'm still going to force you to use your own judgment a little. So sue me.

ARIES

The **Sun in Aries** likes to be in movement—straight, fast, forward movement only, please—no turning around, no asking for directions. Astro-Buddy Rick Levine, the proud owner of a whole bunch of Aries planets, says the best Aries slogan around is "Ready—Fire...Aim!!"—and I've got to agree. Remember, the Aries "style" of action is Like A Bullet. Aries planets are also better at Big Beginnings than at Finishes—of any kind. After all, bullets aren't required to go back and clean up their messes. Like bullets, Aries planets also love to be involved in a "battle" of some kind. High Adventure. Stress. That's what life's all about. If there isn't any stress, they'll make some...

The **Moon in Aries** is dressed in red. She's Mars-powered, and dressed for action. So she displays her emotions impulsively. In other words, when she's upset, it's no secret—she screams, yells, and threatens your life. Once she's let you know she won't take it anymore, she forgets the offense—and maybe your name, too. She won't "let" you or anyone else hurt her feelings—not more than once, anyway. When she's happy, she's jump-up-and-down-all-kinds-of-happy, and wants you to be happy, too.

If you think the Sun in Aries is impatient, you ain't seen nothing yet. Take **Mercury**, the planet that moves the fastest anyway, and put it in the sign that hates to wait the most. What do you get? Zero tolerance for lines, busy signals, red lights, and waiting to be served in a restaurant. This Mercury wants In—and Out—first. It taps pencils, drums on desks, and interrupts, if necessary, to say what it needs to say. It's a mind that's naturally competitive.

Venus in Aries gets your attention with a technique similar to that of a Flamenco dancer all done up in red. She stomps her feet, smiles brilliantly, and makes sure you can't take your eyes off of her. Once she has your attention, however, and the mission's been accomplished, she may turn the other way. Passion is the name of the game with her, relationship-wise. She needs to feel like you're still not quite hers, still not "caught"—and she won't turn away from competition over your affections, either.

Mars in Aries is The Red Planet in one of his two favorite outfits. (Scorpio's the other.) Planets in Aries garb are all decked out in red—bright red—and this one's the reddest. Here's anger and self-assertion at its most honest. This is the type of Mars that's in the front line of battle, the type of Mars who gets mad, gets it out, and gets over it. No time for long-term steaming or pouting over something—they just scream, holler, hit a wall, whatever. Once it's out, they forget it. This Mars is quite formidable, at the moment, but you'll never have to worry about a Hidden Agenda.

TAURUS

The **Sun in Taurus** combines the physical warmth of the Sun with the cozy warmth of The Lady Venus, Taurus's lovely patron saint. The Creative Force behind these folks is Comfort—with a capital "C." Earthly Pleasures-R-Us, that is. They love to be in Venusian situations, like restaurants, art galleries, and beautiful homes. They also like to be surrounded by Venusian folks—those they love—doing Venusian things. They're primarily concerned with how things **feel** physically. They're here to experience and share the pleasures of each of the senses.

Taurus Moon kids are the ones with the most friends in college, because they've always got the best rooms in the dorm, equipped for the ultimate in comfort, complete with refrigerators, blenders, warm, fuzzy quilts, artwork, and great snacks—at all times. This carries into their adult lives, and these folks unfailingly have great nests. They can also fall into emotional ruts because they get "settled" into feeling a particular familiar way and can't seem to stop feeling.

Mercury in Taurus just loves to read. Catalogues, cookbooks, and Consumer Digests, that is. Practical stuff, about stuff you need, if you're going to live in comfort on the planet, that is. They take their time arriving at all decisions, love to "sleep on it," and need solid, tangible, physical proof to really Believe anything. They think in terms of worth—so if you're trying to "sell" them on something, make sure you impress them with the value of the item.

Talk about a happy planet! Picture The Goddess in her softest, silkiest, most form-fitting gown—all earthy greens and browns. That's **Venus in Taurus**. These people are the TouchMeisters—specially trained by The Goddess herself to give the best back rubs, bake the best cookies, and pick out the most expensive items in the boutique. They love whom and what they love completely and totally, and believe that relationships can last forever. Sometimes their relationships last well past the point they should, matter of fact. Old habits, as they say, die hard for Taurus, and they keep thinking of all the time they've got "invested" in you.

Mars in Taurus (with Mars in Scorpio) are the slow boilers of the zodiac. They put up with it, put up with it, and put up with it some more—whatever "IT" is—until you don't even think they're capable of getting angry. Don't think that. All of a sudden, you'll notice their head is down, bull-style, and their hands are on their hips. Ever been charged by a determined, angry animal? Your best bet is to get out of the room immediately and try to remember not to goad them with the red cape again. As a style of action, Mars in Taurus is ready to go the distance, take their time, and be thorough. They pride themselves on Doing It Right The First Time—no matter what It is.

GEMINI

The **Sun in Gemini** marches down the runway in a coat of many colors—because they just can't bring themselves to wear one color or "do" one of anything. Gemini Suns need movement, and communication—and Just A Taste of everything. They're at their most chipper in high-activity, people-oriented places. If you ever want to get rid of a Sun in Gemini, by the way, just tell it to Sit Still and Be Quiet. Not being able to dash around and ask questions is worse than death to these folks. Life is a wonderful game, and words are game-pieces. Geminis are really, really good at Creatively Interpreting—and explaining—the rules of the game, too.

The **Moon in Gemini** likes to stay in motion. As a result, she never lives in one town long enough to know which cable channels match which networks, and she isn't ever 100% sure what her telephone area code is. Still, after only a month or two in town, she's the best short-cut finder around, and she knows everyone at every business she frequents. Despite all that dashing about, she still finds time to read, daily. This Moon may literally have twin children, be a twin, or have "two mothers," too.

Ask **Mercury in Gemini** a question, and you'd better get comfy. They'll tell you every possible detail concerning the story, including the part about how Grandma's favorite apron got stained the day she and grampa went to lunch before they went to look for the library book she left in the green car her sister used to have—and the life history of the librarian who didn't charge them a fine. Lots of their stories go back to High School days, or earlier, when they first discovered that amazing fondness they have for the telephone. Regardless of the topic, they're Word Wizards, with the ability to wind any tale so well that it's like a good book you don't want to finish. Luckily.

Think of **Venus in Gemini** as a High-School cheer-leader. She's charming in a youthful, shy kind of way, full of energy, and very Involved with her friends. No matter what her age, she believes in the Gemini credo—that Variety truly is The Spice Of Life—because you'll never know what you like if you don't try a little bit of everything. That includes objects, foods, experiences, and people. Especially people. Now, that doesn't make this Venus fickle exactly, she just insists on being amused—or she won't be able to help herself from looking over your shoulder at whoever that was who just came into the room. This Venus also tends to be drawn towards younger partners—probably because she gets to laugh with them.

Picture **Mars in Gemini** as Mars, the Warrior, dressed as a clown. He may be smilin', but he's still got an Attitude, and he's still got his sword. This Mars is spontaneous, funny, and quick-witted. He's got a glib answer for everything, puts an amazing amount of energy into puzzles and mind-games, and is known to be scanning several books at once. He's the originator of the ever-popular Drive-Away-Mad tactic, and he's good at it. If he does stick around to yell at you, he'll tell you off—but good—and re-tell the story so that even you will believe it was all your fault, anyway. Even if you're not convinced, forget about getting a word in edgewise—it's all over when this Mars goes off.

CANCER

Cancer folks are known for the value they place on their privacy. That's one of those traditional Sun-sign descriptions that really does work. They're moody, too, much as they'll try to deny it. But they're supposed to be—emotions are their job. Contrary to popular opinion, they don't necessarily focus on having children. They do focus on Mom. Theirs, and the whole idea in general. Many of them see Mothers as omnipotent, matter of fact. They relish re-creating the safety of The Womb Experience through hanging out in safe places with safe people. Like their symbol, the crab, these folks are excellent side-steppers, too. They won't be seen when they don't want to be seen—and they won't show up at all if you don't make them feel needed.

Moon in Cancer owners are undeniably the best huggers around. Really. Try it. Next time you need a squeeze, go look up one up and hug them. It's automatic therapy, and it lasts. These folks were born with The Queen of Feelings in her very favorite sign, and they're very, very good at expressing emotions. They tend to be very tight with their Moms and/or their children, and more into security and privacy than even the Sun in Cancer is. Because the Moon operates so purely here, these folks are driven primarily by their emotions—by how something "hits" them, on a gut level. They operate on instinct—on memories of how things feel.

Owners of this **Mercury** quite literally think with their hearts—so whatever you say to them, don't use That Tone when you say it, or they won't hear you. They read your meaning through how your words "feel," so whatever they hear has to get past their feelings long before it can ever make the journey up the Synapse Highway to their brains. Their emotions tend to "leak out" through their voices, and they can soothe you with their words like a Mama singing a lullaby to her child.

Venus in Cancer says I Love You by feeding you, fussing over you, making you "a nice cup of tea," and rubbing your shoulders when you need it. She makes you feel so loved, matter of fact, you won't realize you've forgotten all about loving her back until it dawns on you that she hasn't been around for a few days. A word of advice: don't forget to say "I Love You." This Venus really needs to hear it. She can be a little on the thin-skinned side, and if she does withdraw into her lovely Venusian nest, it will take a good long while to coax her back out.

Folks with **Mars in Cancer** have energy levels that seem to rise and fall with their moods. If they're happy, they're energetic. When they're unhappy, they suffer from low energy. These folks are emotional beasts, Big Time. Since Mars is The Way We Take Action, when their hearts are involved, they can accomplish anything. Since Mars is the planet that rules the expression of anger, they can also be really, really good at pouting—and even better at whining. When they're angry, they're more liable to cry than to yell. They won't tell you when they're upset, but you'll notice because they'll sigh a lot.

LEO

The **Sun in Leo** is the ultimate in fire—the happiest planet around. Wouldn't you be, if you were the Sun in your favorite outfit? Think of how strong and powerful the Sun shines in August, at the very peak of Summer, and you'll understand how warm and toasty these folks are. Of course, the Sun is pretty hard to ignore when it's noon on an August afternoon, and that describes Leo, too. Sure, they crave attention. Sure, it may seem like they want you to absolutely worship them. Think of it this way: what they really want is to be appreciated. It's not a lot to ask for all that warmth and light they're willing to give you in exchange. So say Thank You, and hug them. Remember, Leo rules the heart, and hearts don't just pump blood.

The **Moon in Leo** displays her emotions dramatically. In English, that means she's liable to throw a tantrum when she's mad, and an elaborate cocktail party in your honor when she's not. Keep in mind that she acts this way because she also feels this way. She's a Queen who absolutely demands deep respect. Like the other fire Moons, she also dresses in red—or anything else that will get your attention and hold it. She's got the heart of a performer, and the soul of a romantic. She wants her feelings to be noticed, above all else, but she also wants to be appreciated for what she is—on the inside.

Talk about entertainment. Take **Mercury**'s urge to communicate, add a little Leo, and shake. What you end up with is a performer who'll do what it takes to get your ear, your attention, and your admiration—one way or another. Doesn't matter if they have to use a saxophone, a table-top, or a real stage to do it. They rival Mercury in Gemini with their ability to tell a tale. They love happy endings. They also love audiences. When they clear their throat, just look at them and smile.

When **Venus in Leo** cares, she'll make sure you know about it. You and everybody else, that is. These folks just love Big Entrances, high drama, and scenes. Leo is, after all, the sign of the performer, so your Leo Venus needs to give—and hear—applause. Maybe she'll call in a skywriter to tell you she loves you— or maybe she'll just tuck the rose and the ring under a white linen napkin and have the waiter bring it to your table. Whatever. Venus in this sign just loves good, old-fashioned Romance, and she's an expert at it.

With **Mars in Leo**, you never have to wonder if they're mad about something. Whatever it is, if it hurts their pride, they storm out of the house, slam the door, screech their tires, and peal out of the driveway, all the while screaming about how they never want to see you again. Then they call you, crying, from the phone booth four blocks away. Go figure. This is Mars in its child-state, complete with tantrums—and very dramatic Big Exits. When it's doing what it wants to do, rather than being angry, however, this Mars is absolutely tireless—especially when they're playing a game or a sport they love.

VIRGO

Folks born with the **Sun in Virgo** hardly ever turn to these pages in astrology books, because they're sick and tired of being told how "picky" they are. Well, I'd like to tell you that it's all just a rumor, but I can't. It's true. Virgos are "picky." They have to be—they're the trouble-shooters of the zodiac, and no sign is more adept at seeing imperfections. They really are meticulous, too, but not necessarily neat. Regardless of how neat they are or aren't, they have the ability to locate whatever they're looking for in a matter of seconds. What they're less famous for is their strongest trait: they originated the Commit Random Acts of Kindness bumper-sticker, and they're always willing to help, no matter what the task.

No matter how much she protests that it's not true, The **Moon in Virgo** really does love her home to be clean and orderly. She'll think about cleaning places the rest of us wouldn't ever even think of looking at, much less touching. The spot between the counter and the stove, for example, or the underside of the kitchen chairs. Now, she may not necessarily get down on her hands and knees and clean it herself, you understand, but she'll want it done by somebody. These folks can be really tough on themselves, but they're gentle, compassionate soul.

You'll know when you're hearing **Mercury in Virgo** speak. They have a knack for saying exactly what they want to say, without ever needing to use any more than just exactly the right amount of words to say it. In addition to a quick, dry wit, this Mercury comes equipped with an incredible eye for detail and the neatest handwriting you've ever seen. Owners are also skilled with their hands, which often means they're expert craftspeople.

All that stuff you've heard about **Venus in Virgo** being "cold" or "antiseptic"? It's not true. They won't stop in the middle of a kiss to wipe off your lipstick or brush their teeth, either. They'll make sure that happens well before you get together. This Venus has spent far too long finding you to let anything interrupt the physical pleasure she's found in touching you. Remember, this is Venus in an earth sign, and Venus likes earth an awful lot. This Venus is particular—that much is true—but that discretion allows her to be grounded in her relationships. It also gives her the sense to pick out exactly what she needs, rather than settling for Almosts. So, if you've been Chosen, accept my congratulations, and go wash up.

Mars in Virgo has an interesting tactic. He attacks his opponents by undermining their credentials, by pointing out to you just how flawed The Opponent really is. This Mars is a sword that picks you to death a little at a time, rather than Having At you all at once, more an eagle-eyed criminal lawyer than a soldier. He "wins" his battles by proving blame, and follows directions better than any other Mars, both on paper and in person.

LIBRA

Libra Suns are the Relationships-R-Us specialists of the zodiac. No, they don't want to go alone. Not anywhere, not ever. They're the most charming critters around, here to share experiences with Lucky You. Of course, they're also on a lifelong quest, in search of The Other, the perfect partner. They're said to be the Balance experts of the zodiac, and they are—but their specialty is restoring balance, not necessarily being balanced. As a result, they often find themselves in situations where they're called upon to use their "powers" to mediate, negotiate, and act as go-betweens.

The **Moon in Libra** is lovely to associate with, but tough to own. This Moon needs emotionally balanced situations to feel stable herself, so she's an expert at sensing out what The Other needs, and delivering it up in most accommodating fashion. She knows instinctively what it takes to keep everyone happy—except, usually, herself—and she knows how to avoid conflict, too.

Folks with **Mercury in Libra** are natural-born mediators. They arrive on the planet with the built-in curse/blessing of being able to understand—and make a case for—both sides of an issue. Now, this is really tough on them because it can turn even the smallest decision into hell. On the other hand, their mouths come equipped with a Libran charm that shows up in the sweetest, nicest small-talk you'll ever hear. These folks could exchange pleasantries with The Queen, if need be—no problem. If it's you they've been chatting with, you won't realize you didn't really talk about anything until well after the conversation's over. Even then, it won't matter. They're just so darned nice, who cares? This is a mind that tends to think in terms of fairness and equality.

Well, here's another very happy lady—**Venus in Libra**. Venus loves Libra as much as she loves Taurus, but here her Manners are emphasized—and hers are impeccable. She'll please and thank you to pieces and somehow manage to say and do just the right thing, no matter how difficult the situation. These folks are matchmakers—they're the Cruise Directors of the zodiac, ready to usher you aboard The Love Boat and find you your perfect match.

Mars in Libra is constantly in a State of Argument with some-one, constantly telling you—sweetly—how unreasonable their last opponent really was, all the while assuring you that they know you're nothing like Them. Even if you are, you'd rather die than show it, and that's how Mars in Libra wins. They're sweet and they smile a lot, but they wrote the book on Killing You With Kindness.

SCORPIO

Sun in Scorpio—These folks are the quiet powerhouses of the zodiac, perfectly able to act, wait, or just assemble a plan. They watch everything out of the corners of their eyes, know exactly what's going on around them at all times, and don't feel the need to share any of it—until they're ready. Now, to be fair, they're the most thorough people around—yes, even obsessive. But if you're going to be really, really good at something, you've got to Obsess on it. They're natural investigators and diggers—and they don't ever do anything spontaneously.

The **Moon in Scorpio** has first, last, and middle say about everything that goes on in The House—or there'll be a torture session at 10 PM sharp. They're the emotional controllers of the zodiac, who feel everything—everything—deeply, or not at all. They can love you just as intensely as they can hate you—at the same time—and you'll never know which it is they're feeling at the moment. The good news is that if they do love you, they'll fire-walk for you.

Take one dose of Pluto, and one dose of **Mercury**, and shake well. What do you get? The ultimate in Persuasion. These are the people who could sell ice cubes to Eskimos—and might, just to see if it could be done. They're also expert at torturing them-selves, at lying awake all night wondering What She Meant By That, and re-running what happened this afternoon, to search for clues. It's exhausting—but it makes for great detectives. Don't ever try to put one over on them. You'll only embarrass yourself.

Venus in Scorpio is magnetic, mysterious, and beautiful—all done up in black. She sees, she stalks, she conquers. No, you don't have a choice. If she wants you, she'll get you. If she can't have you, she'll kill you. Okay, maybe she's not really all that bad, but this is the stuff that Fatal Attraction was modeled after, you know, and this Venus is definitely one Fixed lady. But, seri-ously—kind of—these folks excel in the Depth and Passion Departments, relationships-wise. If you're looking for a truly soulful exchange, for a relationship that will change both your lives forever—this is the one. Just remember—you can check out any time you want, but you can never leave.

When folks with **Mars in Scorpio** are angry, a couple of things can happen. First off, if they're really angry, you'll never know about it. But they won't forget. It might take a while, but they'll get you—or they'll pay someone else to get you, while they're in a public place with a perfectly formed alibi. They can wait, too—a month, a year, or ten years. Doesn't matter. These are the plotters and planners of the zodiac, with at least six chess moves planned in advance. If, on the other hand, they're not really, really mad, they'll allow you to see it, and you'll feel anger roll off of them in scary waves. However, these folks have more drive, physical stamina and ability to recover from physical strain than anybody out there.

SAGITTARIUS

If you're at all familiar with the tarot card The Fool, you know the **Sun in Sagittarius**—complete with the dog, usually. This Sun sign is owned and operated by a card-carrying member of the Ultimate Optimist Club. Combine the creative urge of the Sun with the outgoing, expansive, Devil-Take-It anyway attitude of Jupiter, and you get exactly what you might expect: a cheerful risk-taker who tends to be a bit too scattered and a bit too idealistic at times, but so much fun so that no one minds. Sags are the stand-up comics of the zodiac, lucky clowns who stumble—endearingly, at times—with both their feet and their mouths. They're philosophers, preachers, and Democrats.

The **Moon in Sag** is born believing everything will work out just fine, no matter what. She wrote the song "Don't Worry, Be Happy," because it's easy for her to be happy. She's the true emotional optimist of the zodiac, a real giver—an over-extender, matter of fact—who always seems to land on her feet. If she's happy, you're happy, too—but no matter what she feels, she feels it hugely—as with all else that's Jupiter-powered. She also likes to take her home on the road, and she often ends up living far, far away from her birthplace.

Mercury in Sag learns by having The Big Picture explained first. They use far too many words with far too many flourishing gestures to explain everything, knock things over, and talk too

loud. Fortunately, they're funny, bluntly truthful, and so entertaining and down-to-earth, you might not mind. They can also
tell a great story—sometimes on purpose. They love accents, foreign films, ethnic faces, and books.

Venus in Sag just loves for her Others to come with foreign
accents, dogs, and sports accessories in tow. Failing that, she'd
like you to have a degree or two, or be at work on one. She'll run
like crazy if you tell her you want to "take care of her," and the
only way she won't succumb to Sagittarian Grass-Is-Greener-Syn-
drome is if you take her out for long walks, ferry rides, foreign
films, or exotic cuisine. Once she does fall in love, by the way,
she'll love you like Sag does everything—in a very big way. Yes,
that can mean "overboard." Yes, it can also mean she overdoes it
and blows her Beloved away by overwhelming him or her, but,
hey—as far as this Venus is concerned, faint of heart need not
apply.

Mars in Sag expresses anger by being darkly funny, by grit-
ting his teeth and smiling at the same time he's whipping a ma-
chete around—like our friend Jack Nicholson did, for example,
when he poked his head through the door he'd just axed in the
"The Shining" and yelled, "Here's Johnny..." This Mars won't
stay mad long, however—he believes that life is too short to keep
that much energy tied up in one place. He tends towards the ath-
letic, and he makes a great cowboy.

CAPRICORN

Folks born with the **Sun in Capricorn** are the Honorary Princi-
pals, wherever they go. They seem to always be put in charge of
everything, no matter what it is, because they're so darned organized. They're the originators of such phrases as "neither a borrower nor a lender be," and "because it's the right thing to do."
They're career-minded, so much so that they tend to become their
job, but for that reason they also become masters—experts—at
what they do.

The **Moon in Capricorn** was raised on The Work Ethic. She
never thinks she's done enough for her children, possibly because
she may not have them until later on in life, but usually more
because she felt starved for love herself as a child, and feels that
even though she wants to give hers all the love she didn't get,
she's incapable. Contrary to popular opinion, this Moon is not
cold—she's starved for love, and she cries a lot more than anyone

will ever see. She may have been raised on the road by military parents, too.

I have two really good friends with **Mercury in Capricorn**, and neither of them actually write anything. They print—in block letters. Nice and orderly, nice and regimented. They know exactly how many strokes it takes to make each letter, and they assemble their lives with the same precision. They're not much on fiction—in fact, they prefer to hear "Just the facts, ma'am." For that reason, they make excellent strategists, and even better campaign organizers.

Here's the elegant side of **Venus**, the side that loves evening gowns, tuxedos, expensive jewels, and nights out on the town, riding from the theater to the restaurant in a horse-drawn carriage. Sure, she also love antiques—and anything, or anybody, who's been around long enough to show its worth. Contrary to popular opinion, however, she's not especially "stuffy," relationship-wise. Remember, Capricorn planets aren't "cold"—they're starved for something. Venus in Capricorn is starved for love. Hug her whenever you see her, and she'll do anything for you.

Mars in Capricorn—Sure, they'll work over-time. Matter of fact, they'll work all night, if that's what it takes. These folks are the workaholics of the zodiac, usually right at the top of their field because they don't take vacations. Think of this Mars as a military general who only acts on orders, and doesn't take orders from just anybody. When he's angry, he'll send you a letter to tell you about it, and if he's really angry, he'll just stop paying attention to you—permanently.

AQUARIUS

You can spot the **Sun in Aquarius** in any traffic jam—just look for the car with bumper stickers all over the hatch-back, and/or so many bicycle/ski/windsurf-board racks on top, it looks more like a sculpture than a vehicle. These folks are truly The Different Ones out there. They do their own thing, seem remarkably detached as they go about doing it, and then offer to lend you the $500 you need to pay for your classes. They pride themselves on being unique individuals and good friends, and thrive on the company of kindred spirits. Given a chance, they'll rebel rather than buckle, any old time—doesn't matter what The Issue is.

The **Moon in Aquarius** is here to break The Family Pattern, whatever that is. If they all sit around the kitchen table drinking long-necks, smoking 100s, and talking about how they'd never want to leave Rhode Island anyway, she'll want to go to college, travel the world, and work out. If her family is full of millionaires, she'll want to give up her inheritance and work for the Peace Corps in Zimbabwe. Like the Moon in Capricorn, this Moon has often been labeled "cold," but she's not—she won't cry for herself, but she'll cry a river for an underdog. She doesn't often have children of her own, but she's really good at mothering other people's kids.

Folks born with **Mercury in Aquarius** arrive with a genius of some kind. They learn everything the first time they're taught—which is easy when you realize that they're Uranus-powered, and he's Mr. Future. They have the minds of computers and the souls of rebels. They spend their days making plans for The Takeover, and telling everyone to Change—While There's Still Time. They're quirky inventors, computer hacks, and newspaper reporters.

You'll find **Venus in Aquarius** at a science fiction convention looking for her own personal Captain James T. Kirk of the Starship Enterprise. Okay, so she's a bit off-beat. She's not boring and she doesn't want to have a "normal" relationship. She wants a healthy one, complete with personal freedom. She even wants you to have yours, so that she can feel like the two of you are together because you want to be, not because you have to be. Early on, she may bring home people of a race, creed, or gender that will shock her parents, but, then, she might just fall in love with an astrologer.

Mars in Aquarius is the ultimate rebel, with or without a cause. This Mars believes that all Authority Figures are out to get them and, consequently, Bad—unless they're the authority figure, which is what they really need to be. This Mars is wearing a Sci-Fi Super-Hero costume and his sword has magical powers—he can take it out and freeze you with it before you even notice he's angry.

PISCES

Folks with the **Sun in Pisces** like to leave the planet because they don't feel like we're their people, anyway. As a result, you may find them scuba-diving or swimming—for a temporary escape—or listening to music and reading a fantasy novel. These folks have no walls to stop what's Out There from coming In, so they feel everything—good and bad—that's going on around them.

They Just Know an awful lot, too...most Pisces are born with su-per-sensitive antenna where their ears ought to be.

I like to call **Moon in Pisces** folks The Bunny Moons of the zodiac. This Moon whispers, and hides, and cries—all in the pri-vacy of her closet, so don't be surprised if you don't ever know she's hurt. She doesn't even realize herself how sensitive she is, and she doesn't like to show her feelings, anyway. So, even if she's aware of "picking up" on the vibes from an argument going on in the corner, rather than talk about it, she may just withdraw. She's generous to those creatures she sees vulnerability in, offers her help to strangers, and volunteers at shelters. She loves any kind of stray, matter of fact—people, plants, and critters alike.

Contrary to popular opinion, folks with **Mercury in Pisces** are not always notoriously shy—matter of fact, some of them can be so darned chatty they make Mercury in Gemini look quiet. They're dreamers and idealists who just might have the power to read your mind. They're ultra-sensitive, too, and they don't un-derstand why life isn't the way it's supposed to be—the way it is in the movies. Since they're such film buffs, they're also good at making up their own stories—and that rich gift of fiction can be used a number of ways, all the way from inspiration to romanti-cism, to illusion, to fraud.

Venus in Pisces dreams and wishes, and she wants you to dream and wish, too. She believes in fairy tale endings, love at first sight, and living happily ever after, and she won't stop until she's found it. Now, she doesn't want to see the downside of her lovers, so she may be taken advantage of, at least early in life. Balancing the checkbook isn't her strongest suit, but she'll give you anything she owns.

Mars in Pisces isn't especially "focused," but when he's an-gry, you'll know about it. Since there aren't any boundaries be-tween Pisces and what's Out There, there are no limits to what this Mars will do—and say—when it's mad. Of course, this Mars may also choose to express anger only in private—like in the car, when no one but the owner knows about it. Regardless, this Mars is a holy warrior, a crusader of sorts. He's strongest when he's championing a cause.

CHAPTER EIGHT

OTHER STUFF—
DIFFERENT USES FOR ASTROLOGY

Like I said a couple of paragraphs ago, you've just arrived at the end of a journey. You got through the basics, all of them. Signs, planets, houses, aspects—you're a regular expert now, sitting there with a good, solid astrological foundation under your feet; a good IC, you might say. Of course, the end of one journey is just the beginning of another—and in this case, you won't believe the rights and lefts you can take. There are more paths in astrology than you could possibly follow in one lifetime. Matter of fact, I've got to confess—that's why I love it so much. Because you can never come to the end. There's always a new technique, a new discovery, or just a new way of looking at what you already know. You can do anything with astrology, because it's everywhere. It's a symbol set that's alive.

What I'd like to do for you next, then, is to tell you all about the different branches there are in our wonderful craft. If you stick around for awhile, you'll find yourself weaving in and out of different doors until finally you arrive at one with your name on it. Here's just a small sampling of your choices:

Astro*Carto*Graphy
and Astrolocality Maps

Think back for a moment to that blank wheel we used back in Chapter 5 to show you how the position of the Sun in your chart was calculated because of the time of your birth. Remember how the Midheaven represented Noon, the IC was Midnight, the Ascendant was 6 AM, and the Descendant was 6 PM? Well, pretend for a moment that you were born in NYC at noon. That would put your Sun right on the MC. Due to the difference in time zones, however, noon in NYC is 6 PM in Switzerland, so if you'd been born in Lucerne at that same moment, your Sun would have been on the Descendant rather than on the MC—and so your "specialty" might have been relationships, rather than career. If it was Mercury that shifted, your communication abilities would also shift to the Descendant in Switzerland, and you'd find yourself involved more in one-to-one dialogues than in public speaking.

Well, that's how Astro*Carto*Graphy works. A series of lines are printed out on a map of the world, each one showing where in the world each of your planets would have been on each of the four angles at the moment you were born. Astrolocality Maps (from Astro Communications Services) will provide the same information. You can also get Astrolocality Maps for a single continental area only (such as USA, Europe, South America, etc.)—to get more detail and specificity regarding the exact cities involved. What's the significance? Well, we've already talked about the importance of angularity to a planet's career. You don't have to think about using your angular planets. These pieces of you live right on the doorstep, always ready to do their—your—thing, and quite noticeably, too.

Think of what this means: if you were born with your Sun in the 12th house, and you'd like to see what it's like to be a little more "exposed," you might go to your Sun/ASC line and bask in your own rays. Places where your Moon becomes angular are often places where you literally feel very much "at home." Venus spots show places where your focus will be pulled toward relationships, or beauty or self-indulgence.

In a nutshell, what it amounts to is this: your location very much affects your lifestyle. It's why we're so powerfully drawn to places we've never been, why we travel back to the same spots again and again to vacation, why we "just happen" to meet people from one particular place over and over through life, and why we often feel at home 2000 miles away from where we were born. This is a fairly new technique that I promise will knock your socks off. You really must get one of these maps—it will explain an awful lot. (See page 212 for info.)

Electional Astrology

Much as it might sound like it, this branch of astrology really has nothing to do with elections, *per se*—unless you're planning when to hold one. Electional astrology is working backwards, basically. Rather than reading a chart for an event that's already happened or a person that's already here, you get out your Ephemeris and plan. Again, use what you already know to understand it. Take "elective" surgery, for example, which describes a procedure that's done at your convenience, that's planned around your lifestyle. Elective astrology is the same—you search the ephemeris for a date and a time when the Universe is most receptive to your plans. Basically, it's just working with seasons—and that certainly isn't a new concept. Gardeners have been doing it for centuries. Ever hear of anyone in the northern hemisphere putting out a garden in December? No, and you won't either; the natural cycle of the Sun prefers Spring for planting. Elective astrology is the same train of thought. You just use all the planets to plan your "garden."

Now, the beauty of electional is that you can use it for anything: from a marriage, to a business date, to a party. It comes naturally, too. By the time you've been in astrology for a couple of years, you'll be amazed at how much more often you reach for your ephemeris rather than your date book when you're about to make plans. And when people look at you and say, "You don't really plan your life with that stuff, do you?" you'll look at them and say, "You mean you don't?"

Mundane Astrology

Never has such an exciting topic been so well hidden. Say "mundane" and images of wizened old men dozing off behind their newspapers in leather wing-backed chairs appear before your eyes. Apply it to astrology and you've got what certainly sounds like a boring subject. Well, *au contraire*, gang. Mundane astrology is amazing, astounding, and unbelievable. You know the expression, "Truth is stranger than fiction"? It is. And this branch of astrology is more entertaining and enlightening than make-believe ever could be. Mundane astrology deals with events, places, countries, and societal trends. It's a way of looking at A Moment in Time, and that moment's significance in the world.

For example, July 4th, 1776, is our "birthday" here in the US of A, since the Declaration of Independence was signed that day, and so we celebrate our collective birthday every year on that day by waving flags, setting off firecrackers, and raising you-know-what. Although astrologers will likely never settle on what we all consider the "right" time the last signature was set to paper, we do use the positions of the planets on July 4th, 1776 to examine what's going on in the country at any given time. Every country, then, has a birth chart, as do every city and state. Mundane astrologers watch those charts for political results, financial trends, and national health issues. We even use them to attempt to predict who will emerge the victor in an election.

Events also have birth charts. The Challenger explosion, for example. The moment the Berlin Wall began to tumble. The time a peace treaty is signed, or a war is declared. The L.A. Earthquake of January '94. Any event that affects a great segment of the population is grist for a mundane astrologer's mill.

Trends or "fads" also fall into the category of mundane astrology—especially as applied to the outer planets. Pluto's 13 years in Scorpio, for example, symbolized a time when the entire world's attention was drawn to Plutonian/ Scorpionic subjects. The trend was toward mentioning the Unmentionables, as per both Pluto and Scorpio's fondness for symbolically uncovering Secrets. The Right to Die and the abortion issue came to the forefront of our consciousness, like it or not. Hospice care became a valid option for the chronically ill. AIDS—a sexually-transmitted fatal disease—was isolated and reported, too—and just 4 months after Pluto entered Scorpio. Not to mention recycling, which finally became "important" during this trek.

In a nutshell, this particular branch of astrology presents a Macroscopic View of life on the planet. If you're at all interested in the news, The Big Picture, or where the media gets grist for their mills, pick up a couple of books on mundane astrology and get ready to be consistently amazed. (See the index in the back.)

Oh, and by the way—to get started in mundane, you only need to look as far as *Time* or *Newsweek*, and then in your ephemeris. What you see on the covers of news magazines will always, always reflect what you see in your ephemeris. After all—"As above, so below..."

Horary Astrology

Horary Astrology is the oldest branch of our craft. It's done by looking at a chart for the moment a question was asked in order to arrive at the answer to that question. It's quite involved, and there are a number of rules to learn, but it's great fun and it's fascinating and accurate, too. There are some wonderful books listed in the back to get you started, and the names of some of the recognized "experts" in the field, too. Astrologers think of Horary and Electional as cousins.

Experiential Astrology

Ever wanted to **be** Jupiter for a day? Or hear Pluto **speak**, or **see** a Sun/Saturn square hash it out? Well, then, experiential astrology is for you. Also known as "Astro-Drama," this branch of astrology has recently experienced a major upswing in popularity. Typically, it's done by choosing a natal chart from among a group's participants, then appointing members of the group to "be" a particular planet, in it's "costume," or sign. The chart is then acted out, complete with any transits or even with another chart. Some folks bring costumes. It's fun, it's entertaining, and it's a great way to learn.

These are just a few of the branches of astrology out there. In all, kids, the truth is that astrology is just amazing. It provides answers where there were none and allows you to understand The Rhythm of the Universe. Once you learn it, you'll see it everywhere, and you'll wonder what you ever did without it. I know I do.

CHAPTER NINE

PREDICTION

Okay, let's be honest. We humans are obsessed with the future, with needing to know what's going to happen before it actually does. Always have been, always will be. We're fascinated with psychics, fortune-tellers, and the concept of prediction in general—the idea of somehow being able to look forward and see what's coming. Once we get into astrology and figure out that ephemerides are printed for whole centuries, then, and that tomorrow is definitely listed, most of us do a very natural human thing: we leap straight into predictive work before we even know how to do it.

Now, I could tell you not to do all that, and give you all of the reasons why you won't be doing yourself any favors if you obsess on trying to predict your future with your astrology chart. I could say all that, but I won't, because you'd just ignore me, anyway. Besides, I think it takes a good obsession to really learn something thoroughly. I will mention that if you really must do predictions, even though you're new at this, you should at least arm yourself with a couple of good, nonfatalistic books. Take a peek in the back under "Transits" for the ones I find most helpful, most realistic, and least scary—and read the next section carefully.

Stage One: The Standard Disclaimer

The first thing to remember when you're attempting to predict is also the hardest thing to remember. This goes double when you're predicting for yourself, but it works when you're doing unto others, too. The first step, you see, and the one that may even save you all the rest of the time you were about to spend, is to look at the natal chart and see if you can find a description of the event you're wondering about. Because if it's not in there, it's not In There. If it hasn't got an Honorary Mention in your chart, it's not part of The Story of Your Life, and it's not going to happen. So, for example, before you check your transits to find a great time to gamble, make sure you own the type of chart that indicates a win. It might save you a couple of bucks.

Next, choose your weapons. I've outlined the most popular techniques of forecasting for you, but choose the ones that speak to you, personally. And keep on periodically trying the ones that don't.

Transits—Everybody's Favorite

FINDING TRANSITS

Transits are inarguably the number one favorite predictive technique out there in Astrology-Land today. They're great fun to use, they provide an awful lot of answers quickly, and they're easy, too—immediate astrological gratification. So let's try it. Go get your chart—which should be folded and living permanently inside your ephemeris by now. Turn to today, and pencil in each planet's position from in the ephemeris to around the outside of your wheel, in the appropriate signs and degrees. When you're finished, take a look at where, in your chart, each of today's planets is positioned. If Mercury is penciled in just before your Ascendant, for example, we would say that Mercury is transiting through your 12th house, and will soon be transiting your Ascendant and your first house. The same goes for all the other planets and the Moon. Wherever they turn up in your chart is the spot they're currently transiting, i.e., "going across" in your chart. That's how you "find" transits.

Next, look for any aspects the transiting planets might be making to your natal planets. (Don't forget your Midheaven and your Ascendant degree.) Start with Pluto and work backwards to the Moon. By the time you get back to Mercury again, you'll be able to see how quickly The Inner planets move as compared to The Outers. Notice, for example, that while Pluto stays in a degree for up to four months, the Sun travels through a degree in a day, Mercury covers as much as two degrees a day, and the Moon travels about one degree every 2 - 2½ hours.

DELINEATING TRANSITS

Needless to say, a Pluto transit lasts a lot longer than a Moon transit. Makes sense, too. Pluto represents the idea that old forms need to "die" to make way for the new. That's not a quick process. On the other hand, the Moon comes and goes, mirroring our moods and the constant fluctuation of feelings we experience as we move through a single day. Pluto's transits, then, will be a part of your life for an awful lot longer than will the Moon's. We'll discuss the difference between Outer Planet Transits and Inner Planet Transits at length, by the way, in just a few paragraphs. I just wanted to give you an idea of the variety of planetary speeds we're dealing with here.

If you've just gotten into astrology, a good way to learn all about transits is to go back to all the major days in your life and see what was happening. It's educational, and it will take your attention away—a little—from the obsessive task of Scanning the Globe to see what will happen tonight, and tomorrow, and in an hour—once you realize that you really can pick up the "flavor" of a day from the ephemeris. Like I said earlier, this type of obsession is a natural stage. It's like realizing that you can walk, when you're a few months old. You want to walk everywhere—nonstop. It's the same with any new toy. After a while, you'll calm down and resume going about your business without checking the Moon's position—once you realize that Stuff doesn't automatically "Happen" when it "should," nor does it hardly ever happen the way you think it will. Practice, in fact, will show you that the outcome of your transits is usually not nearly as dramatic as you'll imagine.

Still, sitting up all night—doing the "1:00 AM Waltz with the Ephemeris," as I like to call it—is a part of the initiation process, so I'm not about to tell you not to do it—only that you can save yourself a lot of nervous moments if you keep in mind that everything happens just as it should. Everything. And that's all I'm going to say about it. For now.

The Fatalists, "The Natives,"
and The Concept of Antidotes

So how do transits "work"? Well, it's like this: first of all, as we've said before, the planets don't "do" anything—not even Pluto. (Although he'd like you to **think** he does). They just show you where your interest will be drawn at a particular time. So when a transiting planet comes along and makes itself comfortable on one of your planets, you'll find yourself dealing with Symbolic Situations. The transiting planet represents Incoming Issues and possibly Events that your natal planet is asked to handle. The nature of the transiting planet describes the types of Situations ("themes") that will arise, and the nature of **your** planet shows which "piece" of you you're working on at the moment.

Basically, transiting planets are like Exercise Trainers. They coincide with periods where your strength and "fitness" is tested, times when you get to see just exactly what you can handle. In the process, you learn what you're capable of and what you're not—yet. Your natal planet gets a good "workout," in other words.

If your planet is "strong"—that is, if you're already operating that side of you at optimum capacity—the events symbolized by the transiting planet will provide opportunities for you to make your natal planet even stronger. If, on the other hand, your natal planet isn't working at optimum, the weakness in it will be brought to your attention. Either way, you'll find yourself in situations that will provide you with "report cards"—evaluations of your natal planet's performance.

As time goes on and you adjust to your current set of circumstances, your planet will strengthen, as if it's on a workout program designed especially to "build" its muscles. The idea behind transits is to incorporate the qualities associated with the transiting planet into your natal planet. So if your Moon, for example, is about to be conjuncted by Pluto, your emotions, as symbolized by the Moon in your chart, are about to undergo a very, very intense time—via Pluto. You may encounter power struggles with women, you may be forced to move from your home, or you may realize just how intensely you care for someone. At any rate, the point of the transit is to point out to you that your emotional nature is deepening.

Basically, all transits are Growing Cycles. They represent spurts of change. After the transit has passed, your natal planet will be different. Every transit, in fact, adds knowledge and experience to your personality. It's why life itself is the greatest teacher, and why age naturally brings wisdom.

Now, given that we have ephemerides and we can see Pluto sidling up to our Mars, or Mars sidling up to our Pluto—or both—we have the ability to make choices. That's the whole idea behind astrology—to "do" our charts instead of letting Stuff Happen to us. Of course, even astrologers are subject to an awful lot of things that we can't change, situations that we can only affect by our response to them. So what do we do when we see that Pluto/Mars transit coming—and can we really "do" anything?

Well, it's like this: there are two distinct schools of thought on the subject of transits. One is led by those folks who believe that nothing is carved in stone, that we are all In Charge of our own destinies, and that anything can be positive—if you just "use" it right. Which sounds good, except that when something "bad" happens to you, you end up wondering what you did to bring it on. Like maybe, somehow, if you'd only done something differently, maybe that flood wouldn't have carried away your home. Not a happy state of mind.

Then there's the second school of thought—run by The Fatalists, a real fun crew who believe the contrary is true, that you have absolutely no control over your transits—zero. In their minds, everything has been pre-paid in the eyes of the Universe, and that's that. From this perspective, we're all speeding down a mountainside with no brakes, totally out of control, completely at the mercy of the Powersomethings that Be. In which case you've got to wonder why you'd bother to learn astrology at all, if you're really just condemned to be a spectator to what the planets "Do" to you for the rest of your life.

Personally, I tend to "waffle" a bit on this point. I believe you usually get six-of-one and a half-dozen of the other with transits, mainly because although you certainly can make decisions that affect the outcome of any situation in a Major League kind of way, you certainly can't stop other people from doing what they're doing—and sometimes those other people's paths do cross your own. So the best way to handle your transits is to take charge of the situation as much as you can, to be as conscious of what's going on as possible, and to stay aware of what you might expect from others.

Each of your natal planets is a symbolic container where you store all the different energies that come together to form You. Your Mars, for example, is where you store all your Assertion Impulse. Your Moon is where you keep your Emotional Impulse. Each planet is like a glass full of water, sitting right in the middle of a hallway. When you see what looks like a tough transit coming through the door, then, rather than leaving the glass right there in the way, you can run over to your planet, pick it up, and start pouring your energy out, a little at a time. That way, by the time the transiting planet does get to your planet, although there still may be a bit of a spill, it's definitely not going to be as bad as it could have been.

Let's pretend the planet in question is your Mars, and that a long-term Uranus transit that's been "on" for months is about to be "set off," Big Time, by the added oomph of transiting Mars. You look in the ephemeris and see that they're on the way, and you start thinking about all that stuff in the Olde Bookes about being beheaded, dying of the Plague, and so forth. Well, rather than just sitting there waiting for the executioner to arrive, get busy. Get out all your new books and start circling your favorite Uranus/Mars activities, experiences that are the astrological equivalent of a Thunderstorm. Sudden, exciting things. Anything you've never done before qualifies—especially if you never thought you'd dare to try it.

See, when your Mars is being transited, your energy level is high—and you've got to find a way to use that energy. An Antidote, you might say, specially designed to tap it off. Remember, your Mars is the part of you that insists on Action. He's your soldier, your sword—the part of you that wants to Just Do It. So do something. Take action. We all know what it's like to literally be Too Tired To Get Mad, right? You may not be immune to incoming advances from The Outside World, but if you're tired when the transit arrives, you've used too much of your Mars to be as volatile as you would have been. When your Mars is about to get kicked, then, get yourself up off the couch and exercise. It's the best "antidote" I know of for tough Mars transits.

A Quick "Cookbook" on Transits

If you take my advice and look back over key times in your life, you'll see that we act out our transits in amazing ways, none of which are totally "predictable." Still, the idea is to figure out first what the current symbolism circulating in your life is, and next how it can best be put to work in your life—constructively. So here's a quick guide, an idea of what the point of your transit might be. It's not intended as the Be-All-End-All of prediction, because there really is no such work (except for Robert Hand's *Planets In Transit*, maybe...Check the back for the scoop on that marvelous book); but, it will give you some clues when you're wondering what to expect.

SUN TRANSITS:
LET'S TALK ABOUT YOU...
WHAT DO YOU THINK ABOUT ME?

Yes, under Sun transits, the subject is You. And that's all. The transiting Sun is like a traveling spotlight—wherever it is in your chart right now is a spot where you want to "shine," right now, where you want to Be All That You Can Be. Sun transits describe times of public acclaim, times when the light clicks on overhead and we're "recognized" for what we've done. The ultimate Sun transit, of course, is our birthday, the day we all secretly believe really should be Our Day, of course, a day when we shouldn't have to do anything we don't want to do, when everyone treats us like Visiting Royalty. Special. That's what the Sun is all about— our sense that we're Special. Any time the Sun touches a planet in our charts, it's through that planet we want to be noticed, receive approval, and get presents just for being Us. Since the Sun is the yang or masculine principle, Sun transits also point out times when men take the spotlight in our lives.

MOON TRANSITS:
FEELINGS...NOTHING MORE THAN FEELINGS

The subject is emotions. Home, too. And femininity. Moon transits are fun to monitor because they happen quickly enough to be eminently watchable. Since the Moon travels about a degree every 2-2½ hours, it also dashes through a sign in 2½ days. Moon transits reflect the ebb and flow of our moods, the highs and lows we feel that last a day or two, and the "feelings" that we get—our "gut" reactions, that is—about the situations we encounter. When the Moon touches a planet in your chart, you reflect, mull over, and often find yourself quite literally dreaming about those matters. That goes for daydreams, too. Just as Sun transits point to times of increased dealings with men, Moon transits point to times when women and feminine matters get our attention—so your Mom will often get involved, too.

MERCURY TRANSITS:
LIFE IN THE FAST LANE

The subject is communication—all kinds. Letters, phone calls, short trips, errands. When Mercury dashes through your chart, or skips quickly over one of your planets, you won't be able to sit still. You'll be chatty, interested, and ready to learn anything. You'll do a fair share of running around, and you'll often end up doing at least two things at once. Mercury transits show when a letter or call might come—or a good time to place a call, or mail a letter. Mercury transits are typically busy, fun times, when messages can also arrive via Symbolic Events. Lots of times, because of Mercury's love of duality and variety, you'll find that the events surrounding a Mercury transit also happen in twos.

VENUS TRANSITS:
FEELIN' GROOVY

The subject is comfort, although relationships and sociability also play into it. Usually, Venus transits feel "good," to use that antiquated, nearly illegal astrological term. At best, they're like that favorite Aunt of yours planting a kiss on your planet's cheek. At worst, they bring up the subject of relationship, and make it The Topic of The Day—which can be bad or good, depending on the news. Venus touching one of your planets describes times when you're much more social, when being pleasant and practicing Random Acts of Kindness with your natal planet are the order of the day. Venus loves presents, candy, and cushy conditions, too, however, so when she happens along, your natal planet won't be much in the mood for work. Good company, good food, and good times will be more like it.

MARS TRANSITS:
DON'T STEP ON MY BLUE SUEDE SHOES

The subject is assertion. You'll know you're having a Mars transit when, all of a sudden, everyone around you suddenly has An Attitude—and you're absolutely convinced it's not You. Really. If this does happen to you, just for the heck of it, reflect for a moment. See if you might not be mad about something. Maybe everyone's testy because you keep digging a little bit at them rather than seeking out the real owner of your anger—which may be You—and giving it all away at once. Under Mars transits, our energy level runs high. We even feel "hot"—revved, maybe. Even feverish. We're stronger, more restless, amazingly active, and maybe even a tad on the cranky side. Again, if this "feistiness" starts showing up in your relationships—exercise, exercise, exercise. Run. Work it out. Get Tired. Working with weights is the best, because your Mars is the part of you who wants to win, and every time you complete a repetition, you've won. Remember, Mars rules muscles, iron, the color red, and anger. It's up to you to choose your method.

JUPITER TRANSITS: UP, UP AND AWAY

The subject is risk, growth, and New Stuff. These are *Star Trek* transits, real door-openers. With Jupiter, you wake up one day and find you've got an irresistible urge to boldly go where no one wo/man has gone before, to seek out new places, new people, and new ways of tackling old problems. Sometimes that means long-distance travel, literally, and sometimes you just end up in school. Either way, your perspective widens and you grow, personally, from all the new experiences you're suddenly bold enough to try. Sometimes we grow—literally—under Jupiter transits. Weight-wise, that is. Since Jupiter rules the principle of expansion, your ego can get a bit inflated, too. You get to thinking that you can do anything, anything at all. Your natal planet feels so confident and so swelled it makes you downright euphoric. Manic, even. Jupiter transits are like that. But, damn, they feel good. Real good. Addicting, even.

WHAT'S THE DIFFERENCE BETWEEN OUTER PLANET TRANSITS AND INNER PLANET TRANSITS?

Before we go any further, let's chat about the difference between inner and outer planet transits. You were just about to ask, anyway. It's like this: the inner planets move along so quickly that they tend to represent short-term things—moods, events, and fleeting circumstances. The outer planets, however, really set up camp. Pluto, for example, can stay in one degree for four or five months, while the Sun covers about a degree a day, and the Moon travels a degree every 2-2½ hours. All totaled, the outers can hang around a natal planet or point for up to three years. They usually touch a degree three times, but occasionally they touch it as many as five times, depending on where they choose to do their retrograde. Since an lawful lot can happen in three years, the outers set the stage for major change. We end up making decisions, reacting to situations, and responding to outside circumstances in entirely new ways. Honest. In fact, you'll hardly recognize yourself when the planet moves on.

Think of what you were doing three years ago. Or ten years ago. More importantly, think about who you were then, and look at yourself today. It's easy—now—to see that you were in the middle of some major, sweeping changes back then. You didn't realize it, because you were busy living your life from day to day, but whatever you were going through at the time is very much a part of who you are right now. You incorporated those events into your being, and you grew from the experiences. Well, we're always in the middle of one outer planet transit or another—and we're always changing. That's why it's true that experience is the greatest teacher. And speaking of teachers, it's appropriate that we cover Saturn next.

SATURN TRANSITS:
WHAT GOES AROUND, COMES AROUND

The subject is Reality. Just the facts, ma'am. When Saturn comes along, it's time to Wake Up And Smell the Coffee. Reality arrives, with both guns blasting. Now, although these transits are not notoriously Great Times—and I'd be lying to you if I said they were—they're not notoriously Bad times, either. At best, these are personally satisfying, validating times, when all the efforts you've made are evaluated, and if you deserve it, your rewards arrive. At worst, you'll still get the evaluation, but you'll see your shortcomings show up and feel Unworthy, Undeserving, and Inadequate. If this is the case, don't despair. It's much the same technique that's used in the military. Make 'em feel bad about what they did wrong and they'll try harder the next time. And keep in mind that remedies for whatever ails you also find their way into your life under Saturn transits. Firming up your life is the point: taking care of appropriate responsibilities; living within realistic limits; and getting rid of inappropriate responsibilities, burdens, or limits. If you can handle that part of it, Saturn transits don't have to hurt.

Basically, Saturn transits indicate periods when your natal planet is tested and graded. You either receive rewards from your world, or you get pushed back to Go without the $200 bucks. Either way, you Learn A Valuable Lesson—which is how Saturn earned his nickname, "The Cosmic SchoolMaster." This holds true especially during The Mother of all Saturn Transits, the Saturn Return, that is, that comes along at age 29½, when Saturn returns to its natal placement. At this time the foundation you've laid out for your life will be stressed—from within—by itself. See, over the first 29½ years of your stay here on the planet, you're in training on How To Be A Grown-Up, how to run your own show by your own rules. At 29½ that Young Adult inside you is called out to get to work on the project. It's a serious time, more serious than you've seen in a while. Lots of folks change jobs, get married, get divorced, or get degrees. The best way to deal with any Saturn transit, however, is to work. It's The Right Thing To Do. And don't ever try to get away with anything under Saturn transits. You get what you truly deserve at these times. Nothing more, nothing less. Remember, quality doesn't cost—it pays.

URANUS TRANSITS:
JUST GET YOURSELF FREE

The subject is freedom. Individuality too. Uranus transits are not boring times. Exciting, unusual circumstances happen along, and you truly won't know what to expect—except maybe the unexpected. These are times when The Universe seems absolutely bent on helping you to get yourself free. So if you're feeling "stuck" in your present circumstances, and you see Uranus approaching one of your planets...well, fasten your seat belt and put your tray table in the upright position, because you're about to be liberated. The more "stuck" you feel, the more surprising the transit will be, too. See, sometimes we humans get so embedded in a routine that it takes a good jolt to get us out of it.

Often, temporary people arrive under Uranus transits. I like to call these folks "Uranian Buffers." They walk into your life and trigger you by providing the one thing you just realized was sorely missing from your life. Might be freedom, might be romance, might even be independence. Whatever. They present it to you, get you used to it, and then they're Outta There—no matter what they tell you in the meantime. What you'll discover later is that these folks are "lures," messengers you've chosen to wake you up to the changes you need to make to get on with your next step. And they don't have an easy job, either. Buffers usually bring about a serious tumult in your life—but they're also pretty darned exciting. When they arrive, enjoy them, and think about what they're providing for you. Don't try to hold on when they get up to leave, either. Just enjoy the ride.

In general, during Uranus transits, you may feel like you're inside one of those Winter Snow-Scene ornaments. You feel as if you've been picked up and shaken, by what seems like outside forces. You may get fired "suddenly," for example, and wail about it at first, but later realize it was the best thing that could have happened to you. When something like this happens, it's because you're feeling stifled, but rather than quit and appear irresponsible, you send out tiny "resistance" behaviors, until finally, The Boss decides enough is enough, and you're ousted. You act surprised, but you're really relieved. You're free. Under Uranus, as with any transit, it's really **you** that does the changing. You just do an awful lot of it at these times.

NEPTUNE TRANSITS:
DREAM A LITTLE DREAM OF ME

The subject is escape, romance, and alternate states. Play your cards right, and your Neptune transits will be some of the best times in your life. Now is when your dreams will arrive, when you begin to sense what your purpose is and what will make you most fulfilled. You'll sense these things because you'll feel vaguely dissatisfied. Neptune transits are times of Divine Discontent, times when there's a whole lot of sighin' goin' on—and not a lot of action. But that's all right. You're not supposed to be acting now—just floating—also visualizing, imagining, and playing "what if" in order to help create future.

We meet "Buffers" under Neptune transits, too—but they're very different from Uranian Buffers. These folks are sent along to cast a spell and lure you away from where you are, gradually...no sudden, drastic moves, like Uranus. Nothing is harsh, here, with The Lady Neptune. She whispers, hums, sings you a lullaby, and erases all the rough corners of Your Reality. It's replaced with what you really **are** under those harsh angles. You'll get to know what your dreams are. You won't be able to make them happen immediately, however, and that's where we get into trouble with Neptune transits. We become so wrapped up in The Dream that we start to think we've already got it. We don't. Saturn transits are when you make things "real." Neptune transits are when you decide what you want Real to be.

PLUTO TRANSITS: PASSION PLAYS

The subject is obsession, regeneration, and inevitable change. These are times of Transformation and Rejuvenation, times when we shed our skin and start over—but not without some expense. About two years after the huge fire in Yellowstone Park, I spent three days there. We stayed, of course, in the part of the park untouched by the fire, but drove through the pieces that were. The charred trees were coal-black to about waist-level, then orange, then white. The effect was like a perpetual sunset, and it was eerie, to say the least. Just at the feet of the blackened trees, though, a carpet of fuzzy green babies covered the ground, tiny pine trees and white birch. They marched right through the burned forest, literally covering the ground. Once I spotted them, I wasn't sad any more. I understood The Process. That's what Pluto transits are all about; they're a three stage-process of Life, Death, and Rebirth.

Under Pluto transits, an existing condition in your life dies—one that's outworn its usefulness to you. Something leaves. Period. Yes, it sounds harsh, but you know what? If there wasn't any fire, there wouldn't be little green armies inching their way up towards the sun in Yellowstone. Besides, with Pluto transits, you always know what's got to go. It's just tough to realize that now's the time. If you don't let go, however, whatever it is will probably still leave your life—or you'll learn down the road why it would have been better to let go then. In all, it's best to cooperate with the tide you'll see about to peak in your life. Make plans for Stage Three—Rejuvenation Time—and release what's got to go gracefully.

ASPECTS TRANSITING PLANETS MAKE

Remember the chapter on aspects? The one I had to practically bribe you into reading? If you don't understand it perfectly, go back there right now, because you'll need it to get through this next section. See, different aspects made by transiting planets produce different times. In a nutshell, conjunctions are the most action-oriented transits of all, because a planet has literally barged right into the degree of your natal planet and turned it on. Trines may not bring anything at all, save for a really good feeling—you know how lazy they get. Sextiles show exciting opportunities—muscles that are just dying to be worked. Squares indicate times that may be hectic, overwhelming, or irritating, times when you'd rather be in Philadelphia, but when you'll get a lot done. Oppositions tend to play out in our relationships, since they're 180 degrees apart, and it's often easier to project a part of ourselves on to someone else than to own it. Quincunxes bring up health concerns, and difficult "no win" adjustments—"either-or" situations that require us to "settle" to get along. Semi-sextiles correlate with times when change gets underway—especially when they're exact.

Transits to the Angles
Now, when the "Main Beams" in your chart are transited, especially by the outer planets, the significance can be similar to an earthquake. You may not "be" at the epicenter, but when your "framework" gets touched, all of you reacts. Often, under transits to the angles, we change all four areas associated with these points—our career, our home, our relationship, even our appearance (or sense of who we are). The angles are all about the way that we relate with our world. When they're touched by the outers, especially, you're ready for Big Changes.

The Midheaven
As you know, this highest point in the chart is where the side of you lives that handles your career, status, and reputation. It's straight up—at "High Noon"—and completely exposed. So when a transiting planet arrives, especially by conjunction, it's this side of your life that's exposed: your accomplishments and your reputation. Since this degree is the first one in the tenth house— Saturn's Pad—transiting planets open the doors between Your Public and You. For Better or Worse. For example: Watergate. For example: receiving a promotion. If you don't have a clear life path chosen, transits to your Midheaven will make you want one. If you do, now's your time for Kudos.

Ascendant Transits

These transits indicate times when you'll be much more aware of You. You may begin to dress differently, to show everyone how different you "feel." In fact, when the Ascendant is touched, often we begin literally wearing the "costume" of the planet who's transiting. Under Mars transits you may notice you're wearing an awful lot of red, and stomping your feet a bit more. Under Pluto transits, you'll wear lots of black, and so forth. After you've dressed the part for awhile, you'll begin to act a little differently, too. Your new behavior creates a new facet to your personality, which in turn puts you in different circumstances, and in the company of different people than you're used to. They turn you on to new activities, and all of a sudden, you're not anywhere near the personality type you used to be. You've "added" to You. You're New and Improved. Transits to your Ascendant from Uranus are particularly entertaining. All of a sudden, you get an urge to dye your hair purple—or you cut it all off. Or you change your whole wardrobe. These are invigorating times, specially designed to make You feel good about You. Get involved in the process.

IC Transits

The subject is Home and Family. Now's when you may move, add on to your home, or have a child. Any change in your domestic environment, in fact, will arrive when the IC is transited. Because this is the lowest spot on your chart, the IC also represents how we root ourselves to the planet, emotionally, that is. So transits to this spot can also announce changes in our emotional security—again, For Better Or Worse. Since the IC/MC points are really just two ends of an axis, it's tough to consider transits to one end without seeing both. So think of how tightly linked your home and career are. After all, if you stay put long enough, you end up with a reputation in your community. You're "The Astrologer," for example. Or the Town Select/wo/man. You'll notice transits to either end of an axis more intensely when they're by conjunction, because the transiting planet will have "moved in" to the house.

Descendant Transits

Again, this is just the other end of the Ascendant, so whatever happens here will echo over there, too. And it's true that changes to our physical appearance have an effect on our relationships. If it didn't, we'd never spend as much time as we do in front of the mirror. When a planet enters the seventh, however, the subject is definitely Relationships, and the transiting planet indicates the Situation you're about to start actively seeking out in all your One-On-Ones. Uranus, for example, may describe times when things are much more erratic, or simply that we require more personal freedom in relationships than we ever have before. Jupiter can represent a present, the arrival of a Special Someone—or the end of a confining relationship, or wanting more than is possible—seeking "heaven on earth" from a fellow, fallible human.

TRANSITS THROUGH THE HOUSES

When a planet enters a house, it's moving in. When inners enter a house, our daily activities begin to revolve around those matters—especially since the inners tend to travel in "packs." The farthest Mercury can be from the Sun is 28 degrees, for example, and the Moon makes a loop once a "moonth," too. A "pack" transiting the fourth house may mean we're spending an awful lot of time taking care of our homes—tending to Family Values, you might say.

On the other hand, when an outer enters a house, visiting royalty has just arrived, and for some time, too. Since Uranus has an orbit of 84 years, he spends an average of seven years in a house. This, then, is no ordinary weekend house guest. This guy's here for what's going to seem like forever. Neptune and Pluto stay even longer—up to 20 years in a house, in fact. Needless to say, while the Outer Planet is visiting, we need to make adjustments to accommodate the new energy circulating around us. After awhile, we don't notice its presence any more, but we feel it acutely when the planet first enters the house and then again when it leaves and we've got to clean up after it.

In a nutshell, it's like this: outers move in. They revamp a house to suit their purposes. Inners just stop by for the weekend. Either way, it's really fascinating to watch your focus change.

Progressions—Astrological Time-Lapse Photography

Okay. Get out your ephemeris. Figure out how old you are. If you're thirty, count down thirty days in the ephemeris from the day you were born. If you're twenty-two, count twenty-two days.

Congratulations. Those are your progressed positions. Roughly. For true technical precision, have a progressed chart calculated by a computer. These planets are yours for right now, but they're constantly moving, and if you've got a couple of computer print-outs of progressed charts done at regular intervals, it becomes even more obvious how much the chart actually does move right along. For example, the progressed MC moves at about the same rate of speed as the Sun—a degree a year. The progressed Moon's cycle is about the same as transiting Saturn's orbit. At any rate, it's important to watch your progressed Moon because it shows your inner emotional development.

Progressions are astrological time-lapse photography. They show the stage to which you've evolved, the point in your growth you've reached. Think of a flower unfolding on film, at ultra-slow speed. One frame is like one minute, and not much movement shows. After ten or twenty frames, however, you can not only see movement, you can see a process unfolding. That's how progressions are used—to show the stage you've reached in your inner development. The years that planets change signs or go station to direct or to retrograde by progression are also very important years.

Solar and Lunar Returns

Solar and lunar returns are two other methods of "prediction" that are very useful. Return charts are calculated for the moment when the planet of your choice returned to the spot where it was when you were born. In the case of the Sun, that happens once a year—on your birthday-ish. Lunar returns happen once a month, Mars returns once every two years, and so forth. The symbolism of a transiting planet's conjunction to its natal placement in your chart is very potent. You're about to begin a whole new cycle. So whatever was happening around that returning planet is very important, too, and why the whole return chart is considered, no matter which planet it's done for.

The two most commonly used return charts are Solar Returns and Lunar Returns. Solar Returns, as we said earlier, occur on your birthday—give or take a a day or two. Your birthday is the first day of the next year of your life. Since it's a "first," like any other beginning, it has a birth time. Basically, if you keep in mind that you own your birth chart, you can see how you might "lease" your return charts. They're temporary situations—your quest for the year—or month.

Lunar returns are calculated in the same fashion, by putting up a chart for the moment the Moon returned to her natal spot. You only get to keep these charts for a month—apt symbolism for the quickness with which our feelings change—but they certainly are significant.

Solar Arc Directions

How old are you? Twenty-nine? Well, that's your Solar Arc. Add that number of degrees to every planet in your chart, and to the MC and ASC, too, and see where those planets or points end up. That's it. That's all there is to it. Years when solar arc planets touch natal planets or angles are big years. They almost seem to work like transits. Again, however, solar arcs are symbolic. Since they're found by counting the number of degrees the Sun has "traveled" to this point in our lives, they show how experience has left its mark on each planet—and each Life Department.

Well, that's it. That's the story of Prediction. I suppose now you'll just put this book down and forget all about me for a week or so, you'll be so busy penciling in and erasing your transits, day after day. Try not to get really hung up on it, but, by all means, do get involved. You'll learn more from watching your own chart than you could possible get out of any book.

Oh, and by the way, I put the chapter on relationships next, just to keep your interest up. So when you're done obsessing on your own chart, you can get the chart of your Significant Other and lock yourself away with **that** for a while, too.

CHAPTER TEN

SYNASTRY AND COMPOSITES—
THE ASTROLOGY OF RELATIONSHIPS

What Are You Looking For?

Okay, let's recap. Again. If you're bored with recapping, congratulations. You've learned something. If you're not bored, then concentrate. We're getting close to the end of the book, and you won't hear this lecture again.

All right, then. We've established that each of us is a walking collection of urges and needs. We've seen that horoscope charts are maps that symbolically represent those urges or needs through the planets, signs, and houses, and that by interpreting these magical maps, we can make certain statements about the chart's owner, be it a person, a place, or a thing.

So far, so good?

Great. Now imagine what happens when You and Your volatile little collection bump into Someone Else—with their very own set of urges or needs, likes and dislikes, favorite ice cream flavors, and pet peeves. Doesn't matter who this Other is. They automatically push our planetary buttons in one way or another, and we push theirs. It's a "chemical reaction" of sorts. Sometimes it's a pretty groovy reaction, and we become intoxicated with The Other's presence. That's called Love At First Sight by most folks—Venus to us. Either way, when it happens, it's recordable.

When we're in love, we've technically been "drugged" by the Other (which explained an awful lot to me, I'll tell you). When we're angry, that's chemical, too. It's all about adrenaline, about "getting hot under the collar," and "seeing red"—and yes, that sure is your Mars.

The point is that you've got a lunch box just jam-packed with urges or needs, all of which like nothing better than company—for a variety of reasons. There's Venus, for example (who fell in love last paragraph), the part of you who loves nothing better than Someone to share her chocolates, sunsets, and cushy pillows with.

You've got a Moon, too, who needs to love and be loved, unconditionally, the side of you that needs An Other to cuddle, spoil, nurture, and "emote" to. Your Mercury wants someone there to chat with over dinner. And your Sun (who may not admit it), just loves captive audiences full of Others to tell it how good it did.

In a nutshell, gang, we each need to mingle in some way with Others to truly feel alive.

Needless to say, after coming into contact with Others for awhile, we develop favorites. We begin to choose the Others we spend our time with more and more carefully—especially our mates. (At least, that's the theory—but the jury's still out.) By the time we've had a couple of relationships, we're hooked on them. We need An Other to relate to on an intimate level.

Now, I know that none of you out there spend every unattached waking moment on this planet in an unrelenting search for That Someone Special to partner up with. **You're** far too independent for that. But you may know someone who does. Maybe you went to college with someone like that. At any rate, you know that it takes a great deal of time and energy, this search. It requires the collective efforts of every little corner of ourselves that wants to be heard, loved, or appreciated. The Quest for this Other, in fact, is what gets us up off the couch on a Saturday night to shower, deck ourselves out in gold, and meet yet another Friend of a Friend. This same quest is why we drag ourselves out to loud, smoky clubs till the wee hours, pretending to like the music. It's why we join health clubs, take classes, and go grocery shopping at odd hours.

Yes, we toddle along through life scanning every crowd, searching for That Special Someone who'll set the whole system on

"Alert," who'll Jump-Start us, and get our whole chart going—our bodies, our minds, our spirits, and our hearts. So wouldn't you think, with a wonderful, magical system like astrology, we'd be able to save ourselves some time by just setting a couple of charts down side by side and seeing whose what triggers what?

Well, sure. Good idea. That's called synastry, and it's one of the Top Two methods of Chart Comparison. We'll get to that next. But first, remember this: it's easier to understand how A and B will get along if you get to know A and B well first—because then you'll know what each of them is looking for. So the very first stop to make when you're out looking for relationship potential is to always, always look at each chart separately, before you go anywhere else, and figure out what each individual's expectations are from relationships.

Don't forget to look at the current transits, too. If my Venus is currently being conjuncted by Neptune, for example, well, then, I'm In The Mood for romance, wishes, and daydreams. If it's Saturn who's taken a seat on my Venus, however, I'll want to settle down, have a serious, committed relationship, maybe even build a house.

You get the idea. Individual charts tell you just as much as a comparison will. So even if you've just met an Other, and you're dying to find all the connections you just know are everywhere, try to contain yourself. See what the new Other is shopping for— then start making lists of your planets and their planets, and your asteroids and their asteroids, and your midpoints and their midpoints. (Others, by the way, are going to be at least partially responsible for just about all the new techniques you learn in astrology.)

The Seventh House and the Fifth House, Too

Fine. The lecture worked. You're willing to stall your synastry for four or five minutes, and take a look at your chart—and theirs. Separately. So where do you look for relationship potential in a chart? Well, first off, get yourself over to the seventh house cusp, and have a look at the sign that's there, because, as you already know, that's the Style of Behavior that you display when you're relating one-on-one, the side of you that's reserved for tête-à-tête's. This is the room where we stash the side of us that emerges when

we're in the company of just one Other. It describes the characteristics we want our Other to encourage, support, and enjoy in
us. You remember all that, right?

Of course, the fifth house is important to check, too. It's the
Play Room, remember, where you keep the person you become
when you're doing what you want to do, when you're not duty-
bound or committed in any way, operating only on Wanna's—no
Hafta's. This is the side of you that's eternally young, because it's
always at play. Check here for the qualities you'll need in a playmate. Every relationship needs joy to last. It needs to be "fun" for
each of you to look forward to spending time with the other.

Of course, what's in a house is important, too. We can only
express any of our planets fully when the door of that "room" is
"opened," when we're using that "slice" of our personalities. Folks
with a whole clump of 12th-house placements need to spend time
alone, for example, because they can only "do" those planets fully
when they're alone. If you own seventh-house planets, then, you
can only get those planets "out" when you're in the company of
one other person. Just One.

Needless to say, Saturn in the seventh will have very different expectations from a relationship than will the Moon. He'll
want a commitment. On paper, too. Saturn will also want some
rules laid down, some Guidelines to follow, and a copy of your
most recent financial statement. The Moon, however, wants to
dream, nurture, and take care of The Other. She wants to rub
your feet and hug you. If you're looking for a hugger, and you've
got someone who wants to take charge of your financial affairs,
no amount of Neptune's pink dust will change those basic differences.

Venus and Mars and The Moon—Oh My!

And then there's Venus to consider. She's the head of the Department of Love, Beauty, and Relationships, after all, so this is also
a primary stop to make in the search for expectations from a relationship. Now, the Lady knows what she likes—and what she
doesn't. Venus describes how you give and receives love, and
whether or not you see yourself as "worthy" of a "good" relationship. If you're looking for physical passion, stop off at Mars, and
check the Moon for willingness to trust.

Chemistry and Synastry

All right. You've covered the essential first step. You have an idea of what you're looking for from An Other, and you're ready to branch out. Suppose you've already met An Other and managed to get not just their birthdate but, somehow, their birth time out of them. Well, assuming you've dutifully made all the stops we just talked about before you put the two of your charts anywhere near each other, it's time to move along to the Top Two chart comparison techniques out there: Synastry and Composites.

We'll start with synastry—which is truly great stuff. The beauty of synastry is that it happens just about automatically when you take up the study of astrology. Quick, too. You start out by learning your own chart—and then the chart of at least one Significant Other. Sometimes you learn their chart first, matter of fact. Then you discover romantic, idealistic Neptune in your seventh, and you understand why.

One fine day you look at your chart and their chart, and you notice you've got an awful lot of planets in the same degrees—or signs—or houses. You see that you're connected with this person. Shuffling through your pile of Friends and Family charts, you begin to compare all of them to your own, and you discover that you're connected with everyone you know—Big Time. Keep looking and you'll find that the amount of connections you've got with others will match the depth of the bond you feel with them. You'll even have similar connections with several people. Like I said, we know what we like—and when we find it, we gather it up.

And here's the best part: you'll find that you're even connected to people you've never actually encountered—celebrities, for example. We've all been affected in most magical ways by movie stars we've never met, but just love, and in distinctly Un-Magical ways by Politicians we've also never physically encountered.

At any rate, as soon as you begin to notice connections, you're teaching yourself Synastry without even knowing it. Once you look at A in This Corner, and at B in This Corner, and consider how they might affect one another when they get together, once you "plug" one chart into another, by putting your planets in their chart, and their planets in yours—once you see how somebody else can "trigger" you—and vice-versa—that's synastry. Synastry shows how one set of personality traits affects another. It's like Chemistry, which *Webster's* calls "The study of the composition, structure, and properties of substances, and of the changes these substances undergo when they are exposed to outside influences"—like Each Other, for example. If you think about "chemistry" in terms of what happens when two people first meet, and fall in love—well, it's a very powerful physical reaction. It doesn't stop with the two people involved, either. Everyone in the room can feel it. Same goes for what happens when we're in the same space with two people who don't like each other—or when we're with someone we just don't like. As I said, we all know Mars.

You'll be doing synastry, then, forever, asking people not just for their Sun-signs, but for complete birthdata. Get used to it. It's how you'll **really** learn astrology. And pay attention to certain degrees that turn up time and again in the charts of the Others you select to surround yourself with, for whatever reasons. These degrees are a great way to understand You a little better, by seeing what it is that literally Turns You On. (See Chapter 12, Where To Find It, for some books on Synastry.)

OUTER PLANET "HITS"

One final thing about Synastry. It takes awhile before you really understand the cycles of the planets—before you really "get a feel" for them. You'll eventually see that you share similar Outer Planet positions with just about everyone born within a few years of you. Now, before they realize this, most folks go dashing off at least once thinking they've finally found the perfect soul-mate because "our Plutos are conjunct!" I wanted to save you that embarrassment. Now, I'm not saying that Outer Planet conjunctions aren't important; they are. They show Generational Trends, and they're the reason you share a bit of a larger mind-set with others in your age-group. But Inner Planet connections—to both The Other's Inner and Outer planets—are what you're looking for.

ALCHEMY AND COMPOSITES

Now, whether or not you can actually put this thing together long enough to maintain a third entity, which is what a relationship really becomes, is seen best through a third technique, called the Composite Chart. Composites are different from synastry, in that they're built from You and the Other (or Others). Composites take You and Them, find the degree at the midpoint of all your pairs of planets—your Venus and their Venus, your Sun and their

Sun, and so forth—and create a whole new chart. So Composite Charts don't compare the way that Synastry does—they combine. Alchemy, then, as opposed to Chemistry, equates nicely with Composites. The technical definition of Alchemy (also from *Webster's*) is, "A Medieval science with 3 objectives: 1)—to turn base metals into gold, 2)—to find a universal cure for disease, and 3)—to prolong life indefinitely."

Makes sense, too. When we have a relationship with someone, we're Transforming Something Base—or "ordinary," that is—into something precious: an Us. We come together and create a Twosome that makes us feel much more "special" than we do when we're alone, a Relationship that has needs and wants of its very own. When we're with a new Beloved, we're exploring our new composite together. Maybe that explains why we forget about the rest of the world for a while when we become involved.

It's also interesting that Alchemy was a search for a universal cure for dis-ease, since that's something else we all believe a good Relationship can do for us—find a cure for whatever ails us. And as far as prolonging life indefinitely goes, well, being with the "right" person certainly does make us feel immortal, and partnerships birth events and produce children of all kinds—"brain-children" included—that keep the chain of life going, whether it's by carrying on a family name or by immortalizing what we've done together on paper.

Casting the Composite—A Quick How-To

Now, just in case you don't have access to a computer, here's how composites are calculated. It's easy. All you need are the charts you want to "blend," and a *Book of Tables*. If you don't have a *Book of Tables*, you can approximate by using Equal Houses. Here goes:

1. **Find Midpoints of Each Pair of Planets.** Okay. If you've got an aspectarian, get it out—or maybe you just want to count degrees. Regardless of how you want to find it, let's say you've got a Sun at 4 Aries 30 and another at 5 Sagittarius 50. The Degree Axis that turns up at the exact middle of those two spots is 5 Aquarius 10; that's the composite Sun. Always take the midpoint that's closest to each pair of planets—at the "short end" of the circle, that is. And that's all there is to it. When you've finished with each pair of planets, find the midpoint of the two Midheavens.

2. **Find Composite Midheaven in Book of Houses**. All right, now get out that *Book of Tables* we talked about. (Koch and Placidus are the most commonly used systems, and the easiest tables to find.) Locate the Composite Midheaven you've calculated in your *Book of Tables*.

3. **Find Latitude of Residence**. What's the latitude of the town where the two of you live? If you don't know, look in the back of the *Book of Tables*. Most have the geographical coordinates listed for many of the larger cities. If your town isn't listed, find the city you're closest to and use that latitude.

4. **Use All House Cusps at that Location**. Take the house cusps listed under your Composite Midheaven degree, at the latitude where you live.

(As I've already said, by the way, if you don't have a *Book Of Tables*, don't let that stop you. You can approximate by using the same degree that appears on the Midheaven on each house cusp and applying the signs in their usual order, counterclockwise. This is called an equal house chart, and it will do quite nicely until you can get to a *Book of Tables*. If you're using Equal Houses, by the way, and a planet or two falls close to a house cusp, be sure to read the planet as if it were in both houses until you're sure of where it really does live.)

5. **Insert Planets Around the Wheel**. Once you've got your Composite house cusps, set your composite planets inside the wheel.

6. **Delineate**. Congratulations. Introduce yourself to the entity the two of you create when you come together. Now let's talk about how to understand it.

So How Do These Things "Work"?

Initially, it's easy to underestimate the importance of a Composite. After all, it's not "real." Well, don't underestimate it. It's very real. Composites are collections of midpoints, and midpoints get awfully "hot" when they're activated. Remember that wood stove we talked about back in the aspects chapter? Well, if you and I were to stand in a room about eight feet apart, with that same wood stove exactly four feet from both of us, if the thing were on, we'd be equally warm, and if it were off, we'd be equally cold. Whatever happens to that one particular degree that's exactly between us happens to both of us equally, and that's a very tight bond.

PLANETS IN COMPOSITES

Planets in composites "act" just the way planets "act" in other kinds of charts; they're each at the head of a Department. Each department is where you keep your impulse toward expressing a particular urge or need. For example, the Moon is where you keep your ability to express feelings and determine what's safe. She's the Head of Security in your chart. Mercury is where your communication ability lies—the Head of your Department of Letters, Phone Calls, and Gestures. In a composite chart, all the same holds true, except the planet involved holds a whole separate set of urges or needs that the entity itself has. So if your Composite Sun is Sagittarius, but you're a Virgo and your lover is a Pisces, you'll have to find some Sagittarian activities to "feed" your relationship—travel, classes, and so forth.

HOUSES IN COMPOSITES

Dramatic Composites point to relationships that are interesting, and interesting relationships last. So it's not uncommon to find stellia in Composites. These packets will show what the couple likes to "do" together—what they "specialize" in. Lots of planets in the ninth-house of a composite, for example, will show a relationship that stimulates your imagination, and makes you wonder. You'll philosophize and explore together. You may have met at a class, or one or both of you may function as teacher to the other, literally or figuratively. Houses in composites show where you'll end up "doing" things together, too—the places and types of Life Situations that will draw you, that is—as described by the houses—and the types of people you'll attract, too.

ASPECTS IN COMPOSITES

As we said earlier, a relationship needs to be interesting to keep both parties involved. That means there's got to be a certain amount of excitement built right in—and that means squares. Although trines and sextiles are lovely, and definitely point to special "knacks" you own together, too many trines might point to a Relationship that's "too comfortable." On the other hand, too many squares can also mean that you'll argue a lot. It's like this: however our planets are "wired" to one another, both by synastry and in the composite, if the relationship has value to both of us, we'll work it out. Just remember to feed those "hard" aspects— um, I mean your "difficult but productive aspects." Give them activities, projects to work on together so they're never bored and cranky.

THE ROLE OF THE MOON'S NODES

The Moon's Nodes are very important in Composites, and usually very prominent, too. Now, I know we haven't really covered the Nodes yet, and we're going to go over them again in the next chapter, Exclamation Points, but here's an advance lesson. The Nodes of the Moon are the intersections of two "Great Circles"—the Sun's Apparent Yearly Orbit and the Moon's monthly orbit. The two spots where these circles criss-cross are called the North and South Nodes of the Moon. Since they combine the Sun and Moon, the Nodes operate in your chart like a team of alchemists. They mix and blend two sides of you—the Inside and the Outside—both of which are very "base"—or "ordinary"—without the other, both of which combine to produce a blend of the Future and the Past. Just like the rest of the composite, then, the nodes are "midpoints," but they seem to function (in any type of chart) like gateways, openings through which Others slip in. Which might explain why they're always, always very active spots in the charts of relationships that make a real impact on all parties involved.

The most amazing thing I've found about the nodes in Composites, however, is the frequency with which they seem to come up angular—so often it's not even surprising anymore. In fact, the nodes are so commonly found right on the angles (or, at the very least, in angular houses), that if they're not there, I automatically double-check the birth times of one or both parties. I've also found that the nodes of one or both parties often "hit" exactly with the angles of the composite—or that the angles of the individuals will match the nodal axis of the Composite.

Regardless of where the nodes turn up, however, they'll show you the challenge the universe has presented to the relationship, as per the north node, and the habits or "alibis" the entity will use to avoid things—as per the South Node. So planets attached to the nodes are very important. They'll describe the activities that will help the entity achieve its purpose, as per the "push" of North Node, or hold it back, as per the "pull" of the South Node.

THIS RELATIONSHIP

You'll know you've created a Composite with a life of its own when you find yourself talking about This Relationship—about how It's "good" for you, or "bad" for you, or how much you—or they—have changed as a result of It. Remember, this third entity is a third entity, and you create one with everyone you encounter.

Since it is a whole separate entity, by the way, it stands to reason that the way you experience Our Composite can be quite different from the way I experience it. This is why one partner might see a relationship as "ideal" for them, even if the other doesn't. For this reason, Composites are tough to tame. We can't "control" the Composite chart we create with An Other, because half of it doesn't belong to us. So, although we can change the Synastry between us, and maybe resist reacting to what those Mars squares represent—temporarily, at least—we can't change the composite. We also can't duplicate it with someone else, because there's only one You, baby, and there's only one Me.

Now, how all parties concerned react to The Relationship also depends on the Synastry between your chart and the Composite. So take a peek at how This Relationship and You get along on paper, and you'll find even more answers—and lots more questions—about how and why relationships fascinate us like they do. (Jodie and Stephen Forrest have a great chapter on this in their book, *Skymates*, by the way, which is listed in that now-famous chapter, Where To Find It.)

TRANSITS AND PROGRESSIONS OF COMPOSITE CHARTS

First, Transits

Since, as we've seen, Composites are legitimate entities in their own right, in addition to describing the general tone of The Relationship, your Composite will also experience transits and progressions. This explains why some relationships explode into being as soon as the two of you meet, while others kind of sneak up on you. It's especially amazing to look at transits to composites for when a couple met, got married, had a child, or moved across the country. Matter of fact, transits to the composite usually work noticeably better to time Couple-Oriented Events than transits to the individual's charts. Always check the transits for the First Meeting, too. They'll show what type of start this thing got off to—and it really does matter. We all know how it feels to "Get off on the wrong foot" with someone who we later discover we just love.

Progressed Composites

Progressions show inner change. They point to where a person or thing has evolved to in its development—the stage of growth an entity has symbolically achieved. Composite Charts show Why people or entities come together. Progressed Composites, then, show not just Why, but Why Now. They represent how The Relationship evolves—the changes it undergoes as the two of you settle into it. As with all progressed charts, the role of the progressed Moon is especially important. Watch the aspects it makes to the other progressed planets, and you'll see a symbolic record of changes in the emotional status unfold—and changes in the home environment of co-habitators, too.

If you want to really drive yourself crazy, try this: put transits in your Progressed Composites. Especially watch transits to the progressed Sun, Moon and angles. You won't believe what happens. You'll see when a partnership is ready for Big Change—whether it's relocation, marriage, the birth of a child, divorce, or the beginning of a business. Remember, natal synastry never changes. So when one or the other of you suddenly decide it's time to Get Serious or Move On, it's most often going to show up in your composite.

Calculating Progressed Composites

If you're trying to persuade your computer to do this, be warned—they don't like it. You'll need to trick your computer by progressing each chart separately first, then asking for a composite of the two. If you're calculating by hand, take a Progressed Chart for each individual (again, I strongly advise ordering these from a calculation service), and follow the steps just as you would for two natal charts.

Well, there you have it—your relationship kit, full of How-To's, How-Not-To's, and What to Look For's. Before you take off, however, remember—getting to know your own chart and understanding your own expectations in relationships is the only way to start. Having your head straight about what you really need and learning to recognize what it isn't will save you a whole lot of time in the long run.

CHAPTER ELEVEN

EXCLAMATION POINTS

In addition to the planets, signs, houses, asteroids, and Chiron, there are a few thousand Other Things we use in astrology. Like Fixed Stars, for example, which we'll talk about shortly. Many of these Other Things we use are "points"—spots that we've discovered "work," when stimulated. I like to think of these spots as Exclamation Points. If one of them lands on one of your planets, well, then, as with all exclamation points, the idea is for you to pay attention here—that particular planet or point is especially important, for whatever reason.

Now, some of these points are printed on your computer chart, and some aren't. Here's a bit about the four you'll see most often.

First, The NO, VX, EP, and PF

We'll start with the NO—AKA "The North Node." Now, if, by some unbelievable chance, you somehow have not yet read the chapter on Relationships, go back to that chapter and re-read "The Role of the Moon's Nodes." That will get you started. When you get back and you start looking for the north and south nodes on your chart, be warned that some chart services only print out one node—the **North Node**—AKA "NO"—and they'll assume you know enough to put the South Node directly across from it in your chart, in the opposite sign, but same degree and minute. Now you do. Take a minute here and write it into your chart, just for the heck of it—this is the best way to cement into your overwhelmed little mind that the nodes are a matched set.

Okay. The North and South Nodes are calculated by finding the degrees at the intersection of two Great Circles—the ecliptic (the Sun's Apparent Yearly Orbit), and the Moon's Monthly Orbit. The spots where these two touch forms an axis, and that axis is what's called The Nodes.

The North Node points upward, and symbolically represents where you're going—the direction your life will take. The spot it occupies in your chart shows a very important Point of Becoming—by sign; it's a quality you are totally unfamiliar with but need to learn, to achieve the most from your time down here on Planet #Three. By house, it describes the life circumstances you'll be involved in when Destiny calls. Matter of fact, The North Node is often referred to as "Your Highest Destiny." It's your mission, should you choose to accept it. It's your life's purpose, and the nature of the challenges you'll encounter as you set out to fulfill it. But more than anything, gang, the North Node is what you should be when you grow up.

The South Node, on the other hand, shows the qualities you arrived here with—where you came from. If you're a believer in reincarnation, check this spot out—it's chock full o' information on what you stuffed in your suitcase just before the train took off for this lifetime. It also indicates your heredity—the traits you received from your ancestors, you might say. Might be anything, too—from the ability to play the piano like Mozart to that pollen allergy everyone in your family has had since the 1800's. The South Node is old familiar territory. Since it's so easy to slip back into old habits, the South Node also seems to describe our all-around favorite excuse or alibi for not trying new things—in fact, the South Node has been described brilliantly as the "what if" of the chart, by Donna Van Toen[7].

The idea behind the nodes is to take the best of the South Node—what you already know well—and use it to achieve the best of the North Node—what you're out to learn this time around. When you're working with the nodes, check both house and sign placements, and any planets that aspect the axis, too. And don't forget to watch transits to your North Node. It's at those transit times that life will present opportunities to Be All That You Can Be.

7 Donna Van Toen, *The Astrologers' Node Book*

On to the VX—otherwise known as the **Vertex**. Like the North and South Nodes, this is a point that's calculated. Once again, the Ecliptic is involved, but the Vertex is the spot where the Ecliptic intersects with the Prime Vertical. (Don't ask—just trust me on this.) Anyway...the Vertex seems to show a spot where we encounter Others. Meaningful Others. It's a place where "Fated encounters" occur, it's said. It's fun to check your Vertex to see if it was being "hit" by a transiting planet on a particular day when you met Someone Special—no matter what you think of them now...

And then there's the EP—the **East Point**. Basically, it's seen as a "second Ascendant," because it's "the degree of the zodiac that would be rising if one were born on the equator."[8] It, of course, is opposite to the West Point, which corresponds to a type of "Descendant."

Which brings us to the PF—the **Part of Fortune**. The PF "works" exactly as you'd think it would. It's a spot in your chart where you're supposed to be "lucky." Lots of folks use it when they're figuring out when to buy their lottery tickets. It's calculated by using the following formula: Moon + Ascendant - Sun = Part of Fortune. In other words, your Part of Fortune is the same distance from your Ascendant as your Sun is from your Moon. This one is great fun to work with, and I've had pretty good results with it, personally—as far as "luck" goes, that is. (I'm not, however, living in a mansion on the Riviera, so don't quit your day-job yet, even if Jupiter is going to station on top of your PF.)

Fixed Stars

As you'll remember from science class, there isn't just one Sun out there—there are billions of them—every star, in fact, is a "sun." Now, because they're so far away, they don't seem to be moving, to us, at least—which is why they're called fixed, of course. At any rate, astrologers have been tucking a whole lot of them into charts for years now. Basically, if they're prominent in your chart—closely conjunct to a natal planet or point, that is, by a degree or so—you'll see the qualities of the star symbolically reflected in your planet.

---

8 Robert Hand, pg. 89, *Horoscope Symbols*.

As with all else, I encourage you to play with them, put them in your own chart as you see fit,[9] and experiment. I've given you a few here to start you off, but I'd like to warn you, before you set off to work with them, that most of what was written about them until very recently was very fatalistic, and didn't allow any room for interpretation whatsoever. In fact, in the old books, it's going to seem to you as if just about all of the fixed stars indicate fevers, blindness, and disgrace. They don't. They do, however, add some "oomph" to a planet. Still, please use your common sense when you're hooking them into your chart, and don't expect to be blinded at any moment just because your Mercury is conjunct to Antares or beheaded because your Moon is conjunct to Algol.

A FEW FIXED STARS

Caput Algol: 26 Taurus

Here's the baddest of the bad, the star the ancients associated with "piled-up corpses" and other unappetizing images. This star supposedly signifies losing your head—literally—but if it's prominent in your chart, don't worry. You can "lose your head" in more ways than one!

Spica: 23 Libra

As bad as Algol is, Spica is that good. Here's the star associated with All Good Things—wealth, happiness, and good fortune. Hey, it worked for Bill Clinton: it's conjunct to his Jupiter.

Regulus: 29 Leo

This is The Royal Star, the significator of leaders. Regulus passes out wealth and honors too, and might make you famous in the process.

Antares: 9 Sagittarius

This one's associated with rashness and violence, which seems appropriate. You'll be able to pick Antares out in the sky due to its fiery red color.

9 Astro Communications can provide a one-page lising of the fixed stars prominent in your chart.

CHAPTER TWELVE
WHERE TO FIND IT

One of the things I found most frustrating when I was first trying to learn astrology was the fact that I just couldn't seem to find what I was looking for. I had no idea where to look for organizations, which magazines I might like, or where to find a teacher—a living, breathing person who could answer all those questions you can just imagine I had.

Well. You, friends, will not have those problems. What follows is a list of everything I could possibly think of that you might need to find—conferences, organizations, local groups, magazines, a chart calculation service, software companies, you name it. If it's not here, you don't need it. If you do need it and you can't find it, write to me at my address and I'll get you connected. And, remember, the best way to learn astrology is always going to be by talking to other astrologers about their experiences. We're Cosmic Interpreters, remember, and we all have knowledge to share.

Astrological Organizations

There are lots of really good groups out there, all over the US of A—and all over the world, matter of fact. Membership fees vary, but I've never heard of even a national group that charges more than $40 a year for dues. Most local groups meet once a month and have speakers on a variety of subjects. Usually your membership dues entitle you to attend lectures and workshops for free or for a reduced rate. The lectures are super—it's great to hear other astrologers' Mercurys in action—but the best part of attending meetings is the camaraderie, the feeling that we're all in this together. See, immediately after falling in love with astrology, you'll find yourself craving conversation in The Language. More often than not, you'll end up teaching your friends, too—just so you'll have someone to talk to.

Check with the three major astrological organizations in the country for information on a chapter near you.

THE BIG THREE
AFAN—American Federation for Astrological Networking
This group is devoted to improving astrology's image in the news, protecting the legal and political interests of astrologers, and opening up channels for networking, too. AFAN is based in Beverly Hills, CA, at 8306 Wilshire Boulevard, Suite 537. Write to them for membership and newsletter information.
ISAR—The International Society for Astrological Research
This group focuses on astrological research, and has a wonderful database called IDEA that contains thousands of accurate birth-data by category. Each member receives a list of other members and the particular fields they're interested in. ISAR publishes a quarterly journal called *KOSMOS*, too. For more info, write ISAR, PO Box 38613, Los Angeles, CA, 90038-0613.
NCGR—The National Council for Geocosmic Research
This group has chapters all over the country, most of whom have monthly meetings and sponsor conferences. For information on the *Memberletter*, local chapters, dues, or where to find a teacher in your area, write to the National council for Geocosmic Research, Inc., at 105 Snyder Avenue in Ramsey, NJ, 07446-2720. You fire signs who can't wait a moment longer can send a FAX or use voice-mail at (201) 818-2871.

OTHER GROUPS
AFA—The American Federation of Astrologers
The goals of the AFA are Education, Research, Cooperation, and Progress. They can be reached at PO Box 22949, Tempe, AZ 85285-2040.

Arizona Society of Astrologers
They are located in the Phoenix/Mesa area of Arizona with a
very large, active group (and monthly meetings with lectures
and workshops). Write to ASA, PO Box 9340, Scottsdale, AZ
85252. For more info, contact Charlotte Benson at (602) 952-
1525.

The Astrological Lodge of London
The Lodge was founded in 1915 by Alan Leo. It meets weekly,
on Monday evenings, in London. For information, write to The
Secretary, Astrological Lodge of London, BM Astrolodge,
London WC1N3XX, UK.

Astrological Society of Connecticut
This group is based in Wethersfield, Connecticut. They meet
monthly and frequently have conferences. Write to them at PO
Box 9346, Wethersfield, CT 06109.

Astrological Society of Princeton
Monthly meetings. Contact Ken or Joan Negus at 175 Harrison
Street, Princeton, NJ 08540. Phone (609) 924-4311.

FCA—The Fraternity for Canadian Astrologers
This group is based in Toronto, but there are affiliated groups
all across Canada. The FCA describes itself as "a social community extending a welcome to astrologers at all levels of learning." Write to FCA at 91 Bowmore Road, Toronto, Canada
M4L3J1.

Seacoast Astrological Association
This group is based in Portsmouth, NH. They meet monthly
and sponsor a yearly conference, "Autumn Alchemy." Contact
the SAA at PO Box 4683, Portsmouth, NH 03801-4683.

Washington State Astrological Association.
PO Box 45386, Seattle, WA 98145-0386.

Chart Calculation Services

Astro has been serving the astrological community for over 20 years. They can calculate any kind of horoscope you want, offer the best in astrological references and textbooks, and distribute software if you want to print out charts on your own computer.

Astro can provide Astrolocality Maps to analyze your horoscope anywhere on the earth (see Chapter 8) and fixed star lists and much more.

They have a free Hot Line you can call for astrological information and can help you with just about any astrological need.

Astro Communications Services
5521 Ruffin Rd
San Diego, CA 92123-1314
(800) 888-9983   FAX (619) 492-9917
Astrological Hot Line (M-F, 8 AM-5 PM, Pacific time)
(619) 492-1150.

Children's Chart Interpretations only
Astrograms
PO Box 148076, Chicago, IL 60614. (800)-232-1654.

Software Companies

Each of these companies can sell you software so you can print out charts for yourself, right in the comfort of your home. Call them—shop around.

AIR Software—115 Caya Ave., West Hartford, CT 06110. Phone (800) 629-1AIR. FAX (203) 233-6117.

Astro Communications Services—PO Box 34487, San Diego, CA 92163. Phone (800) 888-9983. FAX (619) 492-9917.

Astrolabe—PO Box 1750-T, Brewster, MA 02631. Phone (800) 843-6682. FAX (508) 896-5289.

Cosmic Patterns—PO Box 14605, Gainesville, FL 32604. Phone (800) 779-2559. FAX (904) 373-8826.

Matrix—315 Marion Avenue, Big Rapids, MI, 49307. (800) PLANETS. FAX (616) 796-3060.

Time Cycles (Macintosh only)—27 Dimmock Road, Waterford, CT 06385. Phone (203) 444-6641. FAX (203) 442-0625.

Magazines

Aspects. Published by Aquarius Workshops. Monthly columns of general astrological interest. Please write to *Aspects* at PO Box 260556, Encino, CA 91426.

Data News. Lots of birthdata—especially for people involved in current happenings. Lois Rodden, 11736 3rd St., Yucaipa, CA 92399.

Dell Horoscope. Available at your grocery store, in the crossword-puzzle section. Subscribe by writing DELL Horoscope Magazine at PO Box 5154, Harlan, IA 51593-5154.

The Horary Practitioner. Traditional horary astrology. Quarterly. 1420 NW Gilman, Suite #2154, Issaquah, WA 98027-5327.

KOSMOS. Published by the International Society for Astrological Research. To subscribe, write to ISAR at the address given above (under Organizations).

The Mercury Hour. Basically consists of letters from astrologers on a variety of topics. Way to keep up with who's saying what to whom. Edith Custer, 3509 Waterlick Road, #C-7, Lynchburg, VA 24502.

The Mountain Astrologer. Published 9 times a year. Focus is general astrological articles of all levels. Write for more information to PO Box 17275, Boulder, CO 80308-0275.

The Mutable Dilemma and *The Asteroid World*. Published 8 times a year. Psychological focus for M.D. and mundane focus for A.W. Write to: 838 S. 5th Ave., Los Angeles, CA 90005.

NCGR Journal. Published by NCGR, for members. To join NCGR, write to the address above (under Organizations).

Sign of the Times. Monthly. Mundane articles & charts. Judy Johns, 8237 Teesdale Ave., North Hollywood, CA 91605-1147.

Welcome to Planet Earth. Monthly Periodical published in Eugene, Oregon. WTPE's focus is Current Events, explained astrologically. Please write for a sample copy. Welcome To Planet Earth, c/o The Great Bear, PO Box 12007, Eugene, OR 97440, or call (503) 683-1760.

Book Publishers

ACS Publications, 5521 Ruffin Road, San Diego, CA 92123. 1-800-888-9983 for orders or (619) 492-9919 for information.

Llewellyn Books, PO Box 64383-126, St. Paul, MN 55164-0383.

Samuel Weiser, Inc.—Box 612, York Beach, ME 03910.

Lecture Tapes

Astrology Et Al—**NORWAC Conference Tapes**—4518 University Way NE, Suite 213, Seattle, WA, 98105.

NCGR Conference Tapes—Contact Arlene Nimark at 1242 E.8th Street, Brooklyn, NY, 11230.

Pegasus Tapes—30358 Highway 78, San Isabel, CA 92070

RKM Enterprises, PO Box 23042, Euclid, OH 44123.

Teachers

NCGR listing—write to NCGR at the above address. Mention that you're looking for a teacher referral.

Local Metaphysical Bookstores—Ask around. They'll know somebody in the area who's working on a book.

Ads in Health-Food Stores—Same thing—just ask.

Alternative Newspapers—Here's where you'll see classes and workshops listed in your area.

Schools

Kepler College—The only liberal arts college in this country where you'll soon be able to get yourself a BA in Astrology. Write for more info at 4518 University Way NE, Suite 213, Seattle, WA, 98105.

Conferences

THE BIG ONE

UAC—A joint effort of NCGR, ISAR, and AFAN, this conference is held every three years at a different location. This, kids, is the Mother of all Conferences—astrologers from all over the world come here to teach, and over 1200 participants attend. Call (800) PTOLEMY for information on the next UAC.

THE OTHERS

ARC—Aquarian Revelation Conference. This conference is only held when Major Astrological Things happen Upstairs. For news about the next one, write to Ray Merriman at SEEK-IT Publications, PO Box 250012, West Bloomfield, MI 48325

ASC—Astrology Southwest Coalition—A joint effort of NCGR, ISAR, and the San Diego Astrological Society.

Autumn Alchemy—Sponsored yearly by the Seacoast Astrological Association of Portsmouth, NH. Write to them at the address above for more information.

Cycles and Symbols—Barbara Morgan, ISIS Institute, San Francisco, CA.

ISAR—Sponsors biennial conferences, featuring research, new techniques, etc. Write to the address above for more info on the next conference.

NCGR—Sponsors frequent conferences at locations all over the country—contact NCGR at the address above or call (800) PTOLEMY for info on the next conference near you.

NORWAC—Held every spring at the Seattle Airport Hilton. Contact: Astrology Et Al for the date of the next NORWAC—(206) 633-4907.

Planet Camp—sponsored by *The Mountain Astrologer*. Contact them at PO Box 17275, Boulder, CO 80308-0275.

Roots—Plainfield, VT. This conference is held each August—it's an astrological camping trip for astrologers of all levels. Contact: Kelley Hunter at HELIA Productions, RR#3, Box 928, Montpelier, VT 05602.

Particular Books on Particular Topics

Basic Textbooks:

This One. Definitely.

Astro Essentials: Planets in Signs, Houses, and Aspects by Maritha Pottenger (ACS)

Astrology for Yourself by Douglas Bloch and Demetra George (Wingbow Press)

Basic Astrology: A Guide for Teachers and Students by Joan Negus (ACS)

Basic Astrology: A Workbook for Students by Joan Negus (ACS)

Character and Fate, by Katherine Merlin. (Penguin Books—Arkana Division)

Complete Horoscope Interpretation by Maritha Pottenger (ACS)

Finding the Person in the Horoscope by Zipporah Dobyns (TIA Publications)

Horoscope Symbols, by Robert Hand (Para Research)

Inner Sky by Steven Forrest (ACS)

The Only Way to Learn Astrology, by Marion March and Joan Mc Evers (ACS)

Your Planetary Personality, by Dennis Oakland (Llewellyn Books)

Asteroids

The Asteroid Ephemeris 1883-1999: Ceres, Pallas, Juno, Vesta by Zipporah Dobyns with Neil F. Michelsen and Rique Pottenger (TIA Publications)

Asteroid Goddesses, by Demetra George (ACS)

The Ultimate Asteroid Book by J. Lee Lehman (Whitford Press)

ASTSIG—(That's short for Asteroid Special Interest Group.) These folks are devoted to studying asteroids, and you can contact them for a listing of over 2000 named asteroids as they were at the time of your birth. Among the esteemed members of this ASTSIG are Jacob Schwartz, Zip Dobyns, Demetra George, and Roxana Muise. They can be reached at PO Box 405, Waldport, OR 97384.

Astrological Exercises and Quizzes
Cosmic Combinations by Joan Negus (ACS)
Encounter Astrology by Maritha Pottenger (ACS)

Astrology and Children
Planets in Youth by Robert Hand (Whitford Press)
Your Magical Child by Maria Kay Simms (ACS)

**Atlases (Latitudes, Longitudes, Time Changes
& Time Zone Information)**
The American Atlas compiled and programmed by Thomas
Shanks (ACS)
The International Atlas compiled and programmed by Thomas
Shanks (ACS)

Calendars
Celestial Guide 1995 by Jim Maynard
Celestial Influences (wall calendar—Eastern or Pacific) 1995 by
Jim Maynard
Celestial Influences Pocket Astrologer (Eastern or Pacific) 1995 by
Jim Maynard
Llewellyn's '95 Astrological Calendar (wall)

Chart Collections *(includes celebrity horoscopes)*
Astro Data II, III, IV, V by Lois Rodden (Data News Press)

Chiron
Chiron, by Maritha Pottenger (ACS)
Chiron and the Healing Journey, by Melanie Reinhart. (Penguin
Books—Arkana Division)
The Continuing Discovery of Chiron, by Erminie Lantero (Sam-
uel Weiser Books)

Dials
Dial Detective by Maria Kay Simms (ACS)

Electional Astrology
The Only Way to Learn About Horary and Electional Astrology by
Marion D. March and Joan McEvers (ACS)
The Timing of Events: Electional Astrology by Bruce Scofield
(Astrolabe)

Ephemerides
The American Ephemeris for the 20th Century, Midnight by Neil F. Michelsen & R. Pottenger (ACS)
The American Ephemeris for the 21st Century by Neil F. Michelsen & R. Pottenger (ACS)

Experiential Astrology
Astrology Alive by Barbara Schermer (Aquarian Press)
Encounter Astrology by Maritha Pottenger (ACS)

History
The Night Speaks: A Meditation on the Astrological Worldview by Steven Forrest (ACS)
Tables of Planetary Phenomena by Neil F. Michelsen (ACS)
Twelve Wings of the Eagle by Maria Kay Simms (ACS)

Horary Astrology
The Only Way to Learn About Horary and Electional Astrology by Marion D. March and Joan McEvers (ACS)

Mundane Astrology
Mundane Astrology, by Michael Baigent, Nicholas Campion, and Charles Harvey. The Aquarian Press, C/O HarperCollins Publishers, 77-85 Fulham Palace Road, Hammersmith, London, UK W6 8JB.
The Book of World Horoscopes, by Nicholas Campion (See Aquarian Press, above)

Planet Series
The Book of Jupiter by Marilyn Waram (ACS)
The Book of Neptune by Marilyn Waram (ACS)
The Book of Pluto by Steven Forrest (ACS)

Relationships
Interpreting Composite & Relationships Charts by Joan Negus (booklet—ACS)
Skymates by Steven & Jodie Forrest (ACS)
The Only Way to Learn About Relationships: Vol. V by Marion D. March and Joan McEvers (ACS)
Your Starway to Love by Maritha Pottenger (ACS)

Relocation
Planets on the Move: Astrology and Relocation by Zipporah Dobyns & Maritha Pottenger (ACS)

Synastry   *See Relationships*

Tables of Houses
The American Book of Tables by Neil F. Michelsen (ACS)
The American Ephemeris 1931-1980 & Book of Tables (cloth) by Neil F. Michelsen (ACS)
The Koch Book of Tables by Neil F. Michelsen (ACS)

Transits and Prediction
Changing Sky by Steven Forrest (ACS)
Modern Transits, by Lois Rodden (AFA)
Planets in Transit, by Robert Hand. (Para Research)
Planets in Solar Returns by Mary Shea (ACS)
The Practice of Prediction, by Nancy Hastings (Samuel Weiser Books)
Roadmap to Your Future by Bernie Ashman (ACS)
Secondary Progressions, by Nancy Hastings (Samuel Weiser Books)

Vertex
The East Point and Antivertex (booklet) by Maritha Pottenger (ACS)

And in Closing, I'd Just Like to Say...

Well, we're done. Hard to believe, huh? We've been through 8 planets, the Sun and Moon, all those asteroids, one big comet, aspects, computer programs, the Part of Fortune, and even Chart Comparison. By now you should be saving your pennies for tuition to Kepler College. If you've been with me since the beginning, I want to thank you for your time. I hope you got what you came for, and I hope you had a couple of good giggles, too. Laughter is the very best teacher.

Here's that list I promised you:

TOP TEN TOPICS TO AVOID AT AN ASTROLOGICAL COCKTAIL PARTY

10. The validity of Sun-Sign astrology
9. Whether or not JFK's death could have been predicted
8. Licensing and Certification for astrologers

7. 900 numbers

6. Fate versus free will

5. House divisions—Koch or Placidus systems
    in particular

4. How to pronounce the name of the planet
    between Saturn and Neptune

3. Orbs

2. Other astrologers

1. The "right" U.S. chart

Before you leave, I'd like to urge you to pursue astrology—whatever branch you feel especially drawn to. It's great stuff you've found here—the very essence of the universe... Thanks again, and we'll see you next time—in *The Lighter Side of Transits*, I'm told...

Ten percent of the author's profits from the sale of this book will be donated to animal welfare organizations, local shelters, environmental groups, and other causes that contribute to the good of the animal kingdom and the earth. Another good chunk will be turned into bird food, and a really good piece of the pie will feed a pack of resident critters, all of whom came from shelters. Anything left over will be used on supplies for the next book, and, maybe, dinner and a movie.

Chiron Locations 1920 - 2010

Jan 1, 1920	02 ♈ 37	May 25, 1921	12 ♈ 48	Oct 17, 1922	14 ♈ 51
Jan 11, 1920	02 ♈ 48	Jun 4, 1921	13 ♈ 11	Oct 27, 1922	14 ♈ 25
Jan 21, 1920	03 ♈ 05	Jun 14, 1921	13 ♈ 30	Nov 6, 1922	14 ♈ 00
Jan 31, 1920	03 ♈ 27	Jun 24, 1921	13 ♈ 44	Nov 16, 1922	13 ♈ 39
Feb 10, 1920	03 ♈ 53	Jul 4, 1921	13 ♈ 54	Nov 26, 1922	13 ♈ 21
Feb 20, 1920	04 ♈ 22	Jul 14, 1921	13 ♈ 58	Dec 6, 1922	13 ♈ 08
Mar 1, 1920	04 ♈ 53	Jul 24, 1921	13 ♈ 58	Dec 16, 1922	13 ♈ 00
Mar 11, 1920	05 ♈ 27	Aug 3, 1921	13 ♈ 52	Dec 26, 1922	12 ♈ 58
Mar 21, 1920	06 ♈ 02	Aug 13, 1921	13 ♈ 41	Jan 5, 1923	13 ♈ 01
Mar 31, 1920	06 ♈ 37	Aug 23, 1921	13 ♈ 25	Jan 15, 1923	13 ♈ 10
Apr 10, 1920	07 ♈ 12	Sep 2, 1921	13 ♈ 06	Jan 25, 1923	13 ♈ 24
Apr 20, 1920	07 ♈ 46	Sep 12, 1921	12 ♈ 43	Feb 4, 1923	13 ♈ 43
Apr 30, 1920	08 ♈ 18	Sep 22, 1921	12 ♈ 18	Feb 14, 1923	14 ♈ 06
May 10, 1920	08 ♈ 48	Oct 2, 1921	11 ♈ 51	Feb 24, 1923	14 ♈ 33
May 20, 1920	09 ♈ 15	Oct 12, 1921	11 ♈ 24	Mar 6, 1923	15 ♈ 03
May 30, 1920	09 ♈ 39	Oct 22, 1921	10 ♈ 57	Mar 16, 1923	15 ♈ 36
Jun 9, 1920	09 ♈ 58	Nov 1, 1921	10 ♈ 33	Mar 26, 1923	16 ♈ 10
Jun 19, 1920	10 ♈ 13	Nov 11, 1921	10 ♈ 11	Apr 5, 1923	16 ♈ 46
Jun 29, 1920	10 ♈ 23	Nov 21, 1921	09 ♈ 53	Apr 15, 1923	17 ♈ 21
Jul 9, 1920	10 ♈ 28	Dec 1, 1921	09 ♈ 39	Apr 25, 1923	17 ♈ 56
Jul 19, 1920	10 ♈ 28	Dec 11, 1921	09 ♈ 31	May 5, 1923	18 ♈ 30
Jul 29, 1920	10 ♈ 23	Dec 21, 1921	09 ♈ 28	May 15, 1923	19 ♈ 02
Aug 8, 1920	10 ♈ 13	Dec 31, 1921	09 ♈ 30	May 25, 1923	19 ♈ 31
Aug 18, 1920	09 ♈ 58	Jan 10, 1922	09 ♈ 38	Jun 4, 1923	19 ♈ 57
Aug 28, 1920	09 ♈ 39	Jan 20, 1922	09 ♈ 51	Jun 14, 1923	20 ♈ 19
Sep 7, 1920	09 ♈ 16	Jan 30, 1922	10 ♈ 10	Jun 24, 1923	20 ♈ 38
Sep 17, 1920	08 ♈ 51	Feb 9, 1922	10 ♈ 32	Jul 4, 1923	20 ♈ 51
Sep 27, 1920	08 ♈ 24	Feb 19, 1922	10 ♈ 59	Jul 14, 1923	20 ♈ 60
Oct 7, 1920	07 ♈ 57	Mar 1, 1922	11 ♈ 29	Jul 24, 1923	21 ♈ 03
Oct 17, 1920	07 ♈ 31	Mar 11, 1922	12 ♈ 01	Aug 3, 1923	21 ♈ 02
Oct 27, 1920	07 ♈ 06	Mar 21, 1922	12 ♈ 35	Aug 13, 1923	20 ♈ 55
Nov 6, 1920	06 ♈ 44	Mar 31, 1922	13 ♈ 10	Aug 23, 1923	20 ♈ 43
Nov 16, 1920	06 ♈ 25	Apr 10, 1922	13 ♈ 45	Sep 2, 1923	20 ♈ 26
Nov 26, 1920	06 ♈ 11	Apr 20, 1922	14 ♈ 20	Sep 12, 1923	20 ♈ 05
Dec 6, 1920	06 ♈ 02	Apr 30, 1922	14 ♈ 54	Sep 22, 1923	19 ♈ 42
Dec 16, 1920	05 ♈ 58	May 10, 1922	15 ♈ 26	Oct 2, 1923	19 ♈ 16
Dec 26, 1920	06 ♈ 00	May 20, 1922	15 ♈ 55	Oct 12, 1923	18 ♈ 48
Jan 5, 1921	06 ♈ 07	May 30, 1922	16 ♈ 21	Oct 22, 1923	18 ♈ 21
Jan 15, 1921	06 ♈ 20	Jun 9, 1922	16 ♈ 44	Nov 1, 1923	17 ♈ 55
Jan 25, 1921	06 ♈ 38	Jun 19, 1922	17 ♈ 03	Nov 11, 1923	17 ♈ 30
Feb 4, 1921	06 ♈ 60	Jun 29, 1922	17 ♈ 17	Nov 21, 1923	17 ♈ 09
Feb 14, 1921	07 ♈ 26	Jul 9, 1922	17 ♈ 26	Dec 1, 1923	16 ♈ 52
Feb 24, 1921	07 ♈ 55	Jul 19, 1922	17 ♈ 30	Dec 11, 1923	16 ♈ 39
Mar 6, 1921	08 ♈ 27	Jul 29, 1922	17 ♈ 28	Dec 21, 1923	16 ♈ 32
Mar 16, 1921	09 ♈ 01	Aug 8, 1922	17 ♈ 22	Dec 31, 1923	16 ♈ 31
Mar 26, 1921	09 ♈ 35	Aug 18, 1922	17 ♈ 11	Jan 10, 1924	16 ♈ 35
Apr 5, 1921	10 ♈ 11	Aug 28, 1922	16 ♈ 55	Jan 20, 1924	16 ♈ 44
Apr 15, 1921	10 ♈ 46	Sep 7, 1922	16 ♈ 35	Jan 30, 1924	16 ♈ 59
Apr 25, 1921	11 ♈ 19	Sep 17, 1922	16 ♈ 11	Feb 9, 1924	17 ♈ 18
May 5, 1921	11 ♈ 52	Sep 27, 1922	15 ♈ 46	Feb 19, 1924	17 ♈ 42
May 15, 1921	12 ♈ 21	Oct 7, 1922	15 ♈ 19	Feb 29, 1924	18 ♈ 10

Chiron Locations 1920 - 2010

Date	Location	Date	Location	Date	Location
Mar 10, 1924	18 ♈ 41	Aug 2, 1925	28 ♈ 22	Dec 25, 1926	27 ♈ 37
Mar 20, 1924	19 ♈ 14	Aug 12, 1925	28 ♈ 20	Jan 4, 1927	27 ♈ 32
Mar 30, 1924	19 ♈ 48	Aug 22, 1925	28 ♈ 12	Jan 14, 1927	27 ♈ 32
Apr 9, 1924	20 ♈ 24	Sep 1, 1925	27 ♈ 58	Jan 24, 1927	27 ♈ 39
Apr 19, 1924	20 ♈ 60	Sep 11, 1925	27 ♈ 41	Feb 3, 1927	27 ♈ 50
Apr 29, 1924	21 ♈ 35	Sep 21, 1925	27 ♈ 19	Feb 13, 1927	28 ♈ 08
May 9, 1924	22 ♈ 09	Oct 1, 1925	26 ♈ 55	Feb 23, 1927	28 ♈ 30
May 19, 1924	22 ♈ 41	Oct 11, 1925	26 ♈ 28	Mar 5, 1927	28 ♈ 56
May 29, 1924	23 ♈ 10	Oct 21, 1925	25 ♈ 60	Mar 15, 1927	29 ♈ 26
Jun 8, 1924	23 ♈ 36	Oct 31, 1925	25 ♈ 32	Mar 25, 1927	29 ♈ 58
Jun 18, 1924	23 ♈ 58	Nov 10, 1925	25 ♈ 05	Apr 4, 1927	00 ♉ 33
Jun 28, 1924	24 ♈ 16	Nov 20, 1925	24 ♈ 41	Apr 14, 1927	01 ♉ 10
Jul 8, 1924	24 ♈ 29	Nov 30, 1925	24 ♈ 21	Apr 24, 1927	01 ♉ 47
Jul 18, 1924	24 ♈ 37	Dec 10, 1925	24 ♈ 04	May 4, 1927	02 ♉ 24
Jul 28, 1924	24 ♈ 40	Dec 20, 1925	23 ♈ 53	May 14, 1927	03 ♉ 00
Aug 7, 1924	24 ♈ 38	Dec 30, 1925	23 ♈ 47	May 24, 1927	03 ♉ 35
Aug 17, 1924	24 ♈ 31	Jan 9, 1926	23 ♈ 47	Jun 3, 1927	04 ♉ 08
Aug 27, 1924	24 ♈ 18	Jan 19, 1926	23 ♈ 52	Jun 13, 1927	04 ♉ 37
Sep 6, 1924	24 ♈ 01	Jan 29, 1926	24 ♈ 03	Jun 23, 1927	05 ♉ 04
Sep 16, 1924	23 ♈ 40	Feb 8, 1926	24 ♈ 19	Jul 3, 1927	05 ♉ 26
Sep 26, 1924	23 ♈ 16	Feb 18, 1926	24 ♈ 40	Jul 13, 1927	05 ♉ 44
Oct 6, 1924	22 ♈ 49	Feb 28, 1926	25 ♈ 06	Jul 23, 1927	05 ♉ 56
Oct 16, 1924	22 ♈ 22	Mar 10, 1926	25 ♈ 35	Aug 2, 1927	06 ♉ 04
Oct 26, 1924	21 ♈ 54	Mar 20, 1926	26 ♈ 07	Aug 12, 1927	06 ♉ 06
Nov 5, 1924	21 ♈ 28	Mar 30, 1926	26 ♈ 41	Aug 22, 1927	06 ♉ 02
Nov 15, 1924	21 ♈ 03	Apr 9, 1926	27 ♈ 17	Sep 1, 1927	05 ♉ 53
Nov 25, 1924	20 ♈ 43	Apr 19, 1926	27 ♈ 53	Sep 11, 1927	05 ♉ 39
Dec 5, 1924	20 ♈ 26	Apr 29, 1926	28 ♈ 30	Sep 21, 1927	05 ♉ 21
Dec 15, 1924	20 ♈ 14	May 9, 1926	29 ♈ 06	Oct 1, 1927	04 ♉ 58
Dec 25, 1924	20 ♈ 07	May 19, 1926	29 ♈ 40	Oct 11, 1927	04 ♉ 32
Jan 4, 1925	20 ♈ 06	May 29, 1926	00 ♉ 12	Oct 21, 1927	04 ♉ 04
Jan 14, 1925	20 ♈ 11	Jun 8, 1926	00 ♉ 42	Oct 31, 1927	03 ♉ 36
Jan 24, 1925	20 ♈ 21	Jun 18, 1926	01 ♉ 08	Nov 10, 1927	03 ♉ 07
Feb 3, 1925	20 ♈ 37	Jun 28, 1926	01 ♉ 30	Nov 20, 1927	02 ♉ 40
Feb 13, 1925	20 ♈ 57	Jul 8, 1926	01 ♉ 48	Nov 30, 1927	02 ♉ 16
Feb 23, 1925	21 ♈ 22	Jul 18, 1926	02 ♉ 00	Dec 10, 1927	01 ♉ 56
Mar 5, 1925	21 ♈ 50	Jul 28, 1926	02 ♉ 08	Dec 20, 1927	01 ♉ 40
Mar 15, 1925	22 ♈ 21	Aug 7, 1926	02 ♉ 10	Dec 30, 1927	01 ♉ 29
Mar 25, 1925	22 ♈ 55	Aug 17, 1926	02 ♉ 07	Jan 9, 1928	01 ♉ 24
Apr 4, 1925	23 ♈ 30	Aug 27, 1926	01 ♉ 59	Jan 19, 1928	01 ♉ 25
Apr 14, 1925	24 ♈ 06	Sep 6, 1926	01 ♉ 45	Jan 29, 1928	01 ♉ 32
Apr 24, 1925	24 ♈ 42	Sep 16, 1926	01 ♉ 27	Feb 8, 1928	01 ♉ 45
May 4, 1925	25 ♈ 18	Sep 26, 1926	01 ♉ 05	Feb 18, 1928	02 ♉ 03
May 14, 1925	25 ♈ 52	Oct 6, 1926	00 ♉ 40	Feb 28, 1928	02 ♉ 26
May 24, 1925	26 ♈ 24	Oct 16, 1926	00 ♉ 12	Mar 9, 1928	02 ♉ 53
Jun 3, 1925	26 ♈ 53	Oct 26, 1926	29 ♈ 44	Mar 19, 1928	03 ♉ 23
Jun 13, 1925	27 ♈ 19	Nov 5, 1926	29 ♈ 16	Mar 29, 1928	03 ♉ 57
Jun 23, 1925	27 ♈ 41	Nov 15, 1926	28 ♈ 49	Apr 8, 1928	04 ♉ 33
Jul 3, 1925	27 ♈ 59	Nov 25, 1926	28 ♈ 25	Apr 18, 1928	05 ♉ 10
Jul 13, 1925	28 ♈ 12	Dec 5, 1926	28 ♈ 04	Apr 28, 1928	05 ♉ 48
Jul 23, 1925	28 ♈ 20	Dec 15, 1926	27 ♈ 48	May 8, 1928	06 ♉ 26

Chiron Locations 1920 - 2010

Date	Position	Date	Position	Date	Position
May 18, 1928	07 ♉ 03	Oct 10, 1929	13 ♉ 14	Mar 4, 1931	14 ♉ 47
May 28, 1928	07 ♉ 38	Oct 20, 1929	12 ♉ 47	Mar 14, 1931	15 ♉ 12
Jun 7, 1928	08 ♉ 11	Oct 30, 1929	12 ♉ 18	Mar 24, 1931	15 ♉ 42
Jun 17, 1928	08 ♉ 41	Nov 9, 1929	11 ♉ 48	Apr 3, 1931	16 ♉ 16
Jun 27, 1928	09 ♉ 08	Nov 19, 1929	11 ♉ 19	Apr 13, 1931	16 ♉ 53
Jul 7, 1928	09 ♉ 30	Nov 29, 1929	10 ♉ 51	Apr 23, 1931	17 ♉ 32
Jul 17, 1928	09 ♉ 48	Dec 9, 1929	10 ♉ 27	May 3, 1931	18 ♉ 12
Jul 27, 1928	10 ♉ 01	Dec 19, 1929	10 ♉ 06	May 13, 1931	18 ♉ 53
Aug 6, 1928	10 ♉ 09	Dec 29, 1929	09 ♉ 51	May 23, 1931	19 ♉ 34
Aug 16, 1928	10 ♉ 11	Jan 8, 1930	09 ♉ 41	Jun 2, 1931	20 ♉ 14
Aug 26, 1928	10 ♉ 07	Jan 18, 1930	09 ♉ 37	Jun 12, 1931	20 ♉ 52
Sep 5, 1928	09 ♉ 58	Jan 28, 1930	09 ♉ 39	Jun 22, 1931	21 ♉ 28
Sep 15, 1928	09 ♉ 43	Feb 7, 1930	09 ♉ 47	Jul 2, 1931	22 ♉ 00
Sep 25, 1928	09 ♉ 24	Feb 17, 1930	10 ♉ 01	Jul 12, 1931	22 ♉ 29
Oct 5, 1928	09 ♉ 00	Feb 27, 1930	10 ♉ 21	Jul 22, 1931	22 ♉ 54
Oct 15, 1928	08 ♉ 34	Mar 9, 1930	10 ♉ 45	Aug 1, 1931	23 ♉ 14
Oct 25, 1928	08 ♉ 06	Mar 19, 1930	11 ♉ 14	Aug 11, 1931	23 ♉ 28
Nov 4, 1928	07 ♉ 36	Mar 29, 1930	11 ♉ 47	Aug 21, 1931	23 ♉ 36
Nov 14, 1928	07 ♉ 08	Apr 8, 1930	12 ♉ 22	Aug 31, 1931	23 ♉ 38
Nov 24, 1928	06 ♉ 40	Apr 18, 1930	13 ♉ 00	Sep 10, 1931	23 ♉ 35
Dec 4, 1928	06 ♉ 16	Apr 28, 1930	13 ♉ 39	Sep 20, 1931	23 ♉ 25
Dec 14, 1928	05 ♉ 56	May 8, 1930	14 ♉ 19	Sep 30, 1931	23 ♉ 09
Dec 24, 1928	05 ♉ 40	May 18, 1930	14 ♉ 59	Oct 10, 1931	22 ♉ 49
Jan 3, 1929	05 ♉ 30	May 28, 1930	15 ♉ 37	Oct 20, 1931	22 ♉ 24
Jan 13, 1929	05 ♉ 25	Jun 7, 1930	16 ♉ 14	Oct 30, 1931	21 ♉ 55
Jan 23, 1929	05 ♉ 27	Jun 17, 1930	16 ♉ 49	Nov 9, 1931	21 ♉ 25
Feb 2, 1929	05 ♉ 35	Jun 27, 1930	17 ♉ 21	Nov 19, 1931	20 ♉ 54
Feb 12, 1929	05 ♉ 48	Jul 7, 1930	17 ♉ 49	Nov 29, 1931	20 ♉ 23
Feb 22, 1929	06 ♉ 07	Jul 17, 1930	18 ♉ 12	Dec 9, 1931	19 ♉ 54
Mar 4, 1929	06 ♉ 30	Jul 27, 1930	18 ♉ 31	Dec 19, 1931	19 ♉ 29
Mar 14, 1929	06 ♉ 58	Aug 6, 1930	18 ♉ 45	Dec 29, 1931	19 ♉ 07
Mar 24, 1929	07 ♉ 30	Aug 16, 1930	18 ♉ 53	Jan 8, 1932	18 ♉ 52
Apr 3, 1929	08 ♉ 05	Aug 26, 1930	18 ♉ 55	Jan 18, 1932	18 ♉ 42
Apr 13, 1929	08 ♉ 41	Sep 5, 1930	18 ♉ 51	Jan 28, 1932	18 ♉ 38
Apr 23, 1929	09 ♉ 19	Sep 15, 1930	18 ♉ 41	Feb 7, 1932	18 ♉ 41
May 3, 1929	09 ♉ 58	Sep 25, 1930	18 ♉ 26	Feb 17, 1932	18 ♉ 51
May 13, 1929	10 ♉ 37	Oct 5, 1930	18 ♉ 05	Feb 27, 1932	19 ♉ 06
May 23, 1929	11 ♉ 14	Oct 15, 1930	17 ♉ 41	Mar 8, 1932	19 ♉ 28
Jun 2, 1929	11 ♉ 50	Oct 25, 1930	17 ♉ 13	Mar 18, 1932	19 ♉ 54
Jun 12, 1929	12 ♉ 24	Nov 4, 1930	16 ♉ 44	Mar 28, 1932	20 ♉ 25
Jun 22, 1929	12 ♉ 55	Nov 14, 1930	16 ♉ 13	Apr 7, 1932	21 ♉ 00
Jul 2, 1929	13 ♉ 22	Nov 24, 1930	15 ♉ 43	Apr 17, 1932	21 ♉ 38
Jul 12, 1929	13 ♉ 45	Dec 4, 1930	15 ♉ 15	Apr 27, 1932	22 ♉ 18
Jul 22, 1929	14 ♉ 04	Dec 14, 1930	14 ♉ 50	May 7, 1932	22 ♉ 60
Aug 1, 1929	14 ♉ 17	Dec 24, 1930	14 ♉ 29	May 17, 1932	23 ♉ 42
Aug 11, 1929	14 ♉ 24	Jan 3, 1931	14 ♉ 14	May 27, 1932	24 ♉ 24
Aug 21, 1929	14 ♉ 26	Jan 13, 1931	14 ♉ 04	Jun 6, 1932	25 ♉ 06
Aug 31, 1929	14 ♉ 22	Jan 23, 1931	13 ♉ 60	Jun 16, 1932	25 ♉ 45
Sep 10, 1929	14 ♉ 13	Feb 2, 1931	14 ♉ 03	Jun 26, 1932	26 ♉ 23
Sep 20, 1929	13 ♉ 58	Feb 12, 1931	14 ♉ 12	Jul 6, 1932	26 ♉ 57
Sep 30, 1929	13 ♉ 38	Feb 22, 1931	14 ♉ 26	Jul 16, 1932	27 ♉ 27

Chiron Locations 1920 - 2010

Date	Position	Date	Position	Date	Position
Jul 26, 1932	27 ♉ 53	Dec 18, 1933	00 ♊ 12	May 12, 1935	08 ♊ 40
Aug 5, 1932	28 ♉ 13	Dec 28, 1933	29 ♉ 45	May 22, 1935	09 ♊ 27
Aug 15, 1932	28 ♉ 29	Jan 7, 1934	29 ♉ 22	Jun 1, 1935	10 ♊ 15
Aug 25, 1932	28 ♉ 38	Jan 17, 1934	29 ♉ 06	Jun 11, 1935	11 ♊ 03
Sep 4, 1932	28 ♉ 41	Jan 27, 1934	28 ♉ 55	Jun 21, 1935	11 ♊ 50
Sep 14, 1932	28 ♉ 37	Feb 6, 1934	28 ♉ 51	Jul 1, 1935	12 ♊ 37
Sep 24, 1932	28 ♉ 28	Feb 16, 1934	28 ♉ 55	Jul 11, 1935	13 ♊ 20
Oct 4, 1932	28 ♉ 12	Feb 26, 1934	29 ♉ 05	Jul 21, 1935	14 ♊ 01
Oct 14, 1932	27 ♉ 51	Mar 8, 1934	29 ♉ 22	Jul 31, 1935	14 ♊ 38
Oct 24, 1932	27 ♉ 26	Mar 18, 1934	29 ♉ 45	Aug 10, 1935	15 ♊ 10
Nov 3, 1932	26 ♉ 57	Mar 28, 1934	00 ♊ 13	Aug 20, 1935	15 ♊ 36
Nov 13, 1932	26 ♉ 25	Apr 7, 1934	00 ♊ 47	Aug 30, 1935	15 ♊ 57
Nov 23, 1932	25 ♉ 53	Apr 17, 1934	01 ♊ 24	Sep 9, 1935	16 ♊ 11
Dec 3, 1932	25 ♉ 21	Apr 27, 1934	02 ♊ 05	Sep 19, 1935	16 ♊ 19
Dec 13, 1932	24 ♉ 52	May 7, 1934	02 ♊ 48	Sep 29, 1935	16 ♊ 19
Dec 23, 1932	24 ♉ 26	May 17, 1934	03 ♊ 33	Oct 9, 1935	16 ♊ 11
Jan 2, 1933	24 ♉ 04	May 27, 1934	04 ♊ 19	Oct 19, 1935	15 ♊ 57
Jan 12, 1933	23 ♉ 48	Jun 6, 1934	05 ♊ 05	Oct 29, 1935	15 ♊ 37
Jan 22, 1933	23 ♉ 38	Jun 16, 1934	05 ♊ 50	Nov 8, 1935	15 ♊ 10
Feb 1, 1933	23 ♉ 34	Jun 26, 1934	06 ♊ 34	Nov 18, 1935	14 ♊ 40
Feb 11, 1933	23 ♉ 37	Jul 6, 1934	07 ♊ 15	Nov 28, 1935	14 ♊ 06
Feb 21, 1933	23 ♉ 47	Jul 16, 1934	07 ♊ 53	Dec 8, 1935	13 ♊ 30
Mar 3, 1933	24 ♉ 03	Jul 26, 1934	08 ♊ 27	Dec 18, 1935	12 ♊ 55
Mar 13, 1933	24 ♉ 26	Aug 5, 1934	08 ♊ 56	Dec 28, 1935	12 ♊ 22
Mar 23, 1933	24 ♉ 53	Aug 15, 1934	09 ♊ 20	Jan 7, 1936	11 ♊ 51
Apr 2, 1933	25 ♉ 25	Aug 25, 1934	09 ♊ 39	Jan 17, 1936	11 ♊ 26
Apr 12, 1933	26 ♉ 02	Sep 4, 1934	09 ♊ 51	Jan 27, 1936	11 ♊ 07
Apr 22, 1933	26 ♉ 41	Sep 14, 1934	09 ♊ 56	Feb 6, 1936	10 ♊ 55
May 2, 1933	27 ♉ 23	Sep 24, 1934	09 ♊ 54	Feb 16, 1936	10 ♊ 50
May 12, 1933	28 ♉ 06	Oct 4, 1934	09 ♊ 46	Feb 26, 1936	10 ♊ 52
May 22, 1933	28 ♉ 50	Oct 14, 1934	09 ♊ 31	Mar 7, 1936	11 ♊ 03
Jun 1, 1933	29 ♉ 34	Oct 24, 1934	09 ♊ 10	Mar 17, 1936	11 ♊ 20
Jun 11, 1933	00 ♊ 17	Nov 3, 1934	08 ♊ 44	Mar 27, 1936	11 ♊ 44
Jun 21, 1933	00 ♊ 58	Nov 13, 1934	08 ♊ 13	Apr 6, 1936	12 ♊ 14
Jul 1, 1933	01 ♊ 37	Nov 23, 1934	07 ♊ 40	Apr 16, 1936	12 ♊ 50
Jul 11, 1933	02 ♊ 13	Dec 3, 1934	07 ♊ 06	Apr 26, 1936	13 ♊ 30
Jul 21, 1933	02 ♊ 45	Dec 13, 1934	06 ♊ 32	May 6, 1936	14 ♊ 15
Jul 31, 1933	03 ♊ 12	Dec 23, 1934	06 ♊ 00	May 16, 1936	15 ♊ 02
Aug 10, 1933	03 ♊ 34	Jan 2, 1935	05 ♊ 32	May 26, 1936	15 ♊ 51
Aug 20, 1933	03 ♊ 51	Jan 12, 1935	05 ♊ 08	Jun 5, 1936	16 ♊ 42
Aug 30, 1933	04 ♊ 01	Jan 22, 1935	04 ♊ 50	Jun 15, 1936	17 ♊ 33
Sep 9, 1933	04 ♊ 05	Feb 1, 1935	04 ♊ 39	Jun 25, 1936	18 ♊ 23
Sep 19, 1933	04 ♊ 02	Feb 11, 1935	04 ♊ 35	Jul 5, 1936	19 ♊ 12
Sep 29, 1933	03 ♊ 53	Feb 21, 1935	04 ♊ 38	Jul 15, 1936	19 ♊ 59
Oct 9, 1933	03 ♊ 38	Mar 3, 1935	04 ♊ 48	Jul 25, 1936	20 ♊ 43
Oct 19, 1933	03 ♊ 17	Mar 13, 1935	05 ♊ 05	Aug 4, 1936	21 ♊ 23
Oct 29, 1933	02 ♊ 51	Mar 23, 1935	05 ♊ 29	Aug 14, 1936	21 ♊ 59
Nov 8, 1933	02 ♊ 21	Apr 2, 1935	05 ♊ 58	Aug 24, 1936	22 ♊ 29
Nov 18, 1933	01 ♊ 49	Apr 12, 1935	06 ♊ 33	Sep 3, 1936	22 ♊ 52
Nov 28, 1933	01 ♊ 16	Apr 22, 1935	07 ♊ 12	Sep 13, 1936	23 ♊ 10
Dec 8, 1933	00 ♊ 43	May 2, 1935	07 ♊ 54	Sep 23, 1936	23 ♊ 20

Chiron Locations 1920 - 2010

Oct 3, 1936	23 ♊ 22	Feb 25, 1938	25 ♊ 26	Jul 20, 1939	13 ♋ 28
Oct 13, 1936	23 ♊ 17	Mar 7, 1938	25 ♊ 26	Jul 30, 1939	14 ♋ 29
Oct 23, 1936	23 ♊ 04	Mar 17, 1938	25 ♊ 34	Aug 9, 1939	15 ♋ 27
Nov 2, 1936	22 ♊ 45	Mar 27, 1938	25 ♊ 51	Aug 19, 1939	16 ♋ 22
Nov 12, 1936	22 ♊ 19	Apr 6, 1938	26 ♊ 15	Aug 29, 1939	17 ♋ 13
Nov 22, 1936	21 ♊ 48	Apr 16, 1938	26 ♊ 46	Sep 8, 1939	17 ♋ 59
Dec 2, 1936	21 ♊ 13	Apr 26, 1938	27 ♊ 24	Sep 18, 1939	18 ♋ 39
Dec 12, 1936	20 ♊ 37	May 6, 1938	28 ♊ 07	Sep 28, 1939	19 ♋ 12
Dec 22, 1936	19 ♊ 60	May 16, 1938	28 ♊ 55	Oct 8, 1939	19 ♋ 38
Jan 1, 1937	19 ♊ 24	May 26, 1938	29 ♊ 46	Oct 18, 1939	19 ♋ 55
Jan 11, 1937	18 ♊ 52	Jun 5, 1938	00 ♋ 41	Oct 28, 1939	20 ♋ 03
Jan 21, 1937	18 ♊ 25	Jun 15, 1938	01 ♋ 37	Nov 7, 1939	20 ♋ 02
Jan 31, 1937	18 ♊ 04	Jun 25, 1938	02 ♋ 35	Nov 17, 1939	19 ♋ 52
Feb 10, 1937	17 ♊ 50	Jul 5, 1938	03 ♋ 33	Nov 27, 1939	19 ♋ 33
Feb 20, 1937	17 ♊ 44	Jul 15, 1938	04 ♋ 30	Dec 7, 1939	19 ♋ 06
Mar 2, 1937	17 ♊ 45	Jul 25, 1938	05 ♋ 25	Dec 17, 1939	18 ♋ 33
Mar 12, 1937	17 ♊ 55	Aug 4, 1938	06 ♋ 18	Dec 27, 1939	17 ♋ 55
Mar 22, 1937	18 ♊ 12	Aug 14, 1938	07 ♋ 07	Jan 6, 1940	17 ♋ 14
Apr 1, 1937	18 ♊ 37	Aug 24, 1938	07 ♋ 52	Jan 16, 1940	16 ♋ 32
Apr 11, 1937	19 ♊ 08	Sep 3, 1938	08 ♋ 31	Jan 26, 1940	15 ♋ 51
Apr 21, 1937	19 ♊ 44	Sep 13, 1938	09 ♋ 04	Feb 5, 1940	15 ♋ 14
May 1, 1937	20 ♊ 26	Sep 23, 1938	09 ♋ 31	Feb 15, 1940	14 ♋ 43
May 11, 1937	21 ♊ 12	Oct 3, 1938	09 ♋ 50	Feb 25, 1940	14 ♋ 19
May 21, 1937	22 ♊ 02	Oct 13, 1938	10 ♋ 00	Mar 6, 1940	14 ♋ 04
May 31, 1937	22 ♊ 53	Oct 23, 1938	10 ♋ 02	Mar 16, 1940	13 ♋ 57
Jun 10, 1937	23 ♊ 47	Nov 2, 1938	09 ♋ 56	Mar 26, 1940	14 ♋ 00
Jun 20, 1937	24 ♊ 41	Nov 12, 1938	09 ♋ 41	Apr 5, 1940	14 ♋ 12
Jun 30, 1937	25 ♊ 35	Nov 22, 1938	09 ♋ 19	Apr 15, 1940	14 ♋ 33
Jul 10, 1937	26 ♊ 27	Dec 2, 1938	08 ♋ 49	Apr 25, 1940	15 ♋ 03
Jul 20, 1937	27 ♊ 18	Dec 12, 1938	08 ♋ 14	May 5, 1940	15 ♋ 40
Jul 30, 1937	28 ♊ 06	Dec 22, 1938	07 ♋ 36	May 15, 1940	16 ♋ 25
Aug 9, 1937	28 ♊ 50	Jan 1, 1939	06 ♋ 56	May 25, 1940	17 ♋ 15
Aug 19, 1937	29 ♊ 30	Jan 11, 1939	06 ♋ 16	Jun 4, 1940	18 ♋ 11
Aug 29, 1937	00 ♋ 04	Jan 21, 1939	05 ♋ 39	Jun 14, 1940	19 ♋ 11
Sep 8, 1937	00 ♋ 32	Jan 31, 1939	05 ♋ 06	Jun 24, 1940	20 ♋ 14
Sep 18, 1937	00 ♋ 53	Feb 10, 1939	04 ♋ 39	Jul 4, 1940	21 ♋ 19
Sep 28, 1937	01 ♋ 07	Feb 20, 1939	04 ♋ 19	Jul 14, 1940	22 ♋ 25
Oct 8, 1937	01 ♋ 13	Mar 2, 1939	04 ♋ 08	Jul 24, 1940	23 ♋ 32
Oct 18, 1937	01 ♋ 11	Mar 12, 1939	04 ♋ 05	Aug 3, 1940	24 ♋ 38
Oct 28, 1937	01 ♋ 01	Mar 22, 1939	04 ♋ 12	Aug 13, 1940	25 ♋ 43
Nov 7, 1937	00 ♋ 43	Apr 1, 1939	04 ♋ 26	Aug 23, 1940	26 ♋ 45
Nov 17, 1937	00 ♋ 18	Apr 11, 1939	04 ♋ 50	Sep 2, 1940	27 ♋ 44
Nov 27, 1937	29 ♊ 47	Apr 21, 1939	05 ♋ 21	Sep 12, 1940	28 ♋ 37
Dec 7, 1937	29 ♊ 12	May 1, 1939	05 ♋ 59	Sep 22, 1940	29 ♋ 26
Dec 17, 1937	28 ♊ 35	May 11, 1939	06 ♋ 43	Oct 2, 1940	00 ♌ 07
Dec 27, 1937	27 ♊ 56	May 21, 1939	07 ♋ 32	Oct 12, 1940	00 ♌ 41
Jan 6, 1938	27 ♊ 19	May 31, 1939	08 ♋ 26	Oct 22, 1940	01 ♌ 07
Jan 16, 1938	26 ♊ 44	Jun 10, 1939	09 ♋ 23	Nov 1, 1940	01 ♌ 23
Jan 26, 1938	26 ♊ 14	Jun 20, 1939	10 ♋ 23	Nov 11, 1940	01 ♌ 30
Feb 5, 1938	25 ♊ 51	Jun 30, 1939	11 ♋ 24	Nov 21, 1940	01 ♌ 27
Feb 15, 1938	25 ♊ 34	Jul 10, 1939	12 ♋ 26	Dec 1, 1940	01 ♌ 14

Chiron Locations 1920 - 2010

Date	Location	Date	Location	Date	Location
Dec 11, 1940	00 ♌ 52	May 5, 1942	08 ♌ 47	Sep 27, 1943	08 ♍ 23
Dec 21, 1940	00 ♌ 22	May 15, 1942	09 ♌ 18	Oct 7, 1943	09 ♍ 40
Dec 31, 1940	29 ♋ 45	May 25, 1942	09 ♌ 58	Oct 17, 1943	10 ♍ 52
Jan 10, 1941	29 ♋ 04	Jun 4, 1942	10 ♌ 47	Oct 27, 1943	11 ♍ 60
Jan 20, 1941	28 ♋ 21	Jun 14, 1942	11 ♌ 42	Nov 6, 1943	13 ♍ 01
Jan 30, 1941	27 ♋ 37	Jun 24, 1942	12 ♌ 44	Nov 16, 1943	13 ♍ 54
Feb 9, 1941	26 ♋ 57	Jul 4, 1942	13 ♌ 50	Nov 26, 1943	14 ♍ 38
Feb 19, 1941	26 ♋ 20	Jul 14, 1942	15 ♌ 01	Dec 6, 1943	15 ♍ 12
Mar 1, 1941	25 ♋ 51	Jul 24, 1942	16 ♌ 16	Dec 16, 1943	15 ♍ 35
Mar 11, 1941	25 ♋ 30	Aug 3, 1942	17 ♌ 32	Dec 26, 1943	15 ♍ 47
Mar 21, 1941	25 ♋ 18	Aug 13, 1942	18 ♌ 50	Jan 5, 1944	15 ♍ 47
Mar 31, 1941	25 ♋ 15	Aug 23, 1942	20 ♌ 07	Jan 15, 1944	15 ♍ 36
Apr 10, 1941	25 ♋ 23	Sep 2, 1942	21 ♌ 24	Jan 25, 1944	15 ♍ 14
Apr 20, 1941	25 ♋ 40	Sep 12, 1942	22 ♌ 39	Feb 4, 1944	14 ♍ 42
Apr 30, 1941	26 ♋ 07	Sep 22, 1942	23 ♌ 51	Feb 14, 1944	14 ♍ 03
May 10, 1941	26 ♋ 43	Oct 2, 1942	24 ♌ 58	Feb 24, 1944	13 ♍ 18
May 20, 1941	27 ♋ 26	Oct 12, 1942	26 ♌ 00	Mar 5, 1944	12 ♍ 31
May 30, 1941	28 ♋ 16	Oct 22, 1942	26 ♌ 56	Mar 15, 1944	11 ♍ 44
Jun 9, 1941	29 ♋ 13	Nov 1, 1942	27 ♌ 45	Mar 25, 1944	11 ♍ 01
Jun 19, 1941	00 ♌ 14	Nov 11, 1942	28 ♌ 24	Apr 4, 1944	10 ♍ 23
Jun 29, 1941	01 ♌ 20	Nov 21, 1942	28 ♌ 54	Apr 14, 1944	09 ♍ 53
Jul 9, 1941	02 ♌ 28	Dec 1, 1942	29 ♌ 14	Apr 24, 1944	09 ♍ 32
Jul 19, 1941	03 ♌ 39	Dec 11, 1942	29 ♌ 22	May 4, 1944	09 ♍ 22
Jul 29, 1941	04 ♌ 51	Dec 21, 1942	29 ♌ 20	May 14, 1944	09 ♍ 24
Aug 8, 1941	06 ♌ 03	Dec 31, 1942	29 ♌ 06	May 24, 1944	09 ♍ 36
Aug 18, 1941	07 ♌ 15	Jan 10, 1943	28 ♌ 42	Jun 3, 1944	09 ♍ 60
Aug 28, 1941	08 ♌ 24	Jan 20, 1943	28 ♌ 09	Jun 13, 1944	10 ♍ 34
Sep 7, 1941	09 ♌ 31	Jan 30, 1943	27 ♌ 30	Jun 23, 1944	11 ♍ 18
Sep 17, 1941	10 ♌ 34	Feb 9, 1943	26 ♌ 45	Jul 3, 1944	12 ♍ 10
Sep 27, 1941	11 ♌ 31	Feb 19, 1943	25 ♌ 59	Jul 13, 1944	13 ♍ 11
Oct 7, 1941	12 ♌ 23	Mar 1, 1943	25 ♌ 13	Jul 23, 1944	14 ♍ 18
Oct 17, 1941	13 ♌ 07	Mar 11, 1943	24 ♌ 31	Aug 2, 1944	15 ♍ 31
Oct 27, 1941	13 ♌ 43	Mar 21, 1943	23 ♌ 54	Aug 12, 1944	16 ♍ 49
Nov 6, 1941	14 ♌ 10	Mar 31, 1943	23 ♌ 25	Aug 22, 1944	18 ♍ 10
Nov 16, 1941	14 ♌ 27	Apr 10, 1943	23 ♌ 06	Sep 1, 1944	19 ♍ 34
Nov 26, 1941	14 ♌ 34	Apr 20, 1943	22 ♌ 58	Sep 11, 1944	21 ♍ 00
Dec 6, 1941	14 ♌ 30	Apr 30, 1943	22 ♌ 60	Sep 21, 1944	22 ♍ 27
Dec 16, 1941	14 ♌ 16	May 10, 1943	23 ♌ 13	Oct 1, 1944	23 ♍ 52
Dec 26, 1941	13 ♌ 52	May 20, 1943	23 ♌ 37	Oct 11, 1944	25 ♍ 16
Jan 5, 1942	13 ♌ 20	May 30, 1943	24 ♌ 10	Oct 21, 1944	26 ♍ 37
Jan 15, 1942	12 ♌ 42	Jun 9, 1943	24 ♌ 53	Oct 31, 1944	27 ♍ 54
Jan 25, 1942	11 ♌ 58	Jun 19, 1943	25 ♌ 45	Nov 10, 1944	29 ♍ 06
Feb 4, 1942	11 ♌ 13	Jun 29, 1943	26 ♌ 44	Nov 20, 1944	00 ♎ 12
Feb 14, 1942	10 ♌ 28	Jul 9, 1943	27 ♌ 49	Nov 30, 1944	01 ♎ 09
Feb 24, 1942	09 ♌ 47	Jul 19, 1943	29 ♌ 00	Dec 10, 1944	01 ♎ 58
Mar 6, 1942	09 ♌ 11	Jul 29, 1943	00 ♍ 16	Dec 20, 1944	02 ♎ 36
Mar 16, 1942	08 ♌ 43	Aug 8, 1943	01 ♍ 35	Dec 30, 1944	03 ♎ 04
Mar 26, 1942	08 ♌ 23	Aug 18, 1943	02 ♍ 56	Jan 9, 1945	03 ♎ 20
Apr 5, 1942	08 ♌ 13	Aug 28, 1943	04 ♍ 18	Jan 19, 1945	03 ♎ 24
Apr 15, 1942	08 ♌ 14	Sep 7, 1943	05 ♍ 41	Jan 29, 1945	03 ♎ 16
Apr 25, 1942	08 ♌ 26	Sep 17, 1943	07 ♍ 03	Feb 8, 1945	02 ♎ 57

Chiron Locations 1920 - 2010

Feb 18, 1945	02 ♎ 28	Jul 13, 1946	15 ♎ 44	Dec 5, 1947	17 ♏ 38
Feb 28, 1945	01 ♎ 50	Jul 23, 1946	16 ♎ 22	Dec 15, 1947	18 ♏ 54
Mar 10, 1945	01 ♎ 07	Aug 2, 1946	17 ♎ 09	Dec 25, 1947	20 ♏ 06
Mar 20, 1945	00 ♎ 20	Aug 12, 1946	18 ♎ 05	Jan 4, 1948	21 ♏ 11
Mar 30, 1945	29 ♍ 32	Aug 22, 1946	19 ♎ 08	Jan 14, 1948	22 ♏ 10
Apr 9, 1945	28 ♍ 47	Sep 1, 1946	20 ♎ 18	Jan 24, 1948	23 ♏ 00
Apr 19, 1945	28 ♍ 08	Sep 11, 1946	21 ♎ 33	Feb 3, 1948	23 ♏ 42
Apr 29, 1945	27 ♍ 35	Sep 21, 1946	22 ♎ 52	Feb 13, 1948	24 ♏ 13
May 9, 1945	27 ♍ 12	Oct 1, 1946	24 ♎ 15	Feb 23, 1948	24 ♏ 33
May 19, 1945	26 ♍ 60	Oct 11, 1946	25 ♎ 40	Mar 4, 1948	24 ♏ 43
May 29, 1945	26 ♍ 58	Oct 21, 1946	27 ♎ 06	Mar 14, 1948	24 ♏ 41
Jun 8, 1945	27 ♍ 08	Oct 31, 1946	28 ♎ 32	Mar 24, 1948	24 ♏ 29
Jun 18, 1945	27 ♍ 29	Nov 10, 1946	29 ♎ 57	Apr 3, 1948	24 ♏ 07
Jun 28, 1945	28 ♍ 01	Nov 20, 1946	01 ♏ 20	Apr 13, 1948	23 ♏ 36
Jul 8, 1945	28 ♍ 42	Nov 30, 1946	02 ♏ 39	Apr 23, 1948	22 ♏ 59
Jul 18, 1945	29 ♍ 33	Dec 10, 1946	03 ♏ 53	May 3, 1948	22 ♏ 16
Jul 28, 1945	00 ♎ 32	Dec 20, 1946	05 ♏ 01	May 13, 1948	21 ♏ 32
Aug 7, 1945	01 ♎ 39	Dec 30, 1946	06 ♏ 02	May 23, 1948	20 ♏ 48
Aug 17, 1945	02 ♎ 51	Jan 9, 1947	06 ♏ 54	Jun 2, 1948	20 ♏ 06
Aug 27, 1945	04 ♎ 09	Jan 19, 1947	07 ♏ 37	Jun 12, 1948	19 ♏ 29
Sep 6, 1945	05 ♎ 31	Jan 29, 1947	08 ♏ 09	Jun 22, 1948	18 ♏ 60
Sep 16, 1945	06 ♎ 56	Feb 8, 1947	08 ♏ 31	Jul 2, 1948	18 ♏ 38
Sep 26, 1945	08 ♎ 22	Feb 18, 1947	08 ♏ 40	Jul 12, 1948	18 ♏ 27
Oct 6, 1945	09 ♎ 50	Feb 28, 1947	08 ♏ 38	Jul 22, 1948	18 ♏ 25
Oct 16, 1945	11 ♎ 17	Mar 10, 1947	08 ♏ 25	Aug 1, 1948	18 ♏ 34
Oct 26, 1945	12 ♎ 43	Mar 20, 1947	08 ♏ 02	Aug 11, 1948	18 ♏ 53
Nov 5, 1945	14 ♎ 06	Mar 30, 1947	07 ♏ 29	Aug 21, 1948	19 ♏ 21
Nov 15, 1945	15 ♎ 25	Apr 9, 1947	06 ♏ 50	Aug 31, 1948	19 ♏ 59
Nov 25, 1945	16 ♎ 40	Apr 19, 1947	06 ♏ 06	Sep 10, 1948	20 ♏ 45
Dec 5, 1945	17 ♎ 48	Apr 29, 1947	05 ♏ 20	Sep 20, 1948	21 ♏ 39
Dec 15, 1945	18 ♎ 48	May 9, 1947	04 ♏ 34	Sep 30, 1948	22 ♏ 40
Dec 25, 1945	19 ♎ 40	May 19, 1947	03 ♏ 52	Oct 10, 1948	23 ♏ 46
Jan 4, 1946	20 ♎ 21	May 29, 1947	03 ♏ 16	Oct 20, 1948	24 ♏ 57
Jan 14, 1946	20 ♎ 53	Jun 8, 1947	02 ♏ 48	Oct 30, 1948	26 ♏ 11
Jan 24, 1946	21 ♎ 12	Jun 18, 1947	02 ♏ 28	Nov 9, 1948	27 ♏ 28
Feb 3, 1946	21 ♎ 20	Jun 28, 1947	02 ♏ 19	Nov 19, 1948	28 ♏ 46
Feb 13, 1946	21 ♎ 15	Jul 8, 1947	02 ♏ 20	Nov 29, 1948	00 ♐ 03
Feb 23, 1946	20 ♎ 60	Jul 18, 1947	02 ♏ 32	Dec 9, 1948	01 ♐ 20
Mar 5, 1946	20 ♎ 33	Jul 28, 1947	02 ♏ 55	Dec 19, 1948	02 ♐ 35
Mar 15, 1946	19 ♎ 59	Aug 7, 1947	03 ♏ 28	Dec 29, 1948	03 ♐ 46
Mar 25, 1946	19 ♎ 17	Aug 17, 1947	04 ♏ 10	Jan 8, 1949	04 ♐ 53
Apr 4, 1946	18 ♎ 31	Aug 27, 1947	05 ♏ 01	Jan 18, 1949	05 ♐ 54
Apr 14, 1946	17 ♎ 44	Sep 6, 1947	05 ♏ 60	Jan 28, 1949	06 ♐ 48
Apr 24, 1946	16 ♎ 59	Sep 16, 1947	07 ♏ 05	Feb 7, 1949	07 ♐ 35
May 4, 1946	16 ♎ 17	Sep 26, 1947	08 ♏ 16	Feb 17, 1949	08 ♐ 12
May 14, 1946	15 ♎ 43	Oct 6, 1947	09 ♏ 32	Feb 27, 1949	08 ♐ 40
May 24, 1946	15 ♎ 16	Oct 16, 1947	10 ♏ 50	Mar 9, 1949	08 ♐ 58
Jun 3, 1946	15 ♎ 00	Oct 26, 1947	12 ♏ 12	Mar 19, 1949	09 ♐ 06
Jun 13, 1946	14 ♎ 55	Nov 5, 1947	13 ♏ 34	Mar 29, 1949	09 ♐ 03
Jun 23, 1946	15 ♎ 00	Nov 15, 1947	14 ♏ 57	Apr 8, 1949	08 ♐ 50
Jul 3, 1946	15 ♎ 17	Nov 25, 1947	16 ♏ 19	Apr 18, 1949	08 ♐ 27

Chiron Locations 1920 - 2010

Date	Location	Date	Location	Date	Location
Apr 28, 1949	07 ♐ 57	Sep 20, 1950	16 ♐ 24	Feb 12, 1952	09 ♑ 22
May 8, 1949	07 ♐ 21	Sep 30, 1950	16 ♐ 57	Feb 22, 1952	10 ♑ 10
May 18, 1949	06 ♐ 40	Oct 10, 1950	17 ♐ 38	Mar 3, 1952	10 ♑ 52
May 28, 1949	05 ♐ 57	Oct 20, 1950	18 ♐ 25	Mar 13, 1952	11 ♑ 28
Jun 7, 1949	05 ♐ 14	Oct 30, 1950	19 ♐ 19	Mar 23, 1952	11 ♑ 55
Jun 17, 1949	04 ♐ 34	Nov 9, 1950	20 ♐ 17	Apr 2, 1952	12 ♑ 15
Jun 27, 1949	03 ♐ 58	Nov 19, 1950	21 ♐ 19	Apr 12, 1952	12 ♑ 26
Jul 7, 1949	03 ♐ 29	Nov 29, 1950	22 ♐ 24	Apr 22, 1952	12 ♑ 29
Jul 17, 1949	03 ♐ 07	Dec 9, 1950	23 ♐ 32	May 2, 1952	12 ♑ 23
Jul 27, 1949	02 ♐ 55	Dec 19, 1950	24 ♐ 39	May 12, 1952	12 ♑ 09
Aug 6, 1949	02 ♐ 52	Dec 29, 1950	25 ♐ 47	May 22, 1952	11 ♑ 48
Aug 16, 1949	02 ♐ 59	Jan 8, 1951	26 ♐ 52	Jun 1, 1952	11 ♑ 20
Aug 26, 1949	03 ♐ 15	Jan 18, 1951	27 ♐ 55	Jun 11, 1952	10 ♑ 48
Sep 5, 1949	03 ♐ 41	Jan 28, 1951	28 ♐ 55	Jun 21, 1952	10 ♑ 12
Sep 15, 1949	04 ♐ 16	Feb 7, 1951	29 ♐ 49	Jul 1, 1952	09 ♑ 33
Sep 25, 1949	04 ♐ 58	Feb 17, 1951	00 ♑ 38	Jul 11, 1952	08 ♑ 55
Oct 5, 1949	05 ♐ 48	Feb 27, 1951	01 ♑ 20	Jul 21, 1952	08 ♑ 19
Oct 15, 1949	06 ♐ 45	Mar 9, 1951	01 ♑ 55	Jul 31, 1952	07 ♑ 47
Oct 25, 1949	07 ♐ 47	Mar 19, 1951	02 ♑ 21	Aug 10, 1952	07 ♑ 19
Nov 4, 1949	08 ♐ 53	Mar 29, 1951	02 ♑ 38	Aug 20, 1952	06 ♑ 58
Nov 14, 1949	10 ♐ 03	Apr 8, 1951	02 ♑ 47	Aug 30, 1952	06 ♑ 44
Nov 24, 1949	11 ♐ 14	Apr 18, 1951	02 ♑ 46	Sep 9, 1952	06 ♑ 38
Dec 4, 1949	12 ♐ 27	Apr 28, 1951	02 ♑ 36	Sep 19, 1952	06 ♑ 40
Dec 14, 1949	13 ♐ 40	May 8, 1951	02 ♑ 18	Sep 29, 1952	06 ♑ 51
Dec 24, 1949	14 ♐ 51	May 18, 1951	01 ♑ 53	Oct 9, 1952	07 ♑ 09
Jan 3, 1950	16 ♐ 00	May 28, 1951	01 ♑ 21	Oct 19, 1952	07 ♑ 35
Jan 13, 1950	17 ♐ 06	Jun 7, 1951	00 ♑ 45	Oct 29, 1952	08 ♑ 09
Jan 23, 1950	18 ♐ 07	Jun 17, 1951	00 ♑ 06	Nov 8, 1952	08 ♑ 49
Feb 2, 1950	19 ♐ 02	Jun 27, 1951	29 ♐ 26	Nov 18, 1952	09 ♑ 34
Feb 12, 1950	19 ♐ 50	Jul 7, 1951	28 ♐ 48	Nov 28, 1952	10 ♑ 24
Feb 22, 1950	20 ♐ 31	Jul 17, 1951	28 ♐ 12	Dec 8, 1952	11 ♑ 18
Mar 4, 1950	21 ♐ 04	Jul 27, 1951	27 ♐ 41	Dec 18, 1952	12 ♑ 14
Mar 14, 1950	21 ♐ 27	Aug 6, 1951	27 ♐ 16	Dec 28, 1952	13 ♑ 13
Mar 24, 1950	21 ♐ 40	Aug 16, 1951	26 ♐ 59	Jan 7, 1953	14 ♑ 11
Apr 3, 1950	21 ♐ 44	Aug 26, 1951	26 ♐ 49	Jan 17, 1953	15 ♑ 10
Apr 13, 1950	21 ♐ 38	Sep 5, 1951	26 ♐ 48	Jan 27, 1953	16 ♑ 07
Apr 23, 1950	21 ♐ 23	Sep 15, 1951	26 ♐ 56	Feb 6, 1953	17 ♑ 01
May 3, 1950	20 ♐ 60	Sep 25, 1951	27 ♐ 13	Feb 16, 1953	17 ♑ 52
May 13, 1950	20 ♐ 29	Oct 5, 1951	27 ♐ 38	Feb 26, 1953	18 ♑ 39
May 23, 1950	19 ♐ 53	Oct 15, 1951	28 ♐ 11	Mar 8, 1953	19 ♑ 20
Jun 2, 1950	19 ♐ 13	Oct 25, 1951	28 ♐ 50	Mar 18, 1953	19 ♑ 55
Jun 12, 1950	18 ♐ 32	Nov 4, 1951	29 ♐ 37	Mar 28, 1953	20 ♑ 23
Jun 22, 1950	17 ♐ 51	Nov 14, 1951	00 ♑ 28	Apr 7, 1953	20 ♑ 44
Jul 2, 1950	17 ♐ 12	Nov 24, 1951	01 ♑ 24	Apr 17, 1953	20 ♑ 57
Jul 12, 1950	16 ♐ 39	Dec 4, 1951	02 ♑ 23	Apr 27, 1953	21 ♑ 02
Jul 22, 1950	16 ♐ 11	Dec 14, 1951	03 ♑ 24	May 7, 1953	20 ♑ 59
Aug 1, 1950	15 ♐ 51	Dec 24, 1951	04 ♑ 27	May 17, 1953	20 ♑ 49
Aug 11, 1950	15 ♐ 39	Jan 3, 1952	05 ♑ 30	May 27, 1953	20 ♑ 30
Aug 21, 1950	15 ♐ 37	Jan 13, 1952	06 ♑ 32	Jun 6, 1953	20 ♑ 06
Aug 31, 1950	15 ♐ 43	Jan 23, 1952	07 ♑ 32	Jun 16, 1953	19 ♑ 36
Sep 10, 1950	15 ♐ 59	Feb 2, 1952	08 ♑ 29	Jun 26, 1953	19 ♑ 03

Chiron Locations 1920 - 2010

Date	Position	Date	Position	Date	Position
Jul 6, 1953	18 ♑ 27	Nov 28, 1954	25 ♑ 07	Apr 21, 1956	11 ♒ 21
Jul 16, 1953	17 ♑ 50	Dec 8, 1954	25 ♑ 48	May 1, 1956	11 ♒ 35
Jul 26, 1953	17 ♑ 14	Dec 18, 1954	26 ♑ 33	May 11, 1956	11 ♒ 43
Aug 5, 1953	16 ♑ 41	Dec 28, 1954	27 ♑ 22	May 21, 1956	11 ♒ 43
Aug 15, 1953	16 ♑ 12	Jan 7, 1955	28 ♑ 13	May 31, 1956	11 ♒ 37
Aug 25, 1953	15 ♑ 49	Jan 17, 1955	29 ♑ 04	Jun 10, 1956	11 ♒ 25
Sep 4, 1953	15 ♑ 32	Jan 27, 1955	29 ♑ 56	Jun 20, 1956	11 ♒ 06
Sep 14, 1953	15 ♑ 22	Feb 6, 1955	00 ♒ 48	Jun 30, 1956	10 ♒ 42
Sep 24, 1953	15 ♑ 20	Feb 16, 1955	01 ♒ 37	Jul 10, 1956	10 ♒ 14
Oct 4, 1953	15 ♑ 26	Feb 26, 1955	02 ♒ 24	Jul 20, 1956	09 ♒ 43
Oct 14, 1953	15 ♑ 39	Mar 8, 1955	03 ♒ 07	Jul 30, 1956	09 ♒ 10
Oct 24, 1953	16 ♑ 01	Mar 18, 1955	03 ♒ 46	Aug 9, 1956	08 ♒ 37
Nov 3, 1953	16 ♑ 29	Mar 28, 1955	04 ♒ 19	Aug 19, 1956	08 ♒ 06
Nov 13, 1953	17 ♑ 04	Apr 7, 1955	04 ♒ 47	Aug 29, 1956	07 ♒ 36
Nov 23, 1953	17 ♑ 44	Apr 17, 1955	05 ♒ 08	Sep 8, 1956	07 ♒ 11
Dec 3, 1953	18 ♑ 29	Apr 27, 1955	05 ♒ 22	Sep 18, 1956	06 ♒ 50
Dec 13, 1953	19 ♑ 19	May 7, 1955	05 ♒ 30	Sep 28, 1956	06 ♒ 36
Dec 23, 1953	20 ♑ 11	May 17, 1955	05 ♒ 30	Oct 8, 1956	06 ♒ 27
Jan 2, 1954	21 ♑ 05	May 27, 1955	05 ♒ 22	Oct 18, 1956	06 ♒ 26
Jan 12, 1954	22 ♑ 00	Jun 6, 1955	05 ♒ 09	Oct 28, 1956	06 ♒ 31
Jan 22, 1954	22 ♑ 55	Jun 16, 1955	04 ♒ 49	Nov 7, 1956	06 ♒ 44
Feb 1, 1954	23 ♑ 49	Jun 26, 1955	04 ♒ 23	Nov 17, 1956	07 ♒ 03
Feb 11, 1954	24 ♑ 41	Jul 6, 1955	03 ♒ 54	Nov 27, 1956	07 ♒ 28
Feb 21, 1954	25 ♑ 30	Jul 16, 1955	03 ♒ 21	Dec 7, 1956	07 ♒ 59
Mar 3, 1954	26 ♑ 15	Jul 26, 1955	02 ♒ 47	Dec 17, 1956	08 ♒ 34
Mar 13, 1954	26 ♑ 55	Aug 5, 1955	02 ♒ 13	Dec 27, 1956	09 ♒ 14
Mar 23, 1954	27 ♑ 29	Aug 15, 1955	01 ♒ 41	Jan 6, 1957	09 ♒ 57
Apr 2, 1954	27 ♑ 57	Aug 25, 1955	01 ♒ 11	Jan 16, 1957	10 ♒ 42
Apr 12, 1954	28 ♑ 19	Sep 4, 1955	00 ♒ 46	Jan 26, 1957	11 ♒ 28
Apr 22, 1954	28 ♑ 33	Sep 14, 1955	00 ♒ 26	Feb 5, 1957	12 ♒ 15
May 2, 1954	28 ♑ 39	Sep 24, 1955	00 ♒ 12	Feb 15, 1957	13 ♒ 02
May 12, 1954	28 ♑ 38	Oct 4, 1955	00 ♒ 05	Feb 25, 1957	13 ♒ 47
May 22, 1954	28 ♑ 29	Oct 14, 1955	00 ♒ 05	Mar 7, 1957	14 ♒ 30
Jun 1, 1954	28 ♑ 14	Oct 24, 1955	00 ♒ 13	Mar 17, 1957	15 ♒ 10
Jun 11, 1954	27 ♑ 52	Nov 3, 1955	00 ♒ 27	Mar 27, 1957	15 ♒ 46
Jun 21, 1954	27 ♑ 24	Nov 13, 1955	00 ♒ 49	Apr 6, 1957	16 ♒ 17
Jul 1, 1954	26 ♑ 53	Nov 23, 1955	01 ♒ 16	Apr 16, 1957	16 ♒ 43
Jul 11, 1954	26 ♑ 19	Dec 3, 1955	01 ♒ 49	Apr 26, 1957	17 ♒ 03
Jul 21, 1954	25 ♑ 43	Dec 13, 1955	02 ♒ 28	May 6, 1957	17 ♒ 17
Jul 31, 1954	25 ♑ 08	Dec 23, 1955	03 ♒ 10	May 16, 1957	17 ♒ 25
Aug 10, 1954	24 ♑ 35	Jan 2, 1956	03 ♒ 55	May 26, 1957	17 ♒ 26
Aug 20, 1954	24 ♑ 06	Jan 12, 1956	04 ♒ 43	Jun 5, 1957	17 ♒ 21
Aug 30, 1954	23 ♑ 41	Jan 22, 1956	05 ♒ 32	Jun 15, 1957	17 ♒ 09
Sep 9, 1954	23 ♑ 22	Feb 1, 1956	06 ♒ 21	Jun 25, 1957	16 ♒ 51
Sep 19, 1954	23 ♑ 10	Feb 11, 1956	07 ♒ 10	Jul 5, 1957	16 ♒ 29
Sep 29, 1954	23 ♑ 05	Feb 21, 1956	07 ♒ 57	Jul 15, 1957	16 ♒ 02
Oct 9, 1954	23 ♑ 08	Mar 2, 1956	08 ♒ 42	Jul 25, 1957	15 ♒ 32
Oct 19, 1954	23 ♑ 18	Mar 12, 1956	09 ♒ 23	Aug 4, 1957	15 ♒ 00
Oct 29, 1954	23 ♑ 35	Mar 22, 1956	10 ♒ 01	Aug 14, 1957	14 ♒ 28
Nov 8, 1954	23 ♑ 60	Apr 1, 1956	10 ♒ 33	Aug 24, 1957	13 ♒ 57
Nov 18, 1954	24 ♑ 30	Apr 11, 1956	10 ♒ 60	Sep 3, 1957	13 ♒ 28

Chiron Locations 1920 - 2010

Date	Location	Date	Location	Date	Location
Sep 13, 1957	13 ♒ 03	Feb 5, 1959	22 ♒ 07	Jun 29, 1960	02 ♓ 02
Sep 23, 1957	12 ♒ 42	Feb 15, 1959	22 ♒ 51	Jul 9, 1960	01 ♓ 46
Oct 3, 1957	12 ♒ 27	Feb 25, 1959	23 ♒ 34	Jul 19, 1960	01 ♓ 25
Oct 13, 1957	12 ♒ 18	Mar 7, 1959	24 ♒ 15	Jul 29, 1960	01 ♓ 00
Oct 23, 1957	12 ♒ 15	Mar 17, 1959	24 ♒ 55	Aug 8, 1960	00 ♓ 33
Nov 2, 1957	12 ♒ 20	Mar 27, 1959	25 ♒ 32	Aug 18, 1960	00 ♓ 04
Nov 12, 1957	12 ♒ 30	Apr 6, 1959	26 ♒ 05	Aug 28, 1960	29 ♒ 34
Nov 22, 1957	12 ♒ 48	Apr 16, 1959	26 ♒ 34	Sep 7, 1960	29 ♒ 05
Dec 2, 1957	13 ♒ 11	Apr 26, 1959	26 ♒ 59	Sep 17, 1960	28 ♒ 38
Dec 12, 1957	13 ♒ 40	May 6, 1959	27 ♒ 18	Sep 27, 1960	28 ♒ 13
Dec 22, 1957	14 ♒ 13	May 16, 1959	27 ♒ 31	Oct 7, 1960	27 ♒ 53
Jan 1, 1958	14 ♒ 50	May 26, 1959	27 ♒ 38	Oct 17, 1960	27 ♒ 38
Jan 11, 1958	15 ♒ 31	Jun 5, 1959	27 ♒ 39	Oct 27, 1960	27 ♒ 28
Jan 21, 1958	16 ♒ 14	Jun 15, 1959	27 ♒ 34	Nov 6, 1960	27 ♒ 25
Jan 31, 1958	16 ♒ 59	Jun 25, 1959	27 ♒ 23	Nov 16, 1960	27 ♒ 27
Feb 10, 1958	17 ♒ 44	Jul 5, 1959	27 ♒ 07	Nov 26, 1960	27 ♒ 36
Feb 20, 1958	18 ♒ 28	Jul 15, 1959	26 ♒ 46	Dec 6, 1960	27 ♒ 50
Mar 2, 1958	19 ♒ 12	Jul 25, 1959	26 ♒ 21	Dec 16, 1960	28 ♒ 10
Mar 12, 1958	19 ♒ 53	Aug 4, 1959	25 ♒ 53	Dec 26, 1960	28 ♒ 35
Mar 22, 1958	20 ♒ 31	Aug 14, 1959	25 ♒ 23	Jan 5, 1961	29 ♒ 05
Apr 1, 1958	21 ♒ 06	Aug 24, 1959	24 ♒ 52	Jan 15, 1961	29 ♒ 38
Apr 11, 1958	21 ♒ 36	Sep 3, 1959	24 ♒ 22	Jan 25, 1961	00 ♓ 15
Apr 21, 1958	22 ♒ 01	Sep 13, 1959	23 ♒ 55	Feb 4, 1961	00 ♓ 53
May 1, 1958	22 ♒ 21	Sep 23, 1959	23 ♒ 30	Feb 14, 1961	01 ♓ 33
May 11, 1958	22 ♒ 35	Oct 3, 1959	23 ♒ 10	Feb 24, 1961	02 ♓ 14
May 21, 1958	22 ♒ 42	Oct 13, 1959	22 ♒ 54	Mar 6, 1961	02 ♓ 54
May 31, 1958	22 ♒ 43	Oct 23, 1959	22 ♒ 44	Mar 16, 1961	03 ♓ 33
Jun 10, 1958	22 ♒ 38	Nov 2, 1959	22 ♒ 41	Mar 26, 1961	04 ♓ 10
Jun 20, 1958	22 ♒ 27	Nov 12, 1959	22 ♒ 44	Apr 5, 1961	04 ♓ 44
Jun 30, 1958	22 ♒ 10	Nov 22, 1959	22 ♒ 53	Apr 15, 1961	05 ♓ 15
Jul 10, 1958	21 ♒ 48	Dec 2, 1959	23 ♒ 08	Apr 25, 1961	05 ♓ 42
Jul 20, 1958	21 ♒ 22	Dec 12, 1959	23 ♒ 28	May 5, 1961	06 ♓ 05
Jul 30, 1958	20 ♒ 53	Dec 22, 1959	23 ♒ 54	May 15, 1961	06 ♓ 22
Aug 9, 1958	20 ♒ 23	Jan 1, 1960	24 ♒ 25	May 25, 1961	06 ♓ 34
Aug 19, 1958	19 ♒ 52	Jan 11, 1960	24 ♒ 59	Jun 4, 1961	06 ♓ 41
Aug 29, 1958	19 ♒ 21	Jan 21, 1960	25 ♒ 37	Jun 14, 1961	06 ♓ 41
Sep 8, 1958	18 ♒ 53	Jan 31, 1960	26 ♒ 17	Jun 24, 1961	06 ♓ 36
Sep 18, 1958	18 ♒ 28	Feb 10, 1960	26 ♒ 58	Jul 4, 1961	06 ♓ 25
Sep 28, 1958	18 ♒ 07	Feb 20, 1960	27 ♒ 40	Jul 14, 1961	06 ♓ 09
Oct 8, 1958	17 ♒ 52	Mar 1, 1960	28 ♒ 21	Jul 24, 1961	05 ♓ 49
Oct 18, 1958	17 ♒ 42	Mar 11, 1960	29 ♒ 01	Aug 3, 1961	05 ♓ 25
Oct 28, 1958	17 ♒ 39	Mar 21, 1960	29 ♒ 40	Aug 13, 1961	04 ♓ 58
Nov 7, 1958	17 ♒ 42	Mar 31, 1960	00 ♓ 15	Aug 23, 1961	04 ♓ 29
Nov 17, 1958	17 ♒ 52	Apr 10, 1960	00 ♓ 48	Sep 2, 1961	03 ♓ 60
Nov 27, 1958	18 ♒ 08	Apr 20, 1960	01 ♓ 16	Sep 12, 1961	03 ♓ 31
Dec 7, 1958	18 ♒ 30	Apr 30, 1960	01 ♓ 39	Sep 22, 1961	03 ♓ 05
Dec 17, 1958	18 ♒ 57	May 10, 1960	01 ♓ 57	Oct 2, 1961	02 ♓ 41
Dec 27, 1958	19 ♒ 29	May 20, 1960	02 ♓ 10	Oct 12, 1961	02 ♓ 21
Jan 6, 1959	20 ♒ 04	May 30, 1960	02 ♓ 17	Oct 22, 1961	02 ♓ 06
Jan 16, 1959	20 ♒ 43	Jun 9, 1960	02 ♓ 17	Nov 1, 1961	01 ♓ 57
Jan 26, 1959	21 ♒ 25	Jun 19, 1960	02 ♓ 12	Nov 11, 1961	01 ♓ 53

Chiron Locations 1920 - 2010

Date	Location	Date	Location	Date	Location
Nov 21, 1961	01 ♓ 55	Apr 15, 1963	13 ♓ 07	Sep 6, 1964	16 ♓ 35
Dec 1, 1961	02 ♓ 04	Apr 25, 1963	13 ♓ 36	Sep 16, 1964	16 ♓ 07
Dec 11, 1961	02 ♓ 18	May 5, 1963	14 ♓ 02	Sep 26, 1964	15 ♓ 40
Dec 21, 1961	02 ♓ 37	May 15, 1963	14 ♓ 22	Oct 6, 1964	15 ♓ 15
Dec 31, 1961	03 ♓ 02	May 25, 1963	14 ♓ 38	Oct 16, 1964	14 ♓ 53
Jan 10, 1962	03 ♓ 31	Jun 4, 1963	14 ♓ 49	Oct 26, 1964	14 ♓ 35
Jan 20, 1962	04 ♓ 03	Jun 14, 1963	14 ♓ 54	Nov 5, 1964	14 ♓ 21
Jan 30, 1962	04 ♓ 39	Jun 24, 1963	14 ♓ 54	Nov 15, 1964	14 ♓ 13
Feb 9, 1962	05 ♓ 16	Jul 4, 1963	14 ♓ 48	Nov 25, 1964	14 ♓ 10
Feb 19, 1962	05 ♓ 55	Jul 14, 1963	14 ♓ 37	Dec 5, 1964	14 ♓ 13
Mar 1, 1962	06 ♓ 35	Jul 24, 1963	14 ♓ 21	Dec 15, 1964	14 ♓ 21
Mar 11, 1962	07 ♓ 14	Aug 3, 1963	14 ♓ 01	Dec 25, 1964	14 ♓ 35
Mar 21, 1962	07 ♓ 52	Aug 13, 1963	13 ♓ 37	Jan 4, 1965	14 ♓ 54
Mar 31, 1962	08 ♓ 28	Aug 23, 1963	13 ♓ 11	Jan 14, 1965	15 ♓ 18
Apr 10, 1962	09 ♓ 01	Sep 2, 1963	12 ♓ 43	Jan 24, 1965	15 ♓ 46
Apr 20, 1962	09 ♓ 31	Sep 12, 1963	12 ♓ 15	Feb 3, 1965	16 ♓ 17
Apr 30, 1962	09 ♓ 57	Sep 22, 1963	11 ♓ 47	Feb 13, 1965	16 ♓ 51
May 10, 1962	10 ♓ 19	Oct 2, 1963	11 ♓ 22	Feb 23, 1965	17 ♓ 26
May 20, 1962	10 ♓ 35	Oct 12, 1963	10 ♓ 59	Mar 5, 1965	18 ♓ 03
May 30, 1962	10 ♓ 47	Oct 22, 1963	10 ♓ 40	Mar 15, 1965	18 ♓ 40
Jun 9, 1962	10 ♓ 53	Nov 1, 1963	10 ♓ 26	Mar 25, 1965	19 ♓ 16
Jun 19, 1962	10 ♓ 53	Nov 11, 1963	10 ♓ 17	Apr 4, 1965	19 ♓ 52
Jun 29, 1962	10 ♓ 47	Nov 21, 1963	10 ♓ 14	Apr 14, 1965	20 ♓ 25
Jul 9, 1962	10 ♓ 36	Dec 1, 1963	10 ♓ 16	Apr 24, 1965	20 ♓ 56
Jul 19, 1962	10 ♓ 20	Dec 11, 1963	10 ♓ 25	May 4, 1965	21 ♓ 23
Jul 29, 1962	10 ♓ 00	Dec 21, 1963	10 ♓ 39	May 14, 1965	21 ♓ 47
Aug 8, 1962	09 ♓ 36	Dec 31, 1963	10 ♓ 58	May 24, 1965	22 ♓ 06
Aug 18, 1962	09 ♓ 10	Jan 10, 1964	11 ♓ 22	Jun 3, 1965	22 ♓ 20
Aug 28, 1962	08 ♓ 42	Jan 20, 1964	11 ♓ 50	Jun 13, 1965	22 ♓ 29
Sep 7, 1962	08 ♓ 13	Jan 30, 1964	12 ♓ 21	Jun 23, 1965	22 ♓ 34
Sep 17, 1962	07 ♓ 45	Feb 9, 1964	12 ♓ 55	Jul 3, 1965	22 ♓ 32
Sep 27, 1962	07 ♓ 19	Feb 19, 1964	13 ♓ 31	Jul 13, 1965	22 ♓ 26
Oct 7, 1962	06 ♓ 56	Feb 29, 1964	14 ♓ 09	Jul 23, 1965	22 ♓ 14
Oct 17, 1962	06 ♓ 36	Mar 10, 1964	14 ♓ 46	Aug 2, 1965	21 ♓ 57
Oct 27, 1962	06 ♓ 22	Mar 20, 1964	15 ♓ 23	Aug 12, 1965	21 ♓ 37
Nov 6, 1962	06 ♓ 12	Mar 30, 1964	15 ♓ 60	Aug 22, 1965	21 ♓ 13
Nov 16, 1962	06 ♓ 09	Apr 9, 1964	16 ♓ 34	Sep 1, 1965	20 ♓ 47
Nov 26, 1962	06 ♓ 11	Apr 19, 1964	17 ♓ 05	Sep 11, 1965	20 ♓ 20
Dec 6, 1962	06 ♓ 19	Apr 29, 1964	17 ♓ 33	Sep 21, 1965	19 ♓ 52
Dec 16, 1962	06 ♓ 33	May 9, 1964	17 ♓ 58	Oct 1, 1965	19 ♓ 26
Dec 26, 1962	06 ♓ 53	May 19, 1964	18 ♓ 18	Oct 11, 1965	19 ♓ 01
Jan 5, 1963	07 ♓ 17	May 29, 1964	18 ♓ 33	Oct 21, 1965	18 ♓ 39
Jan 15, 1963	07 ♓ 45	Jun 8, 1964	18 ♓ 43	Oct 31, 1965	18 ♓ 21
Jan 25, 1963	08 ♓ 17	Jun 18, 1964	18 ♓ 47	Nov 10, 1965	18 ♓ 08
Feb 4, 1963	08 ♓ 52	Jun 28, 1964	18 ♓ 47	Nov 20, 1965	18 ♓ 00
Feb 14, 1963	09 ♓ 29	Jul 8, 1964	18 ♓ 40	Nov 30, 1965	17 ♓ 58
Feb 24, 1963	10 ♓ 07	Jul 18, 1964	18 ♓ 29	Dec 10, 1965	18 ♓ 01
Mar 6, 1963	10 ♓ 45	Jul 28, 1964	18 ♓ 13	Dec 20, 1965	18 ♓ 10
Mar 16, 1963	11 ♓ 23	Aug 7, 1964	17 ♓ 53	Dec 30, 1965	18 ♓ 24
Mar 26, 1963	11 ♓ 60	Aug 17, 1964	17 ♓ 29	Jan 9, 1966	18 ♓ 44
Apr 5, 1963	12 ♓ 35	Aug 27, 1964	17 ♓ 03	Jan 19, 1966	19 ♓ 07

Chiron Locations 1920 - 2010

Date	Location	Date	Location	Date	Location
Jan 29, 1966	19 ♓ 35	Jun 23, 1967	29 ♓ 47	Nov 14, 1968	29 ♓ 10
Feb 8, 1966	20 ♓ 06	Jul 3, 1967	29 ♓ 50	Nov 24, 1968	28 ♓ 58
Feb 18, 1966	20 ♓ 40	Jul 13, 1967	29 ♓ 47	Dec 4, 1968	28 ♓ 52
Feb 28, 1966	21 ♓ 15	Jul 23, 1967	29 ♓ 40	Dec 14, 1968	28 ♓ 52
Mar 10, 1966	21 ♓ 51	Aug 2, 1967	29 ♓ 27	Dec 24, 1968	28 ♓ 56
Mar 20, 1966	22 ♓ 27	Aug 12, 1967	29 ♓ 10	Jan 3, 1969	29 ♓ 07
Mar 30, 1966	23 ♓ 03	Aug 22, 1967	28 ♓ 49	Jan 13, 1969	29 ♓ 22
Apr 9, 1966	23 ♓ 38	Sep 1, 1967	28 ♓ 25	Jan 23, 1969	29 ♓ 42
Apr 19, 1966	24 ♓ 10	Sep 11, 1967	27 ♓ 59	Feb 2, 1969	00 ♈ 07
Apr 29, 1966	24 ♓ 40	Sep 21, 1967	27 ♓ 32	Feb 12, 1969	00 ♈ 35
May 9, 1966	25 ♓ 07	Oct 1, 1967	27 ♓ 05	Feb 22, 1969	01 ♈ 06
May 19, 1966	25 ♓ 30	Oct 11, 1967	26 ♓ 39	Mar 4, 1969	01 ♈ 39
May 29, 1966	25 ♓ 48	Oct 21, 1967	26 ♓ 15	Mar 14, 1969	02 ♈ 14
Jun 8, 1966	26 ♓ 02	Oct 31, 1967	25 ♓ 54	Mar 24, 1969	02 ♈ 49
Jun 18, 1966	26 ♓ 10	Nov 10, 1967	25 ♓ 38	Apr 3, 1969	03 ♈ 24
Jun 28, 1966	26 ♓ 14	Nov 20, 1967	25 ♓ 26	Apr 13, 1969	03 ♈ 59
Jul 8, 1966	26 ♓ 12	Nov 30, 1967	25 ♓ 19	Apr 23, 1969	04 ♈ 32
Jul 18, 1966	26 ♓ 05	Dec 10, 1967	25 ♓ 18	May 3, 1969	05 ♈ 03
Jul 28, 1966	25 ♓ 53	Dec 20, 1967	25 ♓ 22	May 13, 1969	05 ♈ 31
Aug 7, 1966	25 ♓ 36	Dec 30, 1967	25 ♓ 32	May 23, 1969	05 ♈ 55
Aug 17, 1966	25 ♓ 15	Jan 9, 1968	25 ♓ 47	Jun 2, 1969	06 ♈ 16
Aug 27, 1966	24 ♓ 52	Jan 19, 1968	26 ♓ 07	Jun 12, 1969	06 ♈ 33
Sep 6, 1966	24 ♓ 26	Jan 29, 1968	26 ♓ 31	Jun 22, 1969	06 ♈ 44
Sep 16, 1966	23 ♓ 59	Feb 8, 1968	26 ♓ 59	Jul 2, 1969	06 ♈ 51
Sep 26, 1966	23 ♓ 31	Feb 18, 1968	27 ♓ 29	Jul 12, 1969	06 ♈ 53
Oct 6, 1966	23 ♓ 05	Feb 28, 1968	28 ♓ 03	Jul 22, 1969	06 ♈ 49
Oct 16, 1966	22 ♓ 41	Mar 9, 1968	28 ♓ 37	Aug 1, 1969	06 ♈ 40
Oct 26, 1966	22 ♓ 19	Mar 19, 1968	29 ♓ 13	Aug 11, 1969	06 ♈ 27
Nov 5, 1966	22 ♓ 02	Mar 29, 1968	29 ♓ 48	Aug 21, 1969	06 ♈ 09
Nov 15, 1966	21 ♓ 50	Apr 8, 1968	00 ♈ 23	Aug 31, 1969	05 ♈ 47
Nov 25, 1966	21 ♓ 42	Apr 18, 1968	00 ♈ 57	Sep 10, 1969	05 ♈ 23
Dec 5, 1966	21 ♓ 40	Apr 28, 1968	01 ♈ 28	Sep 20, 1969	04 ♈ 57
Dec 15, 1966	21 ♓ 44	May 8, 1968	01 ♈ 57	Sep 30, 1969	04 ♈ 30
Dec 25, 1966	21 ♓ 53	May 18, 1968	02 ♈ 22	Oct 10, 1969	04 ♈ 03
Jan 4, 1967	22 ♓ 08	May 28, 1968	02 ♈ 43	Oct 20, 1969	03 ♈ 38
Jan 14, 1967	22 ♓ 27	Jun 7, 1968	03 ♈ 00	Oct 30, 1969	03 ♈ 15
Jan 24, 1967	22 ♓ 51	Jun 17, 1968	03 ♈ 13	Nov 9, 1969	02 ♈ 55
Feb 3, 1967	23 ♓ 19	Jun 27, 1968	03 ♈ 20	Nov 19, 1969	02 ♈ 39
Feb 13, 1967	23 ♓ 50	Jul 7, 1968	03 ♈ 22	Nov 29, 1969	02 ♈ 29
Feb 23, 1967	24 ♓ 23	Jul 17, 1968	03 ♈ 19	Dec 9, 1969	02 ♈ 23
Mar 5, 1967	24 ♓ 58	Jul 27, 1968	03 ♈ 11	Dec 19, 1969	02 ♈ 23
Mar 15, 1967	25 ♓ 34	Aug 6, 1968	02 ♈ 58	Dec 29, 1969	02 ♈ 28
Mar 25, 1967	26 ♓ 10	Aug 16, 1968	02 ♈ 41	Jan 8, 1970	02 ♈ 39
Apr 4, 1967	26 ♓ 45	Aug 26, 1968	02 ♈ 19	Jan 18, 1970	02 ♈ 55
Apr 14, 1967	27 ♓ 19	Sep 5, 1968	01 ♈ 55	Jan 28, 1970	03 ♈ 16
Apr 24, 1967	27 ♓ 51	Sep 15, 1968	01 ♈ 29	Feb 7, 1970	03 ♈ 41
May 4, 1967	28 ♓ 20	Sep 25, 1968	01 ♈ 02	Feb 17, 1970	04 ♈ 09
May 14, 1967	28 ♓ 46	Oct 5, 1968	00 ♈ 35	Feb 27, 1970	04 ♈ 40
May 24, 1967	29 ♓ 08	Oct 15, 1968	00 ♈ 10	Mar 9, 1970	05 ♈ 13
Jun 3, 1967	29 ♓ 26	Oct 25, 1968	29 ♓ 46	Mar 19, 1970	05 ♈ 48
Jun 13, 1967	29 ♓ 39	Nov 4, 1968	29 ♓ 26	Mar 29, 1970	06 ♈ 23

Chiron Locations 1920 - 2010

Date	Position		Date	Position		Date	Position
Apr 8, 1970	06 ♈ 58		Aug 31, 1971	13 ♈ 03		Jan 22, 1973	13 ♈ 14
Apr 18, 1970	07 ♈ 33		Sep 10, 1971	12 ♈ 41		Feb 1, 1973	13 ♈ 32
Apr 28, 1970	08 ♈ 05		Sep 20, 1971	12 ♈ 16		Feb 11, 1973	13 ♈ 54
May 8, 1970	08 ♈ 36		Sep 30, 1971	11 ♈ 49		Feb 21, 1973	14 ♈ 20
May 18, 1970	09 ♈ 03		Oct 10, 1971	11 ♈ 22		Mar 3, 1973	14 ♈ 50
May 28, 1970	09 ♈ 28		Oct 20, 1971	10 ♈ 56		Mar 13, 1973	15 ♈ 22
Jun 7, 1970	09 ♈ 48		Oct 30, 1971	10 ♈ 31		Mar 23, 1973	15 ♈ 56
Jun 17, 1970	10 ♈ 04		Nov 9, 1971	10 ♈ 08		Apr 2, 1973	16 ♈ 31
Jun 27, 1970	10 ♈ 15		Nov 19, 1971	09 ♈ 50		Apr 12, 1973	17 ♈ 06
Jul 7, 1970	10 ♈ 21		Nov 29, 1971	09 ♈ 35		Apr 22, 1973	17 ♈ 41
Jul 17, 1970	10 ♈ 22		Dec 9, 1971	09 ♈ 26		May 2, 1973	18 ♈ 15
Jul 27, 1970	10 ♈ 18		Dec 19, 1971	09 ♈ 21		May 12, 1973	18 ♈ 47
Aug 6, 1970	10 ♈ 08		Dec 29, 1971	09 ♈ 23		May 22, 1973	19 ♈ 17
Aug 16, 1970	09 ♈ 54		Jan 8, 1972	09 ♈ 30		Jun 1, 1973	19 ♈ 44
Aug 26, 1970	09 ♈ 36		Jan 18, 1972	09 ♈ 42		Jun 11, 1973	20 ♈ 07
Sep 5, 1970	09 ♈ 14		Jan 28, 1972	09 ♈ 59		Jun 21, 1973	20 ♈ 26
Sep 15, 1970	08 ♈ 50		Feb 7, 1972	10 ♈ 21		Jul 1, 1973	20 ♈ 40
Sep 25, 1970	08 ♈ 23		Feb 17, 1972	10 ♈ 47		Jul 11, 1973	20 ♈ 50
Oct 5, 1970	07 ♈ 56		Feb 27, 1972	11 ♈ 16		Jul 21, 1973	20 ♈ 54
Oct 15, 1970	07 ♈ 30		Mar 8, 1972	11 ♈ 47		Jul 31, 1973	20 ♈ 53
Oct 25, 1970	07 ♈ 04		Mar 18, 1972	12 ♈ 21		Aug 10, 1973	20 ♈ 47
Nov 4, 1970	06 ♈ 42		Mar 28, 1972	12 ♈ 56		Aug 20, 1973	20 ♈ 36
Nov 14, 1970	06 ♈ 22		Apr 7, 1972	13 ♈ 31		Aug 30, 1973	20 ♈ 21
Nov 24, 1970	06 ♈ 07		Apr 17, 1972	14 ♈ 06		Sep 9, 1973	20 ♈ 01
Dec 4, 1970	05 ♈ 57		Apr 27, 1972	14 ♈ 40		Sep 19, 1973	19 ♈ 38
Dec 14, 1970	05 ♈ 52		May 7, 1972	15 ♈ 12		Sep 29, 1973	19 ♈ 12
Dec 24, 1970	05 ♈ 53		May 17, 1972	15 ♈ 42		Oct 9, 1973	18 ♈ 45
Jan 3, 1971	05 ♈ 59		May 27, 1972	16 ♈ 09		Oct 19, 1973	18 ♈ 18
Jan 13, 1971	06 ♈ 11		Jun 6, 1972	16 ♈ 32		Oct 29, 1973	17 ♈ 52
Jan 23, 1971	06 ♈ 27		Jun 16, 1972	16 ♈ 52		Nov 8, 1973	17 ♈ 27
Feb 2, 1971	06 ♈ 49		Jun 26, 1972	17 ♈ 06		Nov 18, 1973	17 ♈ 05
Feb 12, 1971	07 ♈ 14		Jul 6, 1972	17 ♈ 16		Nov 28, 1973	16 ♈ 47
Feb 22, 1971	07 ♈ 42		Jul 16, 1972	17 ♈ 21		Dec 8, 1973	16 ♈ 34
Mar 4, 1971	08 ♈ 14		Jul 26, 1972	17 ♈ 21		Dec 18, 1973	16 ♈ 26
Mar 14, 1971	08 ♈ 47		Aug 5, 1972	17 ♈ 16		Dec 28, 1973	16 ♈ 23
Mar 24, 1971	09 ♈ 22		Aug 15, 1972	17 ♈ 05		Jan 7, 1974	16 ♈ 26
Apr 3, 1971	09 ♈ 57		Aug 25, 1972	16 ♈ 50		Jan 17, 1974	16 ♈ 34
Apr 13, 1971	10 ♈ 32		Sep 4, 1972	16 ♈ 31		Jan 27, 1974	16 ♈ 48
Apr 23, 1971	11 ♈ 06		Sep 14, 1972	16 ♈ 08		Feb 6, 1974	17 ♈ 06
May 3, 1971	11 ♈ 38		Sep 24, 1972	15 ♈ 43		Feb 16, 1974	17 ♈ 29
May 13, 1971	12 ♈ 09		Oct 4, 1972	15 ♈ 16		Feb 26, 1974	17 ♈ 56
May 23, 1971	12 ♈ 36		Oct 14, 1972	14 ♈ 49		Mar 8, 1974	18 ♈ 26
Jun 2, 1971	12 ♈ 60		Oct 24, 1972	14 ♈ 23		Mar 18, 1974	18 ♈ 59
Jun 12, 1971	13 ♈ 19		Nov 3, 1972	13 ♈ 58		Mar 28, 1974	19 ♈ 33
Jun 22, 1971	13 ♈ 35		Nov 13, 1972	13 ♈ 36		Apr 7, 1974	20 ♈ 08
Jul 2, 1971	13 ♈ 45		Nov 23, 1972	13 ♈ 17		Apr 17, 1974	20 ♈ 44
Jul 12, 1971	13 ♈ 51		Dec 3, 1972	13 ♈ 04		Apr 27, 1974	21 ♈ 19
Jul 22, 1971	13 ♈ 51		Dec 13, 1972	12 ♈ 55		May 7, 1974	21 ♈ 53
Aug 1, 1971	13 ♈ 46		Dec 23, 1972	12 ♈ 51		May 17, 1974	22 ♈ 25
Aug 11, 1971	13 ♈ 36		Jan 2, 1973	12 ♈ 53		May 27, 1974	22 ♈ 55
Aug 21, 1971	13 ♈ 22		Jan 12, 1973	13 ♈ 01		Jun 6, 1974	23 ♈ 21

Chiron Locations 1920 - 2010

Date	Location	Date	Location	Date	Location
Jun 16, 1974	23 ♈ 44	Nov 8, 1975	24 ♈ 59	Apr 1, 1977	00 ♉ 11
Jun 26, 1974	24 ♈ 03	Nov 18, 1975	24 ♈ 34	Apr 11, 1977	00 ♉ 47
Jul 6, 1974	24 ♈ 17	Nov 28, 1975	24 ♈ 13	Apr 21, 1977	01 ♉ 24
Jul 16, 1974	24 ♈ 26	Dec 8, 1975	23 ♈ 56	May 1, 1977	02 ♉ 01
Jul 26, 1974	24 ♈ 30	Dec 18, 1975	23 ♈ 44	May 11, 1977	02 ♉ 37
Aug 5, 1974	24 ♈ 29	Dec 28, 1975	23 ♈ 37	May 21, 1977	03 ♉ 11
Aug 15, 1974	24 ♈ 22	Jan 7, 1976	23 ♈ 35	May 31, 1977	03 ♉ 44
Aug 25, 1974	24 ♈ 10	Jan 17, 1976	23 ♈ 40	Jun 10, 1977	04 ♉ 14
Sep 4, 1974	23 ♈ 54	Jan 27, 1976	23 ♈ 49	Jun 20, 1977	04 ♉ 41
Sep 14, 1974	23 ♈ 34	Feb 6, 1976	24 ♈ 05	Jun 30, 1977	05 ♉ 04
Sep 24, 1974	23 ♈ 11	Feb 16, 1976	24 ♈ 25	Jul 10, 1977	05 ♉ 22
Oct 4, 1974	22 ♈ 45	Feb 26, 1976	24 ♈ 49	Jul 20, 1977	05 ♉ 35
Oct 14, 1974	22 ♈ 17	Mar 7, 1976	25 ♈ 17	Jul 30, 1977	05 ♉ 44
Oct 24, 1974	21 ♈ 50	Mar 17, 1976	25 ♈ 49	Aug 9, 1977	05 ♉ 47
Nov 3, 1974	21 ♈ 23	Mar 27, 1976	26 ♈ 22	Aug 19, 1977	05 ♉ 44
Nov 13, 1974	20 ♈ 59	Apr 6, 1976	26 ♈ 57	Aug 29, 1977	05 ♉ 36
Nov 23, 1974	20 ♈ 37	Apr 16, 1976	27 ♈ 34	Sep 8, 1977	05 ♉ 23
Dec 3, 1974	20 ♈ 20	Apr 26, 1976	28 ♈ 10	Sep 18, 1977	05 ♉ 05
Dec 13, 1974	20 ♈ 07	May 6, 1976	28 ♈ 46	Sep 28, 1977	04 ♉ 43
Dec 23, 1974	19 ♈ 59	May 16, 1976	29 ♈ 20	Oct 8, 1977	04 ♉ 18
Jan 2, 1975	19 ♈ 57	May 26, 1976	29 ♈ 52	Oct 18, 1977	03 ♉ 51
Jan 12, 1975	20 ♈ 01	Jun 5, 1976	00 ♉ 22	Oct 28, 1977	03 ♉ 22
Jan 22, 1975	20 ♈ 10	Jun 15, 1976	00 ♉ 49	Nov 7, 1977	02 ♉ 54
Feb 1, 1975	20 ♈ 24	Jun 25, 1976	01 ♉ 11	Nov 17, 1977	02 ♉ 27
Feb 11, 1975	20 ♈ 44	Jul 5, 1976	01 ♉ 30	Nov 27, 1977	02 ♉ 02
Feb 21, 1975	21 ♈ 07	Jul 15, 1976	01 ♉ 43	Dec 7, 1977	01 ♉ 41
Mar 3, 1975	21 ♈ 35	Jul 25, 1976	01 ♉ 52	Dec 17, 1977	01 ♉ 25
Mar 13, 1975	22 ♈ 05	Aug 4, 1976	01 ♉ 55	Dec 27, 1977	01 ♉ 13
Mar 23, 1975	22 ♈ 38	Aug 14, 1976	01 ♉ 53	Jan 6, 1978	01 ♉ 07
Apr 2, 1975	23 ♈ 13	Aug 24, 1976	01 ♉ 45	Jan 16, 1978	01 ♉ 07
Apr 12, 1975	23 ♈ 49	Sep 3, 1976	01 ♉ 33	Jan 26, 1978	01 ♉ 13
Apr 22, 1975	24 ♈ 25	Sep 13, 1976	01 ♉ 15	Feb 5, 1978	01 ♉ 24
May 2, 1975	25 ♈ 00	Sep 23, 1976	00 ♉ 54	Feb 15, 1978	01 ♉ 41
May 12, 1975	25 ♈ 34	Oct 3, 1976	00 ♉ 29	Feb 25, 1978	02 ♉ 03
May 22, 1975	26 ♈ 06	Oct 13, 1976	00 ♉ 03	Mar 7, 1978	02 ♉ 29
Jun 1, 1975	26 ♈ 36	Oct 23, 1976	29 ♈ 35	Mar 17, 1978	02 ♉ 59
Jun 11, 1975	27 ♈ 02	Nov 2, 1976	29 ♈ 07	Mar 27, 1978	03 ♉ 31
Jun 21, 1975	27 ♈ 25	Nov 12, 1976	28 ♈ 40	Apr 6, 1978	04 ♉ 06
Jul 1, 1975	27 ♈ 44	Nov 22, 1976	28 ♈ 15	Apr 16, 1978	04 ♉ 43
Jul 11, 1975	27 ♈ 57	Dec 2, 1976	27 ♈ 54	Apr 26, 1978	05 ♉ 20
Jul 21, 1975	28 ♈ 06	Dec 12, 1976	27 ♈ 37	May 6, 1978	05 ♉ 58
Jul 31, 1975	28 ♈ 10	Dec 22, 1976	27 ♈ 25	May 16, 1978	06 ♉ 35
Aug 10, 1975	28 ♈ 08	Jan 1, 1977	27 ♈ 19	May 26, 1978	07 ♉ 10
Aug 20, 1975	28 ♈ 01	Jan 11, 1977	27 ♈ 18	Jun 5, 1978	07 ♉ 43
Aug 30, 1975	27 ♈ 49	Jan 21, 1977	27 ♈ 23	Jun 15, 1978	08 ♉ 13
Sep 9, 1975	27 ♈ 32	Jan 31, 1977	27 ♈ 34	Jun 25, 1978	08 ♉ 40
Sep 19, 1975	27 ♈ 11	Feb 10, 1977	27 ♈ 50	Jul 5, 1978	09 ♉ 03
Sep 29, 1975	26 ♈ 47	Feb 20, 1977	28 ♈ 11	Jul 15, 1978	09 ♉ 22
Oct 9, 1975	26 ♈ 21	Mar 2, 1977	28 ♈ 36	Jul 25, 1978	09 ♉ 35
Oct 19, 1975	25 ♈ 53	Mar 12, 1977	29 ♈ 05	Aug 4, 1978	09 ♉ 44
Oct 29, 1975	25 ♈ 26	Mar 22, 1977	29 ♈ 37	Aug 14, 1978	09 ♉ 46

Chiron Locations 1920 - 2010

Date	Location	Date	Location	Date	Location
Aug 24, 1978	09 ♉ 43	Jan 16, 1980	09 ♉ 08	Jun 9, 1981	20 ♉ 04
Sep 3, 1978	09 ♉ 35	Jan 26, 1980	09 ♉ 09	Jun 19, 1981	20 ♉ 39
Sep 13, 1978	09 ♉ 21	Feb 5, 1980	09 ♉ 16	Jun 29, 1981	21 ♉ 12
Sep 23, 1978	09 ♉ 03	Feb 15, 1980	09 ♉ 29	Jul 9, 1981	21 ♉ 41
Oct 3, 1978	08 ♉ 41	Feb 25, 1980	09 ♉ 48	Jul 19, 1981	22 ♉ 05
Oct 13, 1978	08 ♉ 15	Mar 6, 1980	10 ♉ 11	Jul 29, 1981	22 ♉ 25
Oct 23, 1978	07 ♉ 47	Mar 16, 1980	10 ♉ 39	Aug 8, 1981	22 ♉ 40
Nov 2, 1978	07 ♉ 18	Mar 26, 1980	11 ♉ 11	Aug 18, 1981	22 ♉ 49
Nov 12, 1978	06 ♉ 49	Apr 5, 1980	11 ♉ 45	Aug 28, 1981	22 ♉ 52
Nov 22, 1978	06 ♉ 22	Apr 15, 1980	12 ♉ 22	Sep 7, 1981	22 ♉ 49
Dec 2, 1978	05 ♉ 57	Apr 25, 1980	13 ♉ 01	Sep 17, 1981	22 ♉ 40
Dec 12, 1978	05 ♉ 36	May 5, 1980	13 ♉ 40	Sep 27, 1981	22 ♉ 25
Dec 22, 1978	05 ♉ 20	May 15, 1980	14 ♉ 19	Oct 7, 1981	22 ♉ 05
Jan 1, 1979	05 ♉ 09	May 25, 1980	14 ♉ 57	Oct 17, 1981	21 ♉ 41
Jan 11, 1979	05 ♉ 03	Jun 4, 1980	15 ♉ 34	Oct 27, 1981	21 ♉ 13
Jan 21, 1979	05 ♉ 04	Jun 14, 1980	16 ♉ 09	Nov 6, 1981	20 ♉ 43
Jan 31, 1979	05 ♉ 10	Jun 24, 1980	16 ♉ 40	Nov 16, 1981	20 ♉ 12
Feb 10, 1979	05 ♉ 22	Jul 4, 1980	17 ♉ 08	Nov 26, 1981	19 ♉ 42
Feb 20, 1979	05 ♉ 40	Jul 14, 1980	17 ♉ 32	Dec 6, 1981	19 ♉ 13
Mar 2, 1979	06 ♉ 02	Jul 24, 1980	17 ♉ 51	Dec 16, 1981	18 ♉ 47
Mar 12, 1979	06 ♉ 29	Aug 3, 1980	18 ♉ 05	Dec 26, 1981	18 ♉ 26
Mar 22, 1979	07 ♉ 00	Aug 13, 1980	18 ♉ 14	Jan 5, 1982	18 ♉ 09
Apr 1, 1979	07 ♉ 34	Aug 23, 1980	18 ♉ 17	Jan 15, 1982	17 ♉ 58
Apr 11, 1979	08 ♉ 10	Sep 2, 1980	18 ♉ 14	Jan 25, 1982	17 ♉ 54
Apr 21, 1979	08 ♉ 47	Sep 12, 1980	18 ♉ 05	Feb 4, 1982	17 ♉ 56
May 1, 1979	09 ♉ 25	Sep 22, 1980	17 ♉ 50	Feb 14, 1982	18 ♉ 04
May 11, 1979	10 ♉ 03	Oct 2, 1980	17 ♉ 31	Feb 24, 1982	18 ♉ 19
May 21, 1979	10 ♉ 41	Oct 12, 1980	17 ♉ 07	Mar 6, 1982	18 ♉ 39
May 31, 1979	11 ♉ 17	Oct 22, 1980	16 ♉ 40	Mar 16, 1982	19 ♉ 04
Jun 10, 1979	11 ♉ 51	Nov 1, 1980	16 ♉ 11	Mar 26, 1982	19 ♉ 34
Jun 20, 1979	12 ♉ 22	Nov 11, 1980	15 ♉ 41	Apr 5, 1982	20 ♉ 08
Jun 30, 1979	12 ♉ 49	Nov 21, 1980	15 ♉ 11	Apr 15, 1982	20 ♉ 45
Jul 10, 1979	13 ♉ 12	Dec 1, 1980	14 ♉ 43	Apr 25, 1982	21 ♉ 24
Jul 20, 1979	13 ♉ 31	Dec 11, 1980	14 ♉ 17	May 5, 1982	22 ♉ 05
Jul 30, 1979	13 ♉ 45	Dec 21, 1980	13 ♉ 56	May 15, 1982	22 ♉ 46
Aug 9, 1979	13 ♉ 53	Dec 31, 1980	13 ♉ 40	May 25, 1982	23 ♉ 28
Aug 19, 1979	13 ♉ 56	Jan 10, 1981	13 ♉ 29	Jun 4, 1982	24 ♉ 09
Aug 29, 1979	13 ♉ 53	Jan 20, 1981	13 ♉ 24	Jun 14, 1982	24 ♉ 48
Sep 8, 1979	13 ♉ 44	Jan 30, 1981	13 ♉ 26	Jun 24, 1982	25 ♉ 25
Sep 18, 1979	13 ♉ 30	Feb 9, 1981	13 ♉ 34	Jul 4, 1982	25 ♉ 58
Sep 28, 1979	13 ♉ 11	Feb 19, 1981	13 ♉ 47	Jul 14, 1982	26 ♉ 29
Oct 8, 1979	12 ♉ 48	Mar 1, 1981	14 ♉ 07	Jul 24, 1982	26 ♉ 54
Oct 18, 1979	12 ♉ 21	Mar 11, 1981	14 ♉ 31	Aug 3, 1982	27 ♉ 15
Oct 28, 1979	11 ♉ 53	Mar 21, 1981	14 ♉ 60	Aug 13, 1982	27 ♉ 31
Nov 7, 1979	11 ♉ 23	Mar 31, 1981	15 ♉ 33	Aug 23, 1982	27 ♉ 40
Nov 17, 1979	10 ♉ 54	Apr 10, 1981	16 ♉ 08	Sep 2, 1982	27 ♉ 44
Nov 27, 1979	10 ♉ 26	Apr 20, 1981	16 ♉ 46	Sep 12, 1982	27 ♉ 41
Dec 7, 1979	10 ♉ 02	Apr 30, 1981	17 ♉ 26	Sep 22, 1982	27 ♉ 32
Dec 17, 1979	09 ♉ 40	May 10, 1981	18 ♉ 06	Oct 2, 1982	27 ♉ 17
Dec 27, 1979	09 ♉ 24	May 20, 1981	18 ♉ 46	Oct 12, 1982	26 ♉ 57
Jan 6, 1980	09 ♉ 13	May 30, 1981	19 ♉ 26	Oct 22, 1982	26 ♉ 32

Chiron Locations 1920 - 2010

Nov 1, 1982	26 ♉ 04	Mar 25, 1984	29 ♉ 02	Aug 17, 1985	13 ♊ 57
Nov 11, 1982	25 ♉ 33	Apr 4, 1984	29 ♉ 34	Aug 27, 1985	14 ♊ 18
Nov 21, 1982	25 ♉ 01	Apr 14, 1984	00 ♊ 11	Sep 6, 1985	14 ♊ 32
Dec 1, 1982	24 ♉ 30	Apr 24, 1984	00 ♊ 50	Sep 16, 1985	14 ♊ 39
Dec 11, 1982	24 ♉ 00	May 4, 1984	01 ♊ 32	Sep 26, 1985	14 ♊ 39
Dec 21, 1982	23 ♉ 34	May 14, 1984	02 ♊ 16	Oct 6, 1985	14 ♊ 32
Dec 31, 1982	23 ♉ 12	May 24, 1984	03 ♊ 01	Oct 16, 1985	14 ♊ 18
Jan 10, 1983	22 ♉ 55	Jun 3, 1984	03 ♊ 46	Oct 26, 1985	13 ♊ 58
Jan 20, 1983	22 ♉ 44	Jun 13, 1984	04 ♊ 30	Nov 5, 1985	13 ♊ 33
Jan 30, 1983	22 ♉ 40	Jun 23, 1984	05 ♊ 13	Nov 15, 1985	13 ♊ 03
Feb 9, 1983	22 ♉ 42	Jul 3, 1984	05 ♊ 53	Nov 25, 1985	12 ♊ 29
Feb 19, 1983	22 ♉ 51	Jul 13, 1984	06 ♊ 31	Dec 5, 1985	11 ♊ 55
Mar 1, 1983	23 ♉ 06	Jul 23, 1984	07 ♊ 04	Dec 15, 1985	11 ♊ 20
Mar 11, 1983	23 ♉ 27	Aug 2, 1984	07 ♊ 33	Dec 25, 1985	10 ♊ 47
Mar 21, 1983	23 ♉ 53	Aug 12, 1984	07 ♊ 57	Jan 4, 1986	10 ♊ 17
Mar 31, 1983	24 ♉ 24	Aug 22, 1984	08 ♊ 15	Jan 14, 1986	09 ♊ 52
Apr 10, 1983	24 ♉ 59	Sep 1, 1984	08 ♊ 27	Jan 24, 1986	09 ♊ 33
Apr 20, 1983	25 ♉ 38	Sep 11, 1984	08 ♊ 33	Feb 3, 1986	09 ♊ 20
Apr 30, 1983	26 ♉ 18	Sep 21, 1984	08 ♊ 31	Feb 13, 1986	09 ♊ 15
May 10, 1983	27 ♉ 01	Oct 1, 1984	08 ♊ 23	Feb 23, 1986	09 ♊ 16
May 20, 1983	27 ♉ 44	Oct 11, 1984	08 ♊ 09	Mar 5, 1986	09 ♊ 26
May 30, 1983	28 ♉ 27	Oct 21, 1984	07 ♊ 49	Mar 15, 1986	09 ♊ 42
Jun 9, 1983	29 ♉ 09	Oct 31, 1984	07 ♊ 23	Mar 25, 1986	10 ♊ 05
Jun 19, 1983	29 ♉ 50	Nov 10, 1984	06 ♊ 54	Apr 4, 1986	10 ♊ 34
Jun 29, 1983	00 ♊ 28	Nov 20, 1984	06 ♊ 21	Apr 14, 1986	11 ♊ 09
Jul 9, 1983	01 ♊ 04	Nov 30, 1984	05 ♊ 47	Apr 24, 1986	11 ♊ 48
Jul 19, 1983	01 ♊ 35	Dec 10, 1984	05 ♊ 14	May 4, 1986	12 ♊ 31
Jul 29, 1983	02 ♊ 02	Dec 20, 1984	04 ♊ 42	May 14, 1986	13 ♊ 17
Aug 8, 1983	02 ♊ 25	Dec 30, 1984	04 ♊ 14	May 24, 1986	14 ♊ 05
Aug 18, 1983	02 ♊ 41	Jan 9, 1985	03 ♊ 50	Jun 3, 1986	14 ♊ 54
Aug 28, 1983	02 ♊ 52	Jan 19, 1985	03 ♊ 32	Jun 13, 1986	15 ♊ 43
Sep 7, 1983	02 ♊ 56	Jan 29, 1985	03 ♊ 20	Jun 23, 1986	16 ♊ 33
Sep 17, 1983	02 ♊ 54	Feb 8, 1985	03 ♊ 16	Jul 3, 1986	17 ♊ 20
Sep 27, 1983	02 ♊ 45	Feb 18, 1985	03 ♊ 18	Jul 13, 1986	18 ♊ 06
Oct 7, 1983	02 ♊ 30	Feb 28, 1985	03 ♊ 27	Jul 23, 1986	18 ♊ 49
Oct 17, 1983	02 ♊ 10	Mar 10, 1985	03 ♊ 43	Aug 2, 1986	19 ♊ 28
Oct 27, 1983	01 ♊ 45	Mar 20, 1985	04 ♊ 06	Aug 12, 1986	20 ♊ 02
Nov 6, 1983	01 ♊ 16	Mar 30, 1985	04 ♊ 34	Aug 22, 1986	20 ♊ 31
Nov 16, 1983	00 ♊ 44	Apr 9, 1985	05 ♊ 07	Sep 1, 1986	20 ♊ 54
Nov 26, 1983	00 ♊ 12	Apr 19, 1985	05 ♊ 45	Sep 11, 1986	21 ♊ 11
Dec 6, 1983	29 ♉ 39	Apr 29, 1985	06 ♊ 26	Sep 21, 1986	21 ♊ 20
Dec 16, 1983	29 ♉ 09	May 9, 1985	07 ♊ 10	Oct 1, 1986	21 ♊ 23
Dec 26, 1983	28 ♉ 42	May 19, 1985	07 ♊ 56	Oct 11, 1986	21 ♊ 17
Jan 5, 1984	28 ♉ 19	May 29, 1985	08 ♊ 43	Oct 21, 1986	21 ♊ 05
Jan 15, 1984	28 ♉ 01	Jun 8, 1985	09 ♊ 30	Oct 31, 1986	20 ♊ 46
Jan 25, 1984	27 ♉ 50	Jun 18, 1985	10 ♊ 16	Nov 10, 1986	20 ♊ 20
Feb 4, 1984	27 ♉ 46	Jun 28, 1985	11 ♊ 01	Nov 20, 1986	19 ♊ 50
Feb 14, 1984	27 ♉ 48	Jul 8, 1985	11 ♊ 44	Nov 30, 1986	19 ♊ 16
Feb 24, 1984	27 ♉ 57	Jul 18, 1985	12 ♊ 24	Dec 10, 1986	18 ♊ 40
Mar 5, 1984	28 ♉ 13	Jul 28, 1985	12 ♊ 60	Dec 20, 1986	18 ♊ 04
Mar 15, 1984	28 ♉ 35	Aug 7, 1985	13 ♊ 31	Dec 30, 1986	17 ♊ 29

Chiron Locations 1920 - 2010

Jan 9, 1987	16 ♊ 58	Jun 2, 1988	28 ♊ 13	Oct 25, 1989	16 ♋ 35
Jan 19, 1987	16 ♊ 31	Jun 12, 1988	29 ♊ 08	Nov 4, 1989	16 ♋ 33
Jan 29, 1987	16 ♊ 10	Jun 22, 1988	00 ♋ 03	Nov 14, 1989	16 ♋ 21
Feb 8, 1987	15 ♊ 56	Jul 2, 1988	00 ♋ 59	Nov 24, 1989	16 ♋ 01
Feb 18, 1987	15 ♊ 49	Jul 12, 1988	01 ♋ 54	Dec 4, 1989	15 ♋ 34
Feb 28, 1987	15 ♊ 50	Jul 22, 1988	02 ♋ 47	Dec 14, 1989	15 ♋ 01
Mar 10, 1987	15 ♊ 59	Aug 1, 1988	03 ♋ 38	Dec 24, 1989	14 ♋ 23
Mar 20, 1987	16 ♊ 16	Aug 11, 1988	04 ♋ 25	Jan 3, 1990	13 ♋ 42
Mar 30, 1987	16 ♊ 39	Aug 21, 1988	05 ♋ 08	Jan 13, 1990	13 ♋ 01
Apr 9, 1987	17 ♊ 09	Aug 31, 1988	05 ♋ 46	Jan 23, 1990	12 ♋ 22
Apr 19, 1987	17 ♊ 44	Sep 10, 1988	06 ♋ 17	Feb 2, 1990	11 ♋ 46
Apr 29, 1987	18 ♊ 25	Sep 20, 1988	06 ♋ 42	Feb 12, 1990	11 ♋ 17
May 9, 1987	19 ♊ 10	Sep 30, 1988	06 ♋ 59	Feb 22, 1990	10 ♋ 54
May 19, 1987	19 ♊ 58	Oct 10, 1988	07 ♋ 08	Mar 4, 1990	10 ♋ 39
May 29, 1987	20 ♊ 48	Oct 20, 1988	07 ♋ 09	Mar 14, 1990	10 ♋ 34
Jun 8, 1987	21 ♊ 40	Oct 30, 1988	07 ♋ 02	Mar 24, 1990	10 ♋ 37
Jun 18, 1987	22 ♊ 32	Nov 9, 1988	06 ♋ 47	Apr 3, 1990	10 ♋ 50
Jun 28, 1987	23 ♊ 24	Nov 19, 1988	06 ♋ 24	Apr 13, 1990	11 ♋ 11
Jul 8, 1987	24 ♊ 16	Nov 29, 1988	05 ♋ 55	Apr 23, 1990	11 ♋ 40
Jul 18, 1987	25 ♊ 05	Dec 9, 1988	05 ♋ 20	May 3, 1990	12 ♋ 17
Jul 28, 1987	25 ♊ 51	Dec 19, 1988	04 ♋ 43	May 13, 1990	13 ♋ 01
Aug 7, 1987	26 ♊ 34	Dec 29, 1988	04 ♋ 03	May 23, 1990	13 ♋ 50
Aug 17, 1987	27 ♊ 12	Jan 8, 1989	03 ♋ 24	Jun 2, 1990	14 ♋ 44
Aug 27, 1987	27 ♊ 45	Jan 18, 1989	02 ♋ 48	Jun 12, 1990	15 ♋ 42
Sep 6, 1987	28 ♊ 12	Jan 28, 1989	02 ♋ 16	Jun 22, 1990	16 ♋ 43
Sep 16, 1987	28 ♊ 32	Feb 7, 1989	01 ♋ 50	Jul 2, 1990	17 ♋ 46
Sep 26, 1987	28 ♊ 44	Feb 17, 1989	01 ♋ 31	Jul 12, 1990	18 ♋ 51
Oct 6, 1987	28 ♊ 50	Feb 27, 1989	01 ♋ 20	Jul 22, 1990	19 ♋ 55
Oct 16, 1987	28 ♊ 47	Mar 9, 1989	01 ♋ 18	Aug 1, 1990	20 ♋ 59
Oct 26, 1987	28 ♊ 36	Mar 19, 1989	01 ♋ 24	Aug 11, 1990	22 ♋ 00
Nov 5, 1987	28 ♊ 19	Mar 29, 1989	01 ♋ 39	Aug 21, 1990	22 ♋ 59
Nov 15, 1987	27 ♊ 54	Apr 8, 1989	02 ♋ 02	Aug 31, 1990	23 ♋ 55
Nov 25, 1987	27 ♊ 24	Apr 18, 1989	02 ♋ 32	Sep 10, 1990	24 ♋ 45
Dec 5, 1987	26 ♊ 50	Apr 28, 1989	03 ♋ 09	Sep 20, 1990	25 ♋ 30
Dec 15, 1987	26 ♊ 13	May 8, 1989	03 ♋ 52	Sep 30, 1990	26 ♋ 09
Dec 25, 1987	25 ♊ 35	May 18, 1989	04 ♋ 40	Oct 10, 1990	26 ♋ 39
Jan 4, 1988	24 ♊ 58	May 28, 1989	05 ♋ 32	Oct 20, 1990	27 ♋ 02
Jan 14, 1988	24 ♊ 25	Jun 7, 1989	06 ♋ 28	Oct 30, 1990	27 ♋ 15
Jan 24, 1988	23 ♊ 56	Jun 17, 1989	07 ♋ 25	Nov 9, 1990	27 ♋ 19
Feb 3, 1988	23 ♊ 32	Jun 27, 1989	08 ♋ 25	Nov 19, 1990	27 ♋ 14
Feb 13, 1988	23 ♊ 16	Jul 7, 1989	09 ♋ 25	Nov 29, 1990	26 ♋ 59
Feb 23, 1988	23 ♊ 08	Jul 17, 1989	10 ♋ 24	Dec 9, 1990	26 ♋ 35
Mar 4, 1988	23 ♊ 08	Jul 27, 1989	11 ♋ 22	Dec 19, 1990	26 ♋ 04
Mar 14, 1988	23 ♊ 16	Aug 6, 1989	12 ♋ 18	Dec 29, 1990	25 ♋ 27
Mar 24, 1988	23 ♊ 32	Aug 16, 1989	13 ♋ 11	Jan 8, 1991	24 ♋ 47
Apr 3, 1988	23 ♊ 55	Aug 26, 1989	13 ♋ 59	Jan 18, 1991	24 ♋ 04
Apr 13, 1988	24 ♊ 25	Sep 5, 1989	14 ♋ 43	Jan 28, 1991	23 ♋ 22
Apr 23, 1988	25 ♊ 02	Sep 15, 1989	15 ♋ 20	Feb 7, 1991	22 ♋ 42
May 3, 1988	25 ♊ 44	Sep 25, 1989	15 ♋ 51	Feb 17, 1991	22 ♋ 08
May 13, 1988	26 ♊ 30	Oct 5, 1989	16 ♋ 14	Feb 27, 1991	21 ♋ 40
May 23, 1988	27 ♊ 20	Oct 15, 1989	16 ♋ 29	Mar 9, 1991	21 ♋ 21

Chiron Locations 1920 - 2010

Date	Location	Date	Location	Date	Location
Mar 19, 1991	21 ♋ 10	Aug 10, 1992	13 ♌ 52	Jan 2, 1994	09 ♍ 11
Mar 29, 1991	21 ♋ 09	Aug 20, 1992	15 ♌ 07	Jan 12, 1994	08 ♍ 55
Apr 8, 1991	21 ♋ 18	Aug 30, 1992	16 ♌ 20	Jan 22, 1994	08 ♍ 28
Apr 18, 1991	21 ♋ 36	Sep 9, 1992	17 ♌ 32	Feb 1, 1994	07 ♍ 53
Apr 28, 1991	22 ♋ 03	Sep 19, 1992	18 ♌ 40	Feb 11, 1994	07 ♍ 11
May 8, 1991	22 ♋ 39	Sep 29, 1992	19 ♌ 43	Feb 21, 1994	06 ♍ 25
May 18, 1991	23 ♋ 22	Oct 9, 1992	20 ♌ 41	Mar 3, 1994	05 ♍ 38
May 28, 1991	24 ♋ 12	Oct 19, 1992	21 ♌ 32	Mar 13, 1994	04 ♍ 53
Jun 7, 1991	25 ♋ 07	Oct 29, 1992	22 ♌ 16	Mar 23, 1994	04 ♍ 12
Jun 17, 1991	26 ♋ 07	Nov 8, 1992	22 ♌ 50	Apr 2, 1994	03 ♍ 37
Jun 27, 1991	27 ♋ 11	Nov 18, 1992	23 ♌ 15	Apr 12, 1994	03 ♍ 11
Jul 7, 1991	28 ♋ 18	Nov 28, 1992	23 ♌ 30	Apr 22, 1994	02 ♍ 55
Jul 17, 1991	29 ♋ 27	Dec 8, 1992	23 ♌ 33	May 2, 1994	02 ♍ 50
Jul 27, 1991	00 ♌ 36	Dec 18, 1992	23 ♌ 26	May 12, 1994	02 ♍ 55
Aug 6, 1991	01 ♌ 46	Dec 28, 1992	23 ♌ 09	May 22, 1994	03 ♍ 12
Aug 16, 1991	02 ♌ 54	Jan 7, 1993	22 ♌ 42	Jun 1, 1994	03 ♍ 40
Aug 26, 1991	04 ♌ 00	Jan 17, 1993	22 ♌ 06	Jun 11, 1994	04 ♍ 18
Sep 5, 1991	05 ♌ 03	Jan 27, 1993	21 ♌ 25	Jun 21, 1994	05 ♍ 04
Sep 15, 1991	06 ♌ 02	Feb 6, 1993	20 ♌ 40	Jul 1, 1994	05 ♍ 60
Sep 25, 1991	06 ♌ 56	Feb 16, 1993	19 ♌ 54	Jul 11, 1994	07 ♍ 02
Oct 5, 1991	07 ♌ 43	Feb 26, 1993	19 ♌ 10	Jul 21, 1994	08 ♍ 11
Oct 15, 1991	08 ♌ 24	Mar 8, 1993	18 ♌ 30	Jul 31, 1994	09 ♍ 25
Oct 25, 1991	08 ♌ 56	Mar 18, 1993	17 ♌ 56	Aug 10, 1994	10 ♍ 43
Nov 4, 1991	09 ♌ 18	Mar 28, 1993	17 ♌ 31	Aug 20, 1994	12 ♍ 05
Nov 14, 1991	09 ♌ 32	Apr 7, 1993	17 ♌ 15	Aug 30, 1994	13 ♍ 29
Nov 24, 1991	09 ♌ 35	Apr 17, 1993	17 ♌ 10	Sep 9, 1994	14 ♍ 53
Dec 4, 1991	09 ♌ 27	Apr 27, 1993	17 ♌ 15	Sep 19, 1994	16 ♍ 18
Dec 14, 1991	09 ♌ 11	May 7, 1993	17 ♌ 31	Sep 29, 1994	17 ♍ 42
Dec 24, 1991	08 ♌ 45	May 17, 1993	17 ♌ 58	Oct 9, 1994	19 ♍ 04
Jan 3, 1992	08 ♌ 11	May 27, 1993	18 ♌ 34	Oct 19, 1994	20 ♍ 22
Jan 13, 1992	07 ♌ 31	Jun 6, 1993	19 ♌ 19	Oct 29, 1994	21 ♍ 35
Jan 23, 1992	06 ♌ 48	Jun 16, 1993	20 ♌ 12	Nov 8, 1994	22 ♍ 43
Feb 2, 1992	06 ♌ 03	Jun 26, 1993	21 ♌ 12	Nov 18, 1994	23 ♍ 44
Feb 12, 1992	05 ♌ 20	Jul 6, 1993	22 ♌ 17	Nov 28, 1994	24 ♍ 37
Feb 22, 1992	04 ♌ 41	Jul 16, 1993	23 ♌ 28	Dec 8, 1994	25 ♍ 20
Mar 3, 1992	04 ♌ 07	Jul 26, 1993	24 ♌ 43	Dec 18, 1994	25 ♍ 53
Mar 13, 1992	03 ♌ 41	Aug 5, 1993	26 ♌ 01	Dec 28, 1994	26 ♍ 15
Mar 23, 1992	03 ♌ 24	Aug 15, 1993	27 ♌ 20	Jan 7, 1995	26 ♍ 25
Apr 2, 1992	03 ♌ 17	Aug 25, 1993	28 ♌ 41	Jan 17, 1995	26 ♍ 23
Apr 12, 1992	03 ♌ 20	Sep 4, 1993	00 ♍ 01	Jan 27, 1995	26 ♍ 09
Apr 22, 1992	03 ♌ 33	Sep 14, 1993	01 ♍ 20	Feb 6, 1995	25 ♍ 45
May 2, 1992	03 ♌ 56	Sep 24, 1993	02 ♍ 37	Feb 16, 1995	25 ♍ 12
May 12, 1992	04 ♌ 29	Oct 4, 1993	03 ♍ 50	Feb 26, 1995	24 ♍ 31
May 22, 1992	05 ♌ 09	Oct 14, 1993	04 ♍ 59	Mar 8, 1995	23 ♍ 45
Jun 1, 1992	05 ♌ 58	Oct 24, 1993	06 ♍ 02	Mar 18, 1995	22 ♍ 58
Jun 11, 1992	06 ♌ 53	Nov 3, 1993	06 ♍ 57	Mar 28, 1995	22 ♍ 11
Jun 21, 1992	07 ♌ 54	Nov 13, 1993	07 ♍ 45	Apr 7, 1995	21 ♍ 23
Jul 1, 1992	09 ♌ 00	Nov 23, 1993	08 ♍ 24	Apr 17, 1995	20 ♍ 52
Jul 11, 1992	10 ♌ 10	Dec 3, 1993	08 ♍ 52	Apr 27, 1995	20 ♍ 24
Jul 21, 1992	11 ♌ 22	Dec 13, 1993	09 ♍ 10	May 7, 1995	20 ♍ 06
Jul 31, 1992	12 ♌ 37	Dec 23, 1993	09 ♍ 16	May 17, 1995	19 ♍ 58

Chiron Locations 1920 - 2010

Date	Position	Date	Position	Date	Position
May 27, 1995	20 ♍ 02	Oct 18, 1996	20 ♎ 58	Mar 12, 1998	18 ♏ 42
Jun 6, 1995	20 ♍ 18	Oct 28, 1996	22 ♎ 25	Mar 22, 1998	18 ♏ 26
Jun 16, 1995	20 ♍ 44	Nov 7, 1996	23 ♎ 50	Apr 1, 1998	17 ♏ 60
Jun 26, 1995	21 ♍ 20	Nov 17, 1996	25 ♎ 12	Apr 11, 1998	17 ♏ 26
Jul 6, 1995	22 ♍ 07	Nov 27, 1996	26 ♎ 30	Apr 21, 1998	16 ♏ 46
Jul 16, 1995	23 ♍ 02	Dec 7, 1996	27 ♎ 43	May 1, 1998	16 ♏ 01
Jul 26, 1995	24 ♍ 04	Dec 17, 1996	28 ♎ 49	May 11, 1998	15 ♏ 16
Aug 5, 1995	25 ♍ 14	Dec 27, 1996	29 ♎ 47	May 21, 1998	14 ♏ 32
Aug 15, 1995	26 ♍ 29	Jan 6, 1997	00 ♏ 36	May 31, 1998	13 ♏ 51
Aug 25, 1995	27 ♍ 48	Jan 16, 1997	01 ♏ 15	Jun 10, 1998	13 ♏ 17
Sep 4, 1995	29 ♍ 11	Jan 26, 1997	01 ♏ 43	Jun 20, 1998	12 ♏ 50
Sep 14, 1995	00 ♎ 37	Feb 5, 1997	02 ♏ 00	Jun 30, 1998	12 ♏ 33
Sep 24, 1995	02 ♎ 04	Feb 15, 1997	02 ♏ 05	Jul 10, 1998	12 ♏ 26
Oct 4, 1995	03 ♎ 32	Feb 25, 1997	01 ♏ 58	Jul 20, 1998	12 ♏ 29
Oct 14, 1995	04 ♎ 58	Mar 7, 1997	01 ♏ 40	Jul 30, 1998	12 ♏ 42
Oct 24, 1995	06 ♎ 23	Mar 17, 1997	01 ♏ 13	Aug 9, 1998	13 ♏ 06
Nov 3, 1995	07 ♎ 44	Mar 27, 1997	00 ♏ 36	Aug 19, 1998	13 ♏ 40
Nov 13, 1995	09 ♎ 01	Apr 6, 1997	29 ♎ 54	Aug 29, 1998	14 ♏ 23
Nov 23, 1995	10 ♎ 13	Apr 16, 1997	29 ♎ 08	Sep 8, 1998	15 ♏ 14
Dec 3, 1995	11 ♎ 17	Apr 26, 1997	28 ♎ 22	Sep 18, 1998	16 ♏ 12
Dec 13, 1995	12 ♎ 14	May 6, 1997	27 ♎ 37	Sep 28, 1998	17 ♏ 17
Dec 23, 1995	13 ♎ 01	May 16, 1997	26 ♎ 57	Oct 8, 1998	18 ♏ 27
Jan 2, 1996	13 ♎ 38	May 26, 1997	26 ♎ 24	Oct 18, 1998	19 ♏ 41
Jan 12, 1996	14 ♎ 04	Jun 5, 1997	25 ♎ 59	Oct 28, 1998	20 ♏ 58
Jan 22, 1996	14 ♎ 18	Jun 15, 1997	25 ♎ 45	Nov 7, 1998	22 ♏ 17
Feb 1, 1996	14 ♎ 20	Jun 25, 1997	25 ♎ 41	Nov 17, 1998	23 ♏ 38
Feb 11, 1996	14 ♎ 10	Jul 5, 1997	25 ♎ 48	Nov 27, 1998	24 ♏ 58
Feb 21, 1996	13 ♎ 49	Jul 15, 1997	26 ♎ 06	Dec 7, 1998	26 ♏ 16
Mar 2, 1996	13 ♎ 18	Jul 25, 1997	26 ♎ 34	Dec 17, 1998	27 ♏ 32
Mar 12, 1996	12 ♎ 39	Aug 4, 1997	27 ♎ 13	Dec 27, 1998	28 ♏ 44
Mar 22, 1996	11 ♎ 55	Aug 14, 1997	28 ♎ 00	Jan 6, 1999	29 ♏ 51
Apr 1, 1996	11 ♎ 08	Aug 24, 1997	28 ♎ 56	Jan 16, 1999	00 ♐ 52
Apr 11, 1996	10 ♎ 21	Sep 3, 1997	29 ♎ 59	Jan 26, 1999	01 ♐ 46
Apr 21, 1996	09 ♎ 37	Sep 13, 1997	01 ♏ 09	Feb 5, 1999	02 ♐ 31
May 1, 1996	08 ♎ 59	Sep 23, 1997	02 ♏ 23	Feb 15, 1999	03 ♐ 07
May 11, 1996	08 ♎ 28	Oct 3, 1997	03 ♏ 42	Feb 25, 1999	03 ♐ 33
May 21, 1996	08 ♎ 06	Oct 13, 1997	05 ♏ 04	Mar 7, 1999	03 ♐ 49
May 31, 1996	07 ♎ 55	Oct 23, 1997	06 ♏ 28	Mar 17, 1999	03 ♐ 54
Jun 10, 1996	07 ♎ 56	Nov 2, 1997	07 ♏ 52	Mar 27, 1999	03 ♐ 48
Jun 20, 1996	08 ♎ 07	Nov 12, 1997	09 ♏ 17	Apr 6, 1999	03 ♐ 32
Jun 30, 1996	08 ♎ 30	Nov 22, 1997	10 ♏ 39	Apr 16, 1999	03 ♐ 07
Jul 10, 1996	09 ♎ 03	Dec 2, 1997	11 ♏ 59	Apr 26, 1999	02 ♐ 34
Jul 20, 1996	09 ♎ 46	Dec 12, 1997	13 ♏ 15	May 6, 1999	01 ♐ 55
Jul 30, 1996	10 ♎ 38	Dec 22, 1997	14 ♏ 26	May 16, 1999	01 ♐ 12
Aug 9, 1996	11 ♎ 38	Jan 1, 1998	15 ♏ 31	May 26, 1999	00 ♐ 28
Aug 19, 1996	12 ♎ 46	Jan 11, 1998	16 ♏ 28	Jun 5, 1999	29 ♏ 45
Aug 29, 1996	13 ♎ 59	Jan 21, 1998	17 ♏ 17	Jun 15, 1999	29 ♏ 06
Sep 8, 1996	15 ♎ 17	Jan 31, 1998	17 ♏ 56	Jun 25, 1999	28 ♏ 32
Sep 18, 1996	16 ♎ 39	Feb 10, 1998	18 ♏ 24	Jul 5, 1999	28 ♏ 05
Sep 28, 1996	18 ♎ 04	Feb 20, 1998	18 ♏ 41	Jul 15, 1999	27 ♏ 46
Oct 8, 1996	19 ♎ 31	Mar 2, 1998	18 ♏ 47	Jul 25, 1999	27 ♏ 37

Chiron Locations 1920 - 2010

Aug 4, 1999	27 ♏ 38	Dec 26, 2000	21 ♐ 51	May 20, 2002	08 ♑ 24
Aug 14, 1999	27 ♏ 49	Jan 5, 2001	22 ♐ 59	May 30, 2002	07 ♑ 55
Aug 24, 1999	28 ♏ 09	Jan 15, 2001	24 ♐ 03	Jun 9, 2002	07 ♑ 22
Sep 3, 1999	28 ♏ 39	Jan 25, 2001	25 ♐ 04	Jun 19, 2002	06 ♑ 44
Sep 13, 1999	29 ♏ 18	Feb 4, 2001	25 ♐ 59	Jun 29, 2002	06 ♑ 05
Sep 23, 1999	00 ♐ 05	Feb 14, 2001	26 ♐ 49	Jul 9, 2002	05 ♑ 27
Oct 3, 1999	00 ♐ 59	Feb 24, 2001	27 ♐ 31	Jul 19, 2002	04 ♑ 51
Oct 13, 1999	01 ♐ 59	Mar 6, 2001	28 ♐ 05	Jul 29, 2002	04 ♑ 18
Oct 23, 1999	03 ♐ 04	Mar 16, 2001	28 ♐ 31	Aug 8, 2002	03 ♑ 51
Nov 2, 1999	04 ♐ 14	Mar 26, 2001	28 ♐ 48	Aug 18, 2002	03 ♑ 31
Nov 12, 1999	05 ♐ 26	Apr 5, 2001	28 ♐ 55	Aug 28, 2002	03 ♑ 18
Nov 22, 1999	06 ♐ 41	Apr 15, 2001	28 ♐ 53	Sep 7, 2002	03 ♑ 13
Dec 2, 1999	07 ♐ 56	Apr 25, 2001	28 ♐ 42	Sep 17, 2002	03 ♑ 17
Dec 12, 1999	09 ♐ 10	May 5, 2001	28 ♐ 22	Sep 27, 2002	03 ♑ 29
Dec 22, 1999	10 ♐ 23	May 15, 2001	27 ♐ 55	Oct 7, 2002	03 ♑ 50
Jan 1, 2000	11 ♐ 34	May 25, 2001	27 ♐ 22	Oct 17, 2002	04 ♑ 18
Jan 11, 2000	12 ♐ 41	Jun 4, 2001	26 ♐ 44	Oct 27, 2002	04 ♑ 53
Jan 21, 2000	13 ♐ 42	Jun 14, 2001	26 ♐ 04	Nov 6, 2002	05 ♑ 35
Jan 31, 2000	14 ♐ 38	Jun 24, 2001	25 ♐ 24	Nov 16, 2002	06 ♑ 23
Feb 10, 2000	15 ♐ 26	Jul 4, 2001	24 ♐ 45	Nov 26, 2002	07 ♑ 15
Feb 20, 2000	16 ♐ 07	Jul 14, 2001	24 ♐ 09	Dec 6, 2002	08 ♑ 10
Mar 1, 2000	16 ♐ 38	Jul 24, 2001	23 ♐ 39	Dec 16, 2002	09 ♑ 09
Mar 11, 2000	17 ♐ 00	Aug 3, 2001	23 ♐ 15	Dec 26, 2002	10 ♑ 09
Mar 21, 2000	17 ♐ 12	Aug 13, 2001	22 ♐ 60	Jan 5, 2003	11 ♑ 09
Mar 31, 2000	17 ♐ 14	Aug 23, 2001	22 ♐ 52	Jan 15, 2003	12 ♑ 09
Apr 10, 2000	17 ♐ 06	Sep 2, 2001	22 ♐ 53	Jan 25, 2003	13 ♑ 08
Apr 20, 2000	16 ♐ 49	Sep 12, 2001	23 ♐ 04	Feb 4, 2003	14 ♑ 03
Apr 30, 2000	16 ♐ 23	Sep 22, 2001	23 ♐ 23	Feb 14, 2003	14 ♑ 56
May 10, 2000	15 ♐ 50	Oct 2, 2001	23 ♐ 50	Feb 24, 2003	15 ♑ 43
May 20, 2000	15 ♐ 12	Oct 12, 2001	24 ♐ 26	Mar 6, 2003	16 ♑ 25
May 30, 2000	14 ♐ 31	Oct 22, 2001	25 ♐ 08	Mar 16, 2003	17 ♑ 01
Jun 9, 2000	13 ♐ 49	Nov 1, 2001	25 ♐ 57	Mar 26, 2003	17 ♑ 30
Jun 19, 2000	13 ♐ 08	Nov 11, 2001	26 ♐ 51	Apr 5, 2003	17 ♑ 51
Jun 29, 2000	12 ♐ 30	Nov 21, 2001	27 ♐ 49	Apr 15, 2003	18 ♑ 04
Jul 9, 2000	11 ♐ 57	Dec 1, 2001	28 ♐ 50	Apr 25, 2003	18 ♑ 08
Jul 19, 2000	11 ♐ 31	Dec 11, 2001	29 ♐ 54	May 5, 2003	18 ♑ 05
Jul 29, 2000	11 ♐ 13	Dec 21, 2001	00 ♑ 59	May 15, 2003	17 ♑ 53
Aug 8, 2000	11 ♐ 04	Dec 31, 2001	02 ♑ 03	May 25, 2003	17 ♑ 34
Aug 18, 2000	11 ♐ 04	Jan 10, 2002	03 ♑ 07	Jun 4, 2003	17 ♑ 09
Aug 28, 2000	11 ♐ 14	Jan 20, 2002	04 ♑ 09	Jun 14, 2003	16 ♑ 38
Sep 7, 2000	11 ♐ 33	Jan 30, 2002	05 ♑ 07	Jun 24, 2003	16 ♑ 04
Sep 17, 2000	12 ♐ 01	Feb 9, 2002	06 ♑ 01	Jul 4, 2003	15 ♑ 27
Sep 27, 2000	12 ♐ 38	Feb 19, 2002	06 ♑ 50	Jul 14, 2003	14 ♑ 50
Oct 7, 2000	13 ♐ 22	Mar 1, 2002	07 ♑ 33	Jul 24, 2003	14 ♑ 14
Oct 17, 2000	14 ♐ 12	Mar 11, 2002	08 ♑ 08	Aug 3, 2003	13 ♑ 40
Oct 27, 2000	15 ♐ 09	Mar 21, 2002	08 ♑ 36	Aug 13, 2003	13 ♑ 12
Nov 6, 2000	16 ♐ 10	Mar 31, 2002	08 ♑ 56	Aug 23, 2003	12 ♑ 49
Nov 16, 2000	17 ♐ 15	Apr 10, 2002	09 ♑ 06	Sep 2, 2003	12 ♑ 32
Nov 26, 2000	18 ♐ 23	Apr 20, 2002	09 ♑ 08	Sep 12, 2003	12 ♑ 23
Dec 6, 2000	19 ♐ 32	Apr 30, 2002	09 ♑ 02	Sep 22, 2003	12 ♑ 22
Dec 16, 2000	20 ♐ 42	May 10, 2002	08 ♑ 47	Oct 2, 2003	12 ♑ 29

Chiron Locations 1920 - 2010

Oct 12, 2003	12 ♑ 44	
Oct 22, 2003	13 ♑ 07	
Nov 1, 2003	13 ♑ 37	
Nov 11, 2003	14 ♑ 13	
Nov 21, 2003	14 ♑ 55	
Dec 1, 2003	15 ♑ 42	
Dec 11, 2003	16 ♑ 33	
Dec 21, 2003	17 ♑ 27	
Dec 31, 2003	18 ♑ 22	
Jan 10, 2004	19 ♑ 19	
Jan 20, 2004	20 ♑ 15	
Jan 30, 2004	21 ♑ 11	
Feb 9, 2004	22 ♑ 04	
Feb 19, 2004	22 ♑ 54	
Feb 29, 2004	23 ♑ 40	
Mar 10, 2004	24 ♑ 20	
Mar 20, 2004	24 ♑ 56	
Mar 30, 2004	25 ♑ 24	
Apr 9, 2004	25 ♑ 46	
Apr 19, 2004	26 ♑ 00	
Apr 29, 2004	26 ♑ 07	
May 9, 2004	26 ♑ 05	
May 19, 2004	25 ♑ 56	
May 29, 2004	25 ♑ 40	
Jun 8, 2004	25 ♑ 18	
Jun 18, 2004	24 ♑ 50	
Jun 28, 2004	24 ♑ 18	
Jul 8, 2004	23 ♑ 43	
Jul 18, 2004	23 ♑ 07	
Jul 28, 2004	22 ♑ 32	
Aug 7, 2004	21 ♑ 58	
Aug 17, 2004	21 ♑ 29	
Aug 27, 2004	21 ♑ 04	
Sep 6, 2004	20 ♑ 46	
Sep 16, 2004	20 ♑ 34	
Sep 26, 2004	20 ♑ 30	
Oct 6, 2004	20 ♑ 33	
Oct 16, 2004	20 ♑ 44	
Oct 26, 2004	21 ♑ 02	
Nov 5, 2004	21 ♑ 28	
Nov 15, 2004	21 ♑ 59	
Nov 25, 2004	22 ♑ 37	
Dec 5, 2004	23 ♑ 20	
Dec 15, 2004	24 ♑ 06	
Dec 25, 2004	24 ♑ 56	
Jan 4, 2005	25 ♑ 48	
Jan 14, 2005	26 ♑ 41	
Jan 24, 2005	27 ♑ 34	
Feb 3, 2005	28 ♑ 27	
Feb 13, 2005	29 ♑ 17	
Feb 23, 2005	00 ♒ 05	
Mar 5, 2005	00 ♒ 49	
Mar 15, 2005	01 ♒ 29	
Mar 25, 2005	02 ♒ 03	
Apr 4, 2005	02 ♒ 31	
Apr 14, 2005	02 ♒ 53	
Apr 24, 2005	03 ♒ 08	
May 4, 2005	03 ♒ 15	
May 14, 2005	03 ♒ 15	
May 24, 2005	03 ♒ 08	
Jun 3, 2005	02 ♒ 54	
Jun 13, 2005	02 ♒ 34	
Jun 23, 2005	02 ♒ 08	
Jul 3, 2005	01 ♒ 38	
Jul 13, 2005	01 ♒ 05	
Jul 23, 2005	00 ♒ 31	
Aug 2, 2005	29 ♑ 56	
Aug 12, 2005	29 ♑ 23	
Aug 22, 2005	28 ♑ 54	
Sep 1, 2005	28 ♑ 28	
Sep 11, 2005	28 ♑ 08	
Sep 21, 2005	27 ♑ 55	
Oct 1, 2005	27 ♑ 48	
Oct 11, 2005	27 ♑ 49	
Oct 21, 2005	27 ♑ 56	
Oct 31, 2005	28 ♑ 12	
Nov 10, 2005	28 ♑ 34	
Nov 20, 2005	29 ♑ 02	
Nov 30, 2005	29 ♑ 36	
Dec 10, 2005	00 ♒ 15	
Dec 20, 2005	00 ♒ 58	
Dec 30, 2005	01 ♒ 45	
Jan 9, 2006	02 ♒ 33	
Jan 19, 2006	03 ♒ 23	
Jan 29, 2006	04 ♒ 14	
Feb 8, 2006	05 ♒ 04	
Feb 18, 2006	05 ♒ 52	
Feb 28, 2006	06 ♒ 38	
Mar 10, 2006	07 ♒ 20	
Mar 20, 2006	07 ♒ 58	
Mar 30, 2006	08 ♒ 31	
Apr 9, 2006	08 ♒ 59	
Apr 19, 2006	09 ♒ 21	
Apr 29, 2006	09 ♒ 36	
May 9, 2006	09 ♒ 43	
May 19, 2006	09 ♒ 44	
May 29, 2006	09 ♒ 38	
Jun 8, 2006	09 ♒ 26	
Jun 18, 2006	09 ♒ 07	
Jun 28, 2006	08 ♒ 43	
Jul 8, 2006	08 ♒ 15	
Jul 18, 2006	07 ♒ 43	
Jul 28, 2006	07 ♒ 10	
Aug 7, 2006	06 ♒ 37	
Aug 17, 2006	06 ♒ 04	
Aug 27, 2006	05 ♒ 35	
Sep 6, 2006	05 ♒ 09	
Sep 16, 2006	04 ♒ 49	
Sep 26, 2006	04 ♒ 34	
Oct 6, 2006	04 ♒ 26	
Oct 16, 2006	04 ♒ 24	
Oct 26, 2006	04 ♒ 30	
Nov 5, 2006	04 ♒ 43	
Nov 15, 2006	05 ♒ 02	
Nov 25, 2006	05 ♒ 28	
Dec 5, 2006	05 ♒ 59	
Dec 15, 2006	06 ♒ 35	
Dec 25, 2006	07 ♒ 16	
Jan 4, 2007	07 ♒ 59	
Jan 14, 2007	08 ♒ 45	
Jan 24, 2007	09 ♒ 33	
Feb 3, 2007	10 ♒ 21	
Feb 13, 2007	11 ♒ 08	
Feb 23, 2007	11 ♒ 54	
Mar 5, 2007	12 ♒ 38	
Mar 15, 2007	13 ♒ 19	
Mar 25, 2007	13 ♒ 55	
Apr 4, 2007	14 ♒ 28	
Apr 14, 2007	14 ♒ 55	
Apr 24, 2007	15 ♒ 16	
May 4, 2007	15 ♒ 30	
May 14, 2007	15 ♒ 38	
May 24, 2007	15 ♒ 40	
Jun 3, 2007	15 ♒ 34	
Jun 13, 2007	15 ♒ 23	
Jun 23, 2007	15 ♒ 05	
Jul 3, 2007	14 ♒ 42	
Jul 13, 2007	14 ♒ 15	
Jul 23, 2007	13 ♒ 45	
Aug 2, 2007	13 ♒ 13	
Aug 12, 2007	12 ♒ 41	
Aug 22, 2007	12 ♒ 10	
Sep 1, 2007	11 ♒ 40	
Sep 11, 2007	11 ♒ 15	
Sep 21, 2007	10 ♒ 54	
Oct 1, 2007	10 ♒ 38	
Oct 11, 2007	10 ♒ 29	
Oct 21, 2007	10 ♒ 27	
Oct 31, 2007	10 ♒ 31	
Nov 10, 2007	10 ♒ 42	
Nov 20, 2007	10 ♒ 59	
Nov 30, 2007	11 ♒ 23	
Dec 10, 2007	11 ♒ 52	

Chiron Locations 1920 - 2010

Date	Location		Date	Location		Date	Location
Dec 20, 2007	12 ≈ 26		Dec 24, 2008	17 ≈ 51		Dec 29, 2009	22 ≈ 56
Dec 30, 2007	13 ≈ 04		Jan 3, 2009	18 ≈ 27		Jan 8, 2010	23 ≈ 30
Jan 9, 2008	13 ≈ 45		Jan 13, 2009	19 ≈ 07		Jan 18, 2010	24 ≈ 08
Jan 19, 2008	14 ≈ 29		Jan 23, 2009	19 ≈ 49		Jan 28, 2010	24 ≈ 48
Jan 29, 2008	15 ≈ 14		Feb 2, 2009	20 ≈ 32		Feb 7, 2010	25 ≈ 30
Feb 8, 2008	15 ≈ 60		Feb 12, 2009	21 ≈ 16		Feb 17, 2010	26 ≈ 12
Feb 18, 2008	16 ≈ 45		Feb 22, 2009	21 ≈ 60		Feb 27, 2010	26 ≈ 55
Feb 28, 2008	17 ≈ 29		Mar 4, 2009	22 ≈ 42		Mar 9, 2010	27 ≈ 36
Mar 9, 2008	18 ≈ 11		Mar 14, 2009	23 ≈ 22		Mar 19, 2010	28 ≈ 15
Mar 19, 2008	18 ≈ 51		Mar 24, 2009	24 ≈ 00		Mar 29, 2010	28 ≈ 51
Mar 29, 2008	19 ≈ 26		Apr 3, 2009	24 ≈ 34		Apr 8, 2010	29 ≈ 24
Apr 8, 2008	19 ≈ 57		Apr 13, 2009	25 ≈ 04		Apr 18, 2010	29 ≈ 53
Apr 18, 2008	20 ≈ 23		Apr 23, 2009	25 ≈ 29		Apr 28, 2010	00 H 17
Apr 28, 2008	20 ≈ 43		May 3, 2009	25 ≈ 49		May 8, 2010	00 H 36
May 8, 2008	20 ≈ 58		May 13, 2009	26 ≈ 03		May 18, 2010	00 H 49
May 18, 2008	21 ≈ 06		May 23, 2009	26 ≈ 11		May 28, 2010	00 H 56
May 28, 2008	21 ≈ 07		Jun 2, 2009	26 ≈ 12		Jun 7, 2010	00 H 58
Jun 7, 2008	21 ≈ 03		Jun 12, 2009	26 ≈ 07		Jun 17, 2010	00 H 53
Jun 17, 2008	20 ≈ 52		Jun 22, 2009	25 ≈ 57		Jun 27, 2010	00 H 43
Jun 27, 2008	20 ≈ 35		Jul 2, 2009	25 ≈ 41		Jul 7, 2010	00 H 27
Jul 7, 2008	20 ≈ 13		Jul 12, 2009	25 ≈ 20		Jul 17, 2010	00 H 06
Jul 17, 2008	19 ≈ 47		Jul 22, 2009	24 ≈ 55		Jul 27, 2010	29 ≈ 42
Jul 27, 2008	19 ≈ 18		Aug 1, 2009	24 ≈ 26		Aug 6, 2010	29 ≈ 14
Aug 6, 2008	18 ≈ 47		Aug 11, 2009	23 ≈ 56		Aug 16, 2010	28 ≈ 45
Aug 16, 2008	18 ≈ 16		Aug 21, 2009	23 ≈ 26		Aug 26, 2010	28 ≈ 15
Aug 26, 2008	17 ≈ 45		Aug 31, 2009	22 ≈ 56		Sep 5, 2010	27 ≈ 46
Sep 5, 2008	17 ≈ 16		Sep 10, 2009	22 ≈ 27		Sep 15, 2010	27 ≈ 18
Sep 15, 2008	16 ≈ 51		Sep 20, 2009	22 ≈ 02		Sep 25, 2010	26 ≈ 53
Sep 25, 2008	16 ≈ 30		Sep 30, 2009	21 ≈ 42		Oct 5, 2010	26 ≈ 33
Oct 5, 2008	16 ≈ 14		Oct 10, 2009	21 ≈ 26		Oct 15, 2010	26 ≈ 17
Oct 15, 2008	16 ≈ 04		Oct 20, 2009	21 ≈ 16		Oct 25, 2010	26 ≈ 07
Oct 25, 2008	16 ≈ 01		Oct 30, 2009	21 ≈ 12		Nov 4, 2010	26 ≈ 03
Nov 4, 2008	16 ≈ 04		Nov 9, 2009	21 ≈ 14		Nov 14, 2010	26 ≈ 05
Nov 14, 2008	16 ≈ 14		Nov 19, 2009	21 ≈ 23		Nov 24, 2010	26 ≈ 13
Nov 24, 2008	16 ≈ 30		Nov 29, 2009	21 ≈ 38		Dec 4, 2010	26 ≈ 27
Dec 4, 2008	16 ≈ 52		Dec 9, 2009	21 ≈ 59		Dec 14, 2010	26 ≈ 47
Dec 14, 2008	17 ≈ 19		Dec 19, 2009	22 ≈ 25		Dec 24, 2010	27 ≈ 12

Also by ACS Publications

All About Astrology Series of booklets
The American Atlas, Expanded Fifth Edition (Shanks)
The American Book of Tables (Michelsen)
The American Ephemeris Series 1901-2000
The American Ephemeris for the 20th Century [Noon or Midnight] 1900 to 2000,
    Revised Fifth Edition
The American Ephemeris for the 21st Century 2001-2050, Revised Second Edition
The American Heliocentric Ephemeris 1901-2000
The American Sidereal Ephemeris 1976-2000
Asteroid Goddesses (George & Bloch)
Astro-Alchemy (Negus)
Astro Essentials (Pottenger)
Astrological Games People Play (Ashman)
Astrological Insights into Personality (Lundsted)
Basic Astrology: A Guide for Teachers & Students (Negus)
Basic Astrology: A Workbook for Students (Negus)
The Book of Jupiter (Waram)
The Book of Neptune (Waram)
The Book of Pluto (Forrest)
The Changing Sky (Forrest)
Complete Horoscope Interpretation (Pottenger)
Cosmic Combinations (Negus)
Dial Detective (Simms)
Easy Tarot Guide (Masino)
Expanding Astrology's Universe (Dobyns)
Finding Our Way Through the Dark (George)
Hands That Heal (Burns)
Healing with the Horoscope (Pottenger)
The Inner Sky (Forrest)
The International Atlas, Revised Third Edition (Shanks)
The Koch Book of Tables (Michelsen)
Midpoints (Munkasey)
New Insights into Astrology (Press)
The Night Speaks (Forrest)
The Only Way to... Learn Astrology, Vols. I-VI (March & McEvers)
    Volume I - Basic Principles
    Volume II - Math & Interpretation Techniques
    Volume III - Horoscope Analysis
    Volume IV- Learn About Tomorrow: Current Patterns
    Volume V - Learn About Relationships: Synastry Techniques
    Volume VI - Learn About Horary and Electional Astrology
Planetary Heredity (M. Gauquelin)
Planetary Planting (Riotte)
Planets in Solar Returns (Shea)
Planets in Work: (Binder)
Planets on the Move (Dobyns/Pottenger)
Psychology of the Planets (F. Gauquelin)
Roadmap to Your Future (Ashman)
Skymates (S. & J. Forrest)
Spirit Guides: We Are Not Alone (Belhayes)
Tables of Planetary Phenomena (Michelsen)
'welve Wings of the Eagle (Simms)
'ur Magical Child (Simms)
'r Starway to Love (Pottenger)